Marketing Planning
2008-2009

Karen Beamish and Ruth Ashford

ELSEVIER

AMSTERDAM • BOSTON • HEIDELBERG • LONDON • NEW YORK • OXFORD
PARIS • SAN DIEGO • SAN FRANCISCO • SINGAPORE • SYDNEY • TOKYO

Butterworth-Heinemann is an imprint of Elsevier

Butterworth-Heinemann is an imprint of Elsevier
Linacre House, Jordan Hill, Oxford OX2 8DP, UK
30 Corporate Drive, Suite 400, Burlington, MA 01803, USA

First edition 2008

Notice
No responsibility is assumed by the publisher for any injury and/or damage to persons
or property as a matter of products liability, negligence or otherwise, or from any use
or operation of any methods, products, instructions or ideas contained in the material
herein.

British Library Cataloguing in Publication Data
A catalogue record for this book is available from the British Library.

Library of Congress Cataloguing in Publication Data
A catalogue record for this book is available from the Library of Congress.

ISBN: 978 0 7506 8986 1

For information on all Butterworth-Heinemann publications
visit our website at http://www.elsevierdirect.com

 Designed and typeset by P.K. McBride

Printed and bound in Italy
08 09 10 11 12   10 9 8 7 6 5 4 3 2 1

Contents

CITY COLLEGE
LEARNING RESOURCE CENTRE

Unit 1
Introduction to marketing planning

Learning objectives

Marketing Planning is the mainstay module of the Professional Diploma, formerly known as the Advanced Certificate in Marketing. It is the backbone of marketing, and builds clearly upon the Fundamentals of Marketing at Certificate level and firmly underpins Planning and Control and Integrated Marketing Communications at Postgraduate Diploma level.

This unit will:

◆ Help you to understand the basis and focus of the Marketing Planning course-book.

◆ Help you to understand the nature of the CIM learning outcomes, and what you should achieve through your studies.

◆ Encourage you to read more broadly around the marketing planning area.

◆ Focus on the nature of the examination.

◆ Explain the synergistic planning process – analysis, planning, implementation and control.

◆ List the components of the marketing plan.

◆ Assess the potential impact of wider macro-environmental forces relating to the role of culture, ethical approach, social responsibility, legal frameworks and sustainability.

Syllabus reference: 1.1, 1.2, 1.3, 1.4, 1.5.

Introduction

The Marketing Planning module within the Professional Diploma, formerly known as the Advanced Certificate, has a very clear focus and is based upon four key elements overall:

◆   The marketing plan and its organizational and wider marketing context (15 per cent)

◆   Marketing planning and budgeting (20 per cent)

◆   The extended marketing mix and related tools (50 per cent)

◆   Marketing in different contexts (15 per cent).

A brief insight into each of these components appears below. You might find it useful at this stage to look closely at the CIM syllabus, which can be found either in the CIM website or in the Student Zone at www.cim.co.uk, as this will put your study into context.

The marketing planning process

This element of the text focuses on the process of effectively 'doing' marketing. It looks at the concepts and applications of 'the marketing planning process', from the marketing audit through to developing objectives and marketing strategies. One of the key success factors (KSF) of marketing is the successful utilization and integration of the marketing mix. The marketing mix is a set of tools for the trade; if they are not carefully managed, in a coordinated and defined way, then the strategy may crumble and the process may fall apart.

Organizations will often be found analysing their capabilities, assessing their true position and overall potential in the marketplace, both home and abroad. This analysis provides the foundations of the planning process, which are critical to the direction of the organization in the future.

Malcolm McDonald, Cranfield University School of Management, defines the overall purpose of planning at this stage as follows:

> The overall purpose of marketing planning and its principal focus is the identification and creation of sustainable competitive advantage. (Quoted in Dibb *et al.*, 2005, p. 689)

Implementing the marketing plan is probably one of the most challenging and often fraught areas of business strategy. Each division and department will be involved in fighting for their share of the budget and appropriate resource allocations in order to achieve the objectives that are the fundamental basis of the future success of the organization. Ultimately this can often result in one of the most dramatic changes of all, that is change in the organizational structure. It is necessary to consider carefully the nature, structure and culture of any organization in order that it can clearly meet the challenges to achieving a sustainable competitive advantage and remain at the heart of the marketplace.

Marketing planning in context

This syllabus has been designed and structured in a logical way to provide marketers with an understanding of the different concepts applicable to operational marketing management. Marketers are required to develop a range of transferable skills that aid creativity, innovation and the potential to exploit and develop new marketing opportunities.

In order that you can successfully achieve some elements of this, the CIM syllabus, and this text in association with it, has presented you with an opportunity to look at marketing in a range of different contexts. Therefore the latter part of your studies will see you starting to apply the 'process' and 'relationship' elements of Marketing Planning, into a range of contextual situations, such as:

◆   Industrial/business-to-business marketing

◆   Services marketing

◆   Small- and medium-sized enterprises (SMEs)

◆   Charity and not-for-profit marketing

◆   International marketing.

Being able to apply marketing in different contexts is vital to your own individual success and continuing professional development. You will be in a much stronger position to add value to your own position within the organization as well as to the organization as a whole.

Like people, organizations are far from perfect. Within many businesses it is clear to see that while the concept is good, the reality has scope for improvement. The purpose of your studies is to prepare you to add value to your organization, with a combination of knowledge, understanding and application abilities and skills that could really make the difference, make your organization stand out from the crowd and achieve 'sustainable competitive advantage'.

The aims and objectives of Marketing Planning and the learning outcomes

Having read the CIM syllabus overview for Marketing Planning, it is clear that the syllabus is broken down into three tiers:

◆   Aims and objectives

◆   Learning outcomes

◆   Indicative content and weighting.

Understanding the role of each of these areas is quite important, as together they culminate in the acquisition of the knowledge and understanding that underpins the examination process.

Aims and objectives

The aims and objectives clearly explain the basis of your learning and what that learning is designed to achieve. It is this basis that this text seeks to promote:

◆   To build on your knowledge and understanding of marketing fundamentals.

◆   To enable you to apply modern marketing theory to the understanding and solution of practical marketing problems and situations.

◆   To provide a sound understanding of the process of marketing planning, analysis, strategy and implementation.

◆   To provide a sound understanding of the marketing mix tools that contribute towards the effective implementation of marketing strategy.

◆   To enable you to evaluate the relative effectiveness and costs of elements of the promotional mix, providing underpinning operational knowledge for progression on to the Postgraduate Diploma in Marketing.

◆   To explore the multiple relationships which need to be formed and maintained to enable successful and ongoing exchange in the marketplace.

◆   To examine the need to adapt Marketing Planning to a variety of different contexts.

Table 1.1 provides a list of key learning outcomes, linked to the units of study, so that it is clear to see how the coursebook provides you with the underpinning knowledge and understanding to support a successful outcome to your studies and, of course, the all-important examination. This should provide you with a useful reference for structuring your learning.

Learning outcomes

Table 1.1: Learning outcomes/unit guide

Learning outcomes	Study units/ syllabus reference
Explain the role of the marketing plan within the context of the organization's strategy and culture and broader marketing environment (ethics, social responsibility, legal frameworks and sustainability)	Unit 1
Conduct a marketing audit considering appropriate internal and external factors	Unit 2
Develop marketing objectives and plans at an operational level	Unit 3
Develop the role of branding and positioning within the marketing plan	Unit 4
Integrate marketing mix tools to achieve effective implementation of plans	Units 4–7
Select an appropriate co-ordinated marketing mix incorporating appropriate stakeholder relationships for a particular marketing context	Units 8–11
Set and justify budgets for marketing plans and mix decisions	Unit 3
Define and use appropriate measurements to evaluate the effectiveness of marketing plans and activities	Unit 3
Make recommendations for changes and innovations to marketing processes based on an understanding of the organizational context and evaluation of past marketing activities	Unit 3
All learning outcomes are designed in order that you can apply marketing in practice in a range of different contexts.	

Indicative content

The third and final tier of the syllabus is the indicative content and weighting. This explains in detail the different elements of the syllabus that you will cover to achieve the learning outcomes. These have been referenced in Table 1.1 for your information.

You should endeavour to familiarize yourself with these key syllabus points as they form the basis of the examination process. The examination questions are formulated by the CIM Senior Examiners and are written with a clear focus upon the indicative content. There is more on examinations later in this book.

The importance of reading

While you might be taking the Marketing Planning module with the sole objective of achieving the Professional Diploma, hopefully you will broaden your horizons considerably along the way.

In order to do this, you should not only use this particular course text, but also read around the subject. CIM have clearly specified a range of recommended reading texts, which are listed in your Study Manual. Many of the texts within the reading list have been used to develop this book and you are encouraged to read and follow up on these and the other references interspersed throughout this text and extend your knowledge.

In addition, you should regularly read various journals, such as *Marketing Week, Marketing* and *Campaign*, which have international accessibility, particularly *Marketing Week*, through www.mad.com. Other suggestions are *The Economist* and broadsheet papers, in particular the weekend versions and equivalents of the *Financial Times* and the *Sunday Times*. Here you will see a range of useful and relevant examples of how all of the components of marketing impact on everyday business in your own country. One of the most useful resources is *Marketing in Business*, the CIM magazine, where you will find many useful case studies that will consolidate your learning.

As e-commerce plays such a pivotal role in everyday life, you will also find a range of different websites referenced. It is recommended that you visit them where appropriate and in the context in which they have been offered. A useful journal to support aspects of e-commerce in relation to Marketing Planning is *connectis* – Europe's e-business magazine.

Study tip

As part of your studies you will be continually referring to a range of promotional activities and international references.

To assist you in preparing for the examination you are advised to set up two separate information files. One is for keeping cuttings relating to marketing mix activities, in respect of both consumer and business-to-business marketing. In the second file, you should keep a range of international-based marketing cuttings.

It is recommended that you follow developments closely in two or three countries and record events over a period of time.

These would be particularly useful when answering examination questions that say 'in a country of your choice' or indeed a 'company of your choice'. With a file of cuttings to fall back on at revision time, you have a range of examples to use.

Approaching the Marketing Planning examination

As already suggested, the examination questions are written based upon the very detailed indicative content. Furthermore they are clearly focused on ensuring that you can achieve the specified 'learning outcomes' referenced earlier in this unit. It is vitally important, therefore, that you pay close attention to the requirements of the syllabus and learning outcomes, in order that you can successfully attempt the CIM examinations. Any one element of the syllabus could be tested, therefore 100 per cent coverage must be achieved through your studies.

CIM provide a range of exam preparation tools within their website. You will be provided with Web addresses, passwords and usernames upon completion of your student registration process. The appropriate website address is www.cim.co.uk. In addition to this, you can also use the new Elsevier Revision Cards, which are summary cards for each of your units of study. This will help consolidate your learning considerably in the final revision stages.

The exam paper questions will be mostly practical in nature, in that the questions will ask you to take on a role, possibly solve a problem, write briefing notes, develop an outline plan or devise the basis of a strategy. Many of the questions will ask you to put different concepts from within Marketing Planning into practice.

Questions will be naturally challenging at this level, and will not require you to regurgitate knowledge but to apply it to real-life situations or scenarios. This is a key requirement at the Professional Diploma level. You are about to prove to the Senior Examiner that you can 'do marketing' at an operational management level. Therefore avoid superficial answers and get straight to the thrust of the question.

In addition to the examination, you will also be able to take 'assignment-based assessments'. The assignments are designed to enable you to apply the concepts and theories relating to Marketing Planning in practice. Assignment-based learning allows you to use your own company or one you know well, to develop your assignment and demonstrate your ability 'to do' marketing in a practical and applied way.

An overview of the strategy and planning hierarchy

The backdrop to the planning process

In the last two decades, the function of marketing has had an increasing influence upon the strategic development of the organization, achieving a much more favourable position, more on a par with the other business functions. This has been an uphill battle, one that has seen marketing gaining a very prominent position in the 1980s, and subsequently being diluted in the early 1990s as a result of the economic recession. Ever since, marketing as a business function has had to fight back in order to establish its position at the heart of the corporate planning process.

Essentially, the marketing function may play a pivotal role in feeding information upwards, to provide substance, guidance, direction and vision to support the corporate planning process. In turn, the significant work that the marketing function undertakes plays a major role in establishing a vision and mission for the organization, a sense of direction as to where it is heading in the short, medium and long term.

To put this into context, it is necessary to understand and conceptualize the strategy and planning hierarchy (Figure 1.1). This highlights the route that strategy and planning takes from the corporate strategy stage down to the marketing function and through to marketing tactics. For example, it is likely as a marketing director that you will have a significant input to the strategic decision-making process, this is commonly known as 'bottom-up planning'. Your role would include providing the board and the corporate strategy team with appropriate levels of information to support corporate level decision-making. Subsequent to this, you would also have a vital role in taking the corporate objectives and corporate strategy, and translating them into marketing objectives and marketing strategy (Figure 1.1).

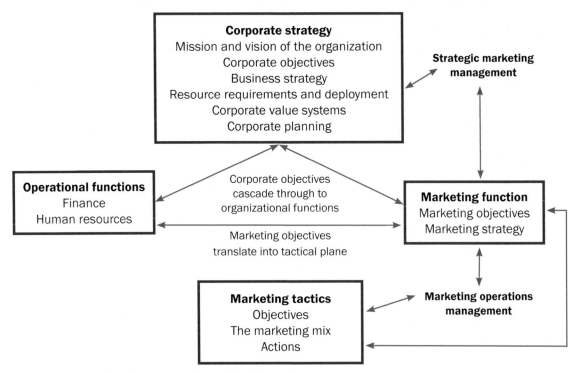

Figure 1.1: Strategy and planning hierarchy

Further down the strategy and planning hierarchy (Figure 1.1), Marketing Planning starts to play a pivotal role in implementing the marketing plans, through a tightly defined marketing programme. This is known as bottom-down planning.

At this stage it is appropriate to consider the various tiers of the strategy and planning hierarchy in a little more detail, in preparation for your studies in Unit 2, 'The marketing audit'.

Corporate planning – what is it?

Corporate planning starts at the very top of the organization. It provides clearly defined objectives for the organization as a whole, which can then be translated down through the hierarchy to each of the business functions, inclusive of marketing, human resources, finance and the operations departments. In turn, each of these business functions has responsibility to deliver the overall corporate objectives, meeting the corporate mission and corporate vision of the organization. They will also have a key role in ensuring that corporate values are deployed and understood by the internal market.

While the business functions will vary in nature, it is essential that they each work together, developing an innovative and integrative approach to delivering corporate objectives. No business unit should work in isolation of the other functional units; ignoring this approach could ultimately have a detrimental effect. It amounts to planning in a vacuum.

A good example of this would be a financial services organization. You will be aware that financial services organizations such as 'Egg', First Direct Bank, American Express or MBNA rely heavily upon 'people' in order to provide the required level of service to meet customer demands and expectations. For any of the above organizations to succeed, both the human resources and the marketing business functions will need to work closely together to achieve an integrated approach to fulfilling the coporate objectives.

Marketing strategy – what is it?

In this unit the words 'strategy' and 'plannin'g often appear linked together in the same sentences. Clearly, however, they are not one and the same, and therefore they must be differentiated.

> Marketing strategy – a strategy indicating the specific target markets and the types of competitive advantages that are to be developed and exploited. (Dibb *et al.*, 2005, p. 656)

> As a strategy, marketing seeks to develop effective responses to changing marketing environments, by defining market segments, developing and positioning product offerings for those target markets. (Webster, 1997, from Hooley *et al.*, 1998, p. 7)

> Strategy is the direction and scope of an organisation over the long term, which achieves advantage in a changing environment through its configuration of resources and competences with the aim of fulfilling stakeholder expectations. (Johnson and Scholes, 2005, p.9)

On close examination of these definitions, it is clear to see that they have a common thread. That is, marketing strategy should create a sense of vision and direction. Nigel Piercy (2001, p. 140) states that:

> Strategy is all about doing best what matters most to the customer.

> and

> Finding new and better ways of looking at important things to get some leverage for changing the way things are done.

Marketing strategy provides the basis of a framework for meeting organizational needs and customer wants in an integrative and innovative way. It communicates to the internal market and its external stakeholders the strategic intent of the organization, where the organization is going, to whom it is taking its products and services and how it proposes to achieve a positive competitive market position.

When developing a strategy, the critical success factor is to ensure that the marketing strategy is robust and focuses on building long-term relationships, creating customer value and sustainable competitive advantage. This is quite important to comprehend, as while organizations are subject to constant change, and as a result often work continually on various contingency plans, there should be some consistency in approach. Therefore, a robust marketing strategy is long term, is strategic in nature and should remain constant. The contingency approach is very much tactical, leading to changes in the marketing mix as a result of changing market conditions.

Piercy (2001) suggests, in his book *Market-Led Strategic Change*, that a robust marketing strategy should have the following characteristics:

◆ Focus on providing superior customer value, but recognize that innovation offers a sustainable advantage.

◆ Make long-term investments in relationships, with suppliers, distributors, employees and customers.

◆ Be built around 100 per cent satisfied customers based on capabilities and motivation of their people.

◆ Build effective supply chains and IT infrastructure to deliver superior operating performance.

Therefore, the key to success is to build a strategy based on these concepts, added to which an organization must strive to ensure that it implements a learning culture, is open to change and is innovative, with a long-term commitment to developing long-lasting customer relationships. Figure 1.2 represents some of the key components of the fundamentals of marketing strategy.

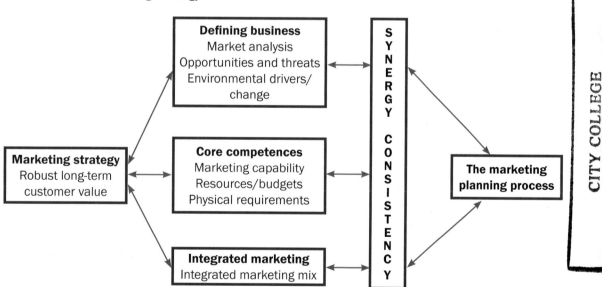

Figure 1.2: The basics of strategy. Adapted from: Drummond *et al.* (2003)

Essentially marketing strategy should identify specific segments of the market, towards which the organization's marketing activities and programmes might be aimed. It should highlight opportunities to be exploited and explicitly state the objectives required in order that the corporate goals of the organization should be achieved.

Ultimately, strategy should ensure synergy across the whole organization without exception. Critical to the success of any strategy is the need to ensure that all business functions and their underpinning activities are working for the same purpose and design, with a common vision, achieving integration and consistency in approach.

Planning – what is it?

Planning is an essential process ensuring that the defined strategy may be successfully implemented, and that the infrastructure required in order to meet the corporate and marketing objectives has been set in place. Planning provides specific direction, activities and timetables, and it creates pathways to achieving competitive advantage. Effectively it becomes a programme of events.

More and more organizations today appear to have an increasing emphasis on the importance of planning, and Johnson and Scholes (2001) suggest a number of reasons why this might be:

◆ Planning provides a structured means of analysing the marketplace, considering the dynamics of it and forcing managers to both question and challenge what they quite often take for granted.

◆ Planning provides a sense of direction, and can be seen as a means of involving employees in the development of a strategy. This provides an opportunity for employees to take ownership of the overall objectives and the planned approach to achieving them.

◆ A plan is a good way of communicating proposed actions/activities expected to be undertaken by the organization, in order that it achieves its corporate objectives.

◆ Having a plan in place provides a sound basis for control, and presents an opportunity to regularly review the organization's progress against objectives.

While there is an emphasis on 'planning' as a key business activity at this stage, your studies will focus on 'marketing planning' at an operational level. Therefore, it is important to highlight a typical marketing planning model at this stage, so that you understand the level for which you are being prepared.

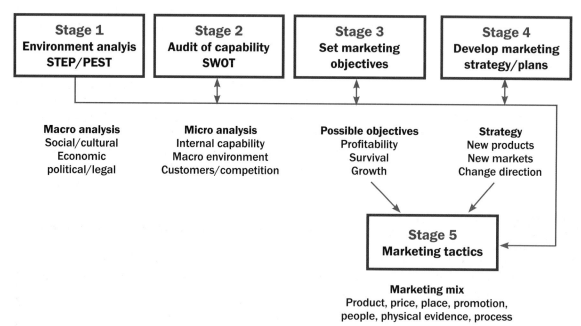

Figure 1.3: The marketing planning process

The 'marketing planning process model' in Figure 1.3 clearly illustrates how planning might take place within a typical marketing function. This model will form the basis of your study within Unit 3.

However, while the focus will be around marketing planning, it is still important to understand the 'bigger picture' of how it all fits together, including the issues and implications of planning.

Barriers to planning

While planning has many positive facets, it can also create many barriers within the organization. It is likely that the majority of people and organizations have faced considerable change as a result of newly defined strategies and have had to come to terms with some of the major repercussions of this level of change. The most prominent factor related to change is that, almost without exception, it is linked with cost cutting and downsizing.

Drummond *et al.* (2003) suggested that barriers to successful planning are:

◆ **The existing culture** may not be amenable to marketing plans, particularly if the organization is not marketing-oriented.

◆ **Power and politics** – All organizations are subject to internal politics and often as a result of this the strategic planning process becomes a boardroom battlefield, where vested interests fight each other's proposals in order to gain resources and status.

◆ **Analysis not action** – Many organizations waste time and energy in analysing data and developing rationales for action, but ultimately fail to act. A further element of this is 'paralysis-by-analysis', too much information, not enough direction.

◆ **Resources** – After years of downsizing, striving for increased efficiencies, many organizations now find themselves resource-starved. When corporate objectives are defined, it is of prime importance that organizations realistically consider the resources required, in order that they can rise to the challenge of achieving the corporate targets.

◆ **Skills** are very closely linked to the challenges of resources. One of the key components of any organization is a highly skilled workforce. As a result of the changes brought about by the economic slowdown in the early 1990s, marketing as a function was cascaded down to managers in the organization who were untrained, unskilled and unable to suddenly carry the mantle of marketing that had now been bestowed upon them. An unskilled workforce could significantly hinder the implementation of marketing plans and ultimately reduce service and performance levels overall.

Question 1.1

Stop for a moment and think about your own organization, or one that you are familiar with. Make a list of specific barriers to planning and the subsequent change that your chosen organization has experienced.

Why do you think these barriers were created?

The influence of change upon the planning process

One of the most certain factors impacting upon the planning process in any organization is change – a by-product of the modern-day world. Planning is now undertaken against the backdrop of constant change, internally and externally. Organizations are challenged to manage through a range of either predictable change or unexpected change, cyclical change or evolutionary change. Either way, the impact upon the organization can be significant, causing a slowdown in the strategy implementation process, or a diversion to develop an unexpected and unanticipated opportunity that is essential to exploit and promote.

Of course, alternatively, change can mean that strategies and plans are no longer relevant or that they will no longer guarantee the levels of success that had previously been anticipated. We live in an era where we continuously receive profit warnings, that is organizations who fail to meet the profit objectives determined by the marketing plan.

Profit warnings by British companies hit their highest level last in October 2005 since the September 11 attacks on America. In 2005, there were over 370 profit warnings by quoted companies, up from 261 in the first nine months of 2004. This continued into 2006, where significant companies suffered real setbacks in business. It continues to this day, particular relating to the oil and gas industry, where there is increasing pressure on organisations due to the impact of the 'credit crunch' and the rising prices for oil, due to the ongoing Middle Eastern conflicts. Also airlines are under immense pressure as the rise in oil prices has had a significant impact on their operational costs.

In today's rapidly changing environment, understanding the key drivers and forces will be of primary importance if an organization is to be prepared to respond to them.

In essence, change means the future is unpredictable, more intense, more competitive, with shorter product life cycles, shorter planning cycles and much uncertainty. In an environment where planning is a key activity, the challenges presented by change will intensify.

Activity 1.1

Taking your own organization, or one that you are familiar with, consider the various changes they have implemented over the past two years. Then think about the key drivers of that change – make a list of them.

Relationship marketing with the wider public and society

In the final stage of this unit, it is important to consider marketing in the broader context of the wider public and society, that is carry out the marketing activity in a way that is socially acceptable, ethically driven and is proactively incorporated into the organization's vision, mission, ethos, culture and day-to-day business dealings.

At times ethics and business seem to be mutually incompatible. However, social and ethical marketing are a very politically correct element of today's society and business at large. A further example of how a social and ethical issue in the context of 'green marketing' has affected a high volume market is McDonald. McDonald's have been involved in a number of social and ethical responsibility issues, in respect of their products and packaging, which they have had to address so as to retain favour with the marketplace. This was a costly exercise and one that was carried out under the spotlight of huge publicity.

Today there are a number of dynamic groups and individuals who engage in social issues, such as human rights and, in particular, green issues. With the introduction of the Kyoto Agreement, there has been a significant impact upon how organizations manage their activities to remain within the framework of reference that the agreement has defined. Failing to redress the balance between where the organization is and where it should be in respect of the Kyoto Agreement has been shown to cause high levels of discomfort.

Recognition of corporate social responsibility (CSR), both as an important part of business behaviour and a key marketing issue, has increased enormously in the last few years. This is because it is not only an issue of ethics but one which has become integral to sustaining the consumer goodwill that feeds sales and profits.

Increasingly people are not just passive consumers insensitive to what is going on around them. The indications are that the upcoming generations are more aware and more likely to buy from companies they see as socially responsible.

Where organizations transgress, as in the case of Esso and Exxon, reputations can be swept away almost overnight, as these and other global corporations have discovered.

The drinks industry is under constant attack and the particular target is alcoholic soft drinks, which took the market by surprise, indeed by storm, in the summer of 1995. In particular, drinks such as Hooch, Lemonheads and Vodka Sauce are the source of constant contention between consumer movements and the brewing industry with regard to the problem of under-age drinking and distinguishing between an alcoholic drink and a soft drink. This has since continued to be a source of contention as there are an increasing number of alco-pop drinks on sale.

Marketing and social responsibility

Corporate social responsibility refers to the attention of business to:

◆ Community involvement

◆ Socially responsible products and processes

◆ Socially responsible employee relation.

Corporate social responsibility has become prominent in the language and strategy of business and by the growth of dedicated CSR organizations nationally, in the European Union and globally. Governments and international governmental organizations are also increasingly encouraging CSR and forming CSR partnerships.

Definition

Social responsibility – The obligations and accountability to society of individuals and organizations above and beyond their primary functions and interests.

A further definition is that of CSR. The European Commission in its 2001 green paper 'Promoting a European Framework for corporate social responsibility' define it as 'a concept whereby companies integrate social and environment concerns in their business operations and in their interaction with their stakeholders on a voluntary basis'. CSR relates to actions which are above and beyond that required by law (McWilliams and Siegel, 2001).

Corporate social responsibility is one of business' contributions to achieving sustainable development. It is about business behaving responsibly towards society and the environment ensuring economic development is sustainable. It is a term describing the way in which businesses take account of the impacts of their operation, processes and products on the economy, society and the environment on a local, regional, national and global level; maximizing benefits to the business as well as society and the environment, whilst minimizing any downsides.

It is voluntary action over and above compliance with the law, integrating socially responsible behaviour into core business values and recognizing the business benefits of doing so.

Others see it more simply as 'doing things right' and a matter of good management which takes a holistic view of an organization's role and responsibilities. A poll of 25 000 citizens across 23 countries on six continents showed that perceptions of companies around the world are more strongly linked with citizenship (56 per cent) than either brand quality (40 per cent) or the perception of business management (34 per cent).

Case study: Egg's corporate social responsibility statement

Our core values at Egg are honesty, integrity and respect for people. We respect our people's individuality and diversity, encouraging them to develop their careers in a stimulating environment in keeping with our values. Our customers are the reason we exist and we constantly look to offer them the products and services that put them in control of their money.

Source: www.egg.com

Manufacturers need to care for consumers in terms of safety. This could involve environmental or health consequences. The social costs and benefits of new products must also be examined. Marketers have to consider their response to, say pharmaceutical products, where the side effects of new drugs must be researched, and often through contentious methods such as testing on animals.

Marketers must also consider other issues important to social marketing, such as environmentalism, legislation, consumerism and consumer pressure.

The accepted wisdom on the value of CSR is that it achieves the following objectives:

- To meet responsibilities
- To put something back
- To manage impacts on society
- To improve reputation
- To meet government expectations.

Some useful websites that you may want to look at to find out more about CSR are:

- Business in the Community – www.bitc.org.uk
- Institute of Business Ethics – www.ibe.org.uk
- Society of Business – www.societyandbusiness.gov.uk.
- Starbucks – www.starbucks.co.uk

Case study: Starbucks

Starbucks maintain that CSR runs deeply through the company, by giving back to communities and the environment and by treating staff with dignity and respect.

Starbucks are taking important measures to help improve the lives of coffee farmers and protect the environment where they grow their beans.

We have examined many issues that farmers face, including economic challenges and environmental concerns. Commitment to origins is Starbucks' way of helping coffee farmers address these challenges while sustaining their farms, being sensitive to the environment and meeting the highest-quality coffee standards.

1   Commitment to origins – by making investments that benefit coffee producer communities and the natural environment.

2   Protecting the environment – by promoting conservation in coffee-growing countries and recycling programmes.

3   In the community – by making contributions to neighbourhoods where Starbucks have outlets.

4   Commitment to partners – by creating a happy work environment where staff are treated with respect.

Environmentalism – green marketing

Wastage, effluent, emissions of fumes and acid rain have to be taken seriously by manufacturers. Due to the high level of industrialization in the modern world, the environment is under constant threat from global warming. In recent times we have experienced severe weather effects, such as heavy rain, gales and significant flooding. All of this relates to environmentalism and as such means that organizations must in the future consider their strategy in relation to these issues.

Organizations such as NIREX, who dispose of atomic waste, are subject to heavy criticism by environmental groups such as the Green Party and by the press. Their contact with the public is minimal; they deal with industry, hence they are little influenced by the public.

Case study: Marks and Spencer go carbon neutral

In January 2007 Marks and Spencer announced a £200 million 'eco-plan' to make it carbon neutral in 5 years, as its contribution to the battle against climate change. By 2012 MS said it would be carbon neutral, send no waste to landfill and 'set new standards in ethical trading'.

Marks and Spencer will also focus on sourcing its food from the UK and Ireland as it looked to reduce air freight costs. Food brought into the UK by plane would be labelled 'flown'.

Marks and Spencer are contributing towards the significant debate about long-term sustainability of business and resources, and aim to cut energy consumption and use renewables. It suggests that the plan they have in place would be consistent with taking 100,000 cars off the road each year.

Marks and Spencer's actions signal the first in a range of changes that see organizations aiming to tackle the enormous challenges of climate change and waste.

This is a very good example of 'green marketing' particularly as Marks and Spencer confirmed that they will continue to sell great quality, stylish and innovative products, but want to increase sales as opposed to costs, making the customer experience as important and valuable but changing business practices to retain profitability.

Source: www.marksandspencer.com

Legislation

Perhaps one of the most dynamic areas for the major political parties when in power has been the introduction of legislation to protect the consumer. This provides external constraints on business, the most significant being that of government policy itself.

The manufacturer and the supplier have legal duties to consumers and a number of laws have been passed over the years to protect the latter, notably the following:

◆   The Trade Descriptions Acts 1968 and 1972

◆   The Consumer Safety Act 1978

◆   The Consumer Credit Act 1974.

The rise in consumerism

A major element of social responsibility is considering the impact of consumerism. Although consumers have had rights, enforceable by law, for many years, they have not really been effective because of the cost of taking legal action. The consumerist movement is a way of taking agreed action for specific purposes, such as opposing the building of an additional terminal at London's Heathrow Airport. Such schemes are often associated with local initiatives. One group that is known nationally is the Consumers' Association, famous for the publication *Which?*

The consumer movement is a diverse collection of independent individuals, groups and organizations seeking to protect the rights of consumers.

It may be useful to consider at this stage two definitions of consumerism.

Definitions

Consumerism – an organized movement of concerned citizens and government to enhance the rights and powers of buyers in relation to sellers (Kotler, 1995).

Consumerism – a social force designed to protect the consumer by organizing legal, moral and economic pressures on business (Cravens and Hills, 1970) .

In both of these definitions, there is a suggestion of an alienation from business and industry, and a feeling that the consumer's point of view is neglected.

Social response to consumerist pressure

Companies have responded in many different ways to the consumer movement and the individual consumer. Some have resisted and actively lobbied against consumerist pressure; others have ignored it and gone about their business as if the consumerist movement did not exist. However, evidence from the United States suggests that those companies which reacted to the consumerist movement positively, increased their market shares and profits quite substantially, and it is now recognized that most companies have to respond to environmental and social issues and accept the new buyer's rights, at least in principle.

It is quite interesting to consider the differing responses of organizations to social and environmental pressures. Below are some of the responses of businesses:

- ◆ **Ignore consumerism** – A reaction that encourages legislation in the marketing area, as companies believe/hope that the consumerism movement is a passing phase.

- ◆ **Counter consumerism** – The stronger elements in the business sector will endeavour to resist consumerist pressures by lobbying the government. This is really a delaying tactic, as a government wins more votes from consumers than from big businesses generally.

- ◆ **Profit from consumerism** – To respond to consumerist pressures by creating new means of profit is the most acceptable alternative long-term strategy for business.

- ◆ **Voluntary adaptation** – This is, in fact, treading the tightrope – meeting consumerist demands, but over a longer period than the government would want. This approach could misfire, indeed backfire.

- ◆ **Accept government intervention** – Business has traditionally resisted government interference, but it is now becoming more acceptable, and certain politicians talk of a government/business partnership.

There is one thing, though, that is certain and that is that consumerism is here to stay. Increasingly it demonstrates against the building of more roads or airport runways, and it shows that people have a high level of determination that can no longer be ignored. The same applies to the 'Green' movement, which aims to preserve the natural order to reduce pollution. Quite often the improvement of processes, which is necessary to reduce pollution, is a once-only capital cost and the process runs at a lower cost afterwards. It is clear that the ideas of consumerism and anti-pollution make some sense, even if manufacturers do not like the details of some of the claims, and it is essential to have a policy on these matters.

Reduction of pollution is a social responsibility, and can often be achieved either through factory processes or in lower-cost wrappings, and this, in turn, is a matter which can be used as a topic for favourable publicity.

For many organizations, it would make sense to run a social audit, in the same way that they may run a marketing audit. The difference would be that the results could be used for publicity purposes, either to show existing good practice or to report progress on matters that need attention.

Most important of all, though, is a declaration of company policy regarding consumerism and social responsibility. When all members of staff at all levels have a clear directive to which they can work, they will feel happier to do the little bit extra that is often needed to work more cleanly. This may look like a matter of ethics and social responsibility, but it will often result in the production of economies and a reduction in selling costs.

Ethical issues for consumers and marketers

We have very much focused on social marketing, of which ethical marketing is an important part. Taking social responsibility often means being ethical in behaviour. We must briefly consider the importance of ethical issues relating to the role of marketing.

Some of the matters that are highlighted by the consumer movement are often taken up because they impinge strongly on the livelihoods of people who are closely involved with the industry. Farmers have to work the land efficiently and effectively, yet intensive farming methods spoil wildlife habitats. These methods include the growth of genetically modified (GM) crops, even when these crops threaten to upset the ecological balance of the agricultural environment.

Instead of just fighting farmers, organizations such as the Royal Society for the Protection of Birds have investigated a range of activities and produced a book to show farmers how they can benefit from looking after wildlife as well as their crops. The government has found itself with a moral and ethical obligation to consider the impact of GM crops more closely also. In turn, codes of practice or legislation will be introduced on the future inclusion of GM crops in the marketplace and the development of associated food products.

This is probably a more acceptable view of consumerism, but at times there are excessive demands from consumers, who continue to bring the consumer movement into disrepute. Therefore, it is necessary, where appropriate and indeed possible, to have codes of ethics by which industry can operate.

Ethical implications for the marketing mix

Should a company be quite serious about acting responsibly at a social and ethical level, then it is likely that there may be some adaptation of the marketing mix. Key issues in the mix are as follows:

Product

- Meeting safety standards
- Dangerous products modified or removed
- Ethical issues relating to planned obsolescence should be considered
- No further testing on animals.

Price

- Consideration given to what is a fair price
- Monopolies and mergers more closely monitored to prevent monopolistic power on prices.

Promotion

- The challenge of promoting materials ethically and taking into account social responsibility for example: advertising to children or the elderly.

Place

◆   A duty to ensure that products are available to all, on an equal cost basis

◆   Environmental transportation concerns are considered.

Summary

As many markets reach maturity, organizations are working significantly harder to achieve and retain sustainable competitive advantage. The varying dynamics of devising strategies and plans require careful and sensitive management, as the organization, that is 'the corporate group' of business functions, seeks to achieve its organizational objectives.

There are many strategic marketing issues that need to be addressed in respect of the future success of an organization and its product/services portfolio. Ideally an organization will need to focus on the brand values, brand statements, customer services, supply chains and, of course, its customers and consumers.

Developing a strategy and associated plans that are innovative, competitive and sustainable is a tremendous challenge. Ultimately the most successful measure of performance is said to be customer satisfaction. Without satisfied customers the organization will struggle to remain competitive and remain at the leading edge in the marketplace, and the challenge will never be fully realized.

According to Nigel Piercy (2001), author of *Market-Led Strategic Change*, you can tell if a company has a strategy and knows where it is going and develops the capability to get there. He suggests 'this is something that stands behind planning and systems and structure – strategy is more fundamental'.

It is therefore clear to see that strategies and plans give focus, structure, outcomes and a planned destiny for the organization. Every organization should have a pathway mapped out that takes it to a state of competitive strength.

In Unit 3 of this book, we look very closely at the setting of appropriate objectives, and the development of appropriate strategies, but prior to looking at this, it is essential to understand the planning framework and where it all fits together.

Study tip

Nobody will be expecting you to produce a fully fledged strategic marketing plan as a result of study for this module. The learning outcome supporting this module is very focused on providing you with an understanding of marketing planning at an operational level. This 'Planning Overview' will have provided you with an insight into the relationship between corporate planning and marketing planning, and therefore the focus of your studies will relate to 'bottom-up' planning, that is operational level marketing, where the responsibility rests for the successful implementation of the marketing plan.

Drummond *et al.* (2003) describe 'bottom-up planning' thus: 'Authority and responsibility for formulation and implementation of strategy is devolved. Senior marketing managers approve, and then monitor, agreed objectives.'

Bibliography

Cravens, D. and Hills, G. (1970) 'Consumerism: A Perspective for Business', *Business Horizons*, 13, 21–3

Dibb. S., Simkin., L, Pride. W. and Ferrell. O. (2005) *Marketing Concepts and Strategies*, Houghton Mifflin, 4th edition

Drummond, G., Ensor, J. and Ashford, R. (2003) *Strategic Marketing: Planning and Control*, Oxford: Elsevier Butterworth-Heinemann

Hooley, G.J., Saunders, N.A. and Piercy, N.F (1998) *Marketing Strategy and Competitive Positioning*, FT Prentice Hall, 3rd edition

Johnson, G. and Scholes, K. (2005) *Exploring Corporate Strategy*, FT Prentice Hall, 6th edition

Kotler, P., (1995) *Strategic Marketing for Non-Profit Organizations*, Prentice Hall, 5th edition

McWilliams, A. and Siegel, D. (2001) *Academy of Management Review*, 26(1) 117–27

Piercy, N. (2001) *Market-Led Strategic Change*, Oxford: Butterworth-Heinemann

Useful websites include:

www.wnim.com

www.cim.com

www.connectedinmarketing.com

www.mad.com

www.marketresearch.org.uk (useful links on ethics and code of conduct)

Unit 2
The marketing audit

Learning objectives

The main focus of this unit is on the development of the marketing strategy and the overall planning function. The learning outcomes associated with this unit will enable you to:

2.1 Explain the constituents of the macro environmental and micro environmental marketing audit.

2.2 Assess the external marketing environment for an organization through a PESTEL audit.

2.3 Assess the internal marketing environment for an organization through an internal audit.

2.4 Critically appraise processes and techniques used for auditing the marketing environments.

2.5 Explain the role of marketing information and research in conducting and analysing the marketing audit.

This unit will serve to provide you with some of the analytical tools of the trade for ensuring that sufficient analysis is undertaken and then used to underpin the marketing decision-making process and overall strategy development.

Introduction

Having worked through the introductory unit, and the overview of the strategy and planning hierarchy, you should now have a good idea about the importance of marketing planning in giving structure and direction to marketing activities.

Principally, in the words of Dibb *et al.* (2005, p. 715):

> Marketing planning is a systematic process involving the assessment of marketing opportunities and resources, the determination of marketing objectives, and the development of a plan for implementation and control.

Therefore, the overall purpose of the marketing plan is to create a blueprint, a map, which provides detailed requirements of the company's marketing activities for the future. It serves a number of purposes:

◆ It provides a pathway along which a company may travel to reach its ultimate destination.

◆ It provides time-lines for marketing activities to be achieved within, for example 6 months, 12 months and so on.

◆ It enables resources to be allocated efficiently and effectively to ensure that high levels of performance are achieved.

◆ It identifies strengths, weaknesses, opportunities and threats, all of which can be addressed, exploited and improved upon.

◆ It ensures that the organization is marketing-oriented and customer-focused, ideally striving to meet customer needs, wants and expectations.

◆ It may shape the organizational structure in order to achieve the corporate objective and marketing objectives.

◆ It assists in the implementation and control of the marketing strategy.

Planning is fundamental to the successful implementation of strategy and achievement of objectives.

Conducting a marketing audit

The marketing audit is of pivotal importance to the planning process, as it provides the backbone analysis that supports both the corporate and marketing decision-making processes.

Its primary objective is to ensure that the decision-making process is an informed one and that the organization is coming from a position of strength in respect of its knowledge of the marketplace, as opposed to 'planning in a vacuum'.

The audit seeks to provide information on two key aspects of the marketing environment, the external and internal environment, otherwise known as the 'macro' and 'micro' environment (Stages 1 and 2 of Figure 1.3).

Primarily the macro environment will provide information in relation to the external conditions in which the company operates, taking into account the following:

◆ The wider **political/legal** environment, not just on a local basis, but on a global basis. For example, the European Union, World Trade Organization (WTO), G8 countries, organizations such as NAFTA. (These will be addressed again in Unit 9, 'International marketing'.)

◆ Key **economic** factors – understanding key economic drivers that affect organizations' ability to achieve high performance and profitability.

◆ **Social/cultural** issues – this element will concentrate on demographics, population trends, birth rates and life expectancy, changing lifestyles and family life cycles and the changing role of women.

One of the most significant influences on modern marketing is the rapid evolution of new technologies. Technological factors are highly influential in today's environment and they enable high levels of innovation, create factors influencing competitive advantage and have enabled the implementation of more efficient and effective manufacturing processes and a wide range of scientific developments. The most radical change in our time is that of the Internet, the World Wide Web (WWW), the information superhighway, which is rapidly changing the way we all do business, broadening business horizons and opening up new opportunities.

The significance of understanding the macro environment should never be underestimated. Understanding important trends, anticipating change, forecasting the organization's future, measuring the impact of strategies and preparing alternative strategies (contingencies) will all be directed by the outcome of the macro-environmental analysis.

The key words are political/legal, economic, social/cultural, technological – these are the key environmental factors, more formally known as PEST. Other acronyms are used, such as SLEPT. For the purpose of this text we will use PESTEL.

◆   **P**olitical

◆   **E**conomic

◆   **S**ocial

◆   **T**echnological

◆   **E**nvironmental

◆   **L**egal.

No organization should ever underestimate the powerful force of external drivers within the marketplace, as they can ultimately hinder the success and indeed aid the failure of many organizations. Changing trends in the marketplace have often seen the demise of business. Take for example the downturn in electronic communications in 2001 through to 2003. As competition intensified, many major corporations cut jobs in a big way.

A further effect of this downturn in hi-tech industries was that banks were being hit by a meltdown in hi-tech deals. They experienced a devastating slump in business in the early part of 2001 and onwards into 2002, and as a result only 50 per cent of the banking deals normally made were experienced.

However, possibly some of the most devastating events of all time, which had an impact of unprecedented measure, were the attacks of September 11th 2001 and subsequently the tsunami on 26 December 2004. Whilst we can see that economic downturn had a significant impact upon the economy earlier in 2001, the events that took place in the United States did untold damage to many industries and many economies, not least of all the airline industry and the US economy, with tens of thousands of jobs being lost as a result, the impact of which is still being felt. Of course the war in Iraq has had a tremendous effect on world stability, and the impact upon tourism, for example, is a strong case in point. In terms of the tsunami, the impact of this event has devastated tourism in some areas for the foreseeable future, for instance parts of Sri Lanka, Indonesia, Thailand and India – this has an impact on countries all over the world and those organizations which sell holidays to exotic locations such as these.

Thinking back to the effects of September 11th 2001, the ongoing effects of terrorism are quite considerable, with threats against the United Kingdom and the United States continuing. In July 2005 the United Kingdom experienced terrorist attacks in London. Even now, in 2007, in Iraq the condition remains highly unstable, impacting continuously upon the cost of oil and gas supplies.

Again as a result of change in the environment in one industry, a range of industries subsequently have to respond also as the downturn may affect their ability to exploit new opportunities as originally planned.

On the other hand, the 'micro environment' looks at a range of internal factors, which relate to the elements of the internal marketplace. Typically this will look at issues relating to marketing processes, suppliers, customers, competitors, stakeholders, and integral to this, issues relating to resourcing and financing the future marketing activities of the organization.

Should organizations fail to respond to changing marketing conditions, or underestimate the internal infrastructure that may be required to support the changing marketing conditions, then they may further fail to understand the changing needs of customers. In addition, they may also fail to understand their customers' increasing expectations, which ultimately means failure to meet growth and profit-related objectives.

External forces are dynamic, the marketplace is volatile, and changes can be rapid. Today it appears that organizations face new levels of uncertainty, more significant threats, but also major opportunities. The key is being prepared to understand and analyse the market, and indeed respond to key drivers that are forcing such rapid rates of change.

Insight: The changing marketing environment for Castrol Oil

All businesses operate within an environment of change. One of the most important aspects of change is change in the marketplace as customers become more demanding.

Castrol oil recognizes that 'marketing is the process which involves identifying existing customer needs and requirements and with anticipating future changes'. It is therefore a dynamic discipline for Castrol. The marketing environment for most, if not all, products changes regularly. The challenge facing the marketer is, therefore, to find out as much as possible about this changing environment so that the business can respond in an appropriate way. This remains true for any company regardless of the industry, from a bottle of car oil to a fast moving consumer good (FMCG), such as a bar of chocolate or a packet of soap powder.

Because Castrol products are designed to complement high quality engines, the company works closely with Original Engine Manufacturers (OEMs) such as BMW, VW/Audi, Ford, Jaguar and Toyota to develop high quality lubricants that are tailored to meet the requirements of modern engines.

Castrol's marketing research therefore involves finding out detailed information from both the OEMs and motor vehicle users.

The desired result of the research is to produce and supply the best quality high technology oils to meet the needs of modern engines.

The marketing environment in which Castrol operates is constantly changing because:

1   New engines are continually being developed by the engine manufacturers with new specifications and requirements.

2   Government regulations regularly change. For example, in recent years UK and European regulations increasingly require engines to be cleaner and to help create a cleaner environment.

3   The world is becoming wealthier, and increasingly modern consumers require more sophisticated motoring products. More and more consumers are buying more luxurious and sophisticated vehicles. To complement this purchase they require the best quality oils.

Castrol's response to these changes is to provide oils which are technically superior to anything else on the market, and which are market focused.

There are two vital activities, therefore, that an organization should be involved in:

1   Environmental analysis

2   Environmental scanning.

Environmental analysis is the process of analysing, assessing and interpreting information collected through the environmental scanning process.

Environmental scanning is the process of actually collecting the information in order that the organization can understand relevant information in relation to external forces and drivers within the marketplace (see Figure 2.1).

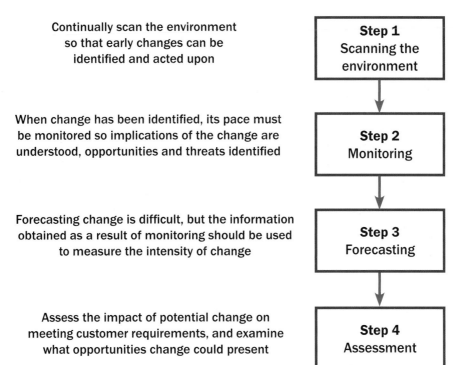

Figure 2.1: Environmental assessment process

Assessing the marketing environment

When undertaking an assessment of the marketing environment, there are critical areas of external information that might be useful to consider.

◆ **Market intelligence** – Looking at change, potential, competitors and associated marketing activities.

◆ **Technical intelligence** – Vital, given the rapid evolution in today's technology. An examination of technological developments that would aid and improve production techniques, increasing quality and efficiency, but also allowing innovation and modernization, is essential.

◆ **Political/economic intelligence** – Looking at political and economic shifts within the external environment.

◆ **Mergers/acquisitions intelligence** – In an era of ever-larger mergers and acquisitions betweens banks, IT organizations, communication networks and so on, it is vital that organizations assess the potential impact and how they might respond to it.

◆ **Supply chain intelligence** – What is the position of the supply chain in terms of supplies of raw materials, available resources and so on.

Assessing the marketing environment is a huge task, but of major importance to the future success of the organization.

Stage 1 – Analysis of the macro environment

In this section you will now be looking at the components of the macro environment and considering in more depth the issues relating to each element of SLEPT.

There are a number of perceived benefits to the organization in undertaking such an activity:

◆ It aids the decision-making process and planning process.

◆ It can provide a sound basis for change and evolution within the organization.

◆ It provides a clear analysis of competitive activities and an understanding of related market share.

◆ It enables organizations to anticipate the opportunities that change in the external environment might present.

◆ Organizations may become more aware of emerging trends and opportunities in international markets that it may be appropriate to pursue.

◆ Organizations may, as a result of the changing external environment, need to consider their resources, both financial and physical, in order that they may implement relevant change strategies.

◆ It enables organizations both to foresee and consider the implications of environmental, regulatory and political changes, and to manage the implementation of such changes successfully.

◆ It can assist organizations in forecasting potential supply and demand from the open market and from their supply chain.

The list could go on. What is important, however, is that understanding the key components of PESTEL is essential to an organization if it is to cope with change and, most important, respond to it.

Political

The twenty-first century is experiencing a new kind of political power that is very broad and very diverse. With increasing moves towards emphasis on globalization, there is more and more influence from global politics and international driving forces. Both national and international governments are increasing their political weight, enforcing greater regulation of a range of industry sectors, in order that customers and organizations alike are protected from irregularities that can bring organizations into disrepute.

Political initiatives at both home and abroad can create many opportunities, while also generating many threats into the political scene. There are political agendas in all areas of business; there is political influence in agriculture, mining and fuels, to name but a few.

Key issues might include:

◆   Increases in taxation, reducing disposable income
◆   Environmental protection (a social and political issue)
◆   Employment law
◆   Health and safety
◆   Foreign trade agreements
◆   Stability of political systems (e.g. Middle East).

Political factors can also often impact in a cyclical manner, and the cause-and-effect scenario sees political influences cross-fertilizing with other elements of the external market analysis.

Economic

One of the key influences in any organization is the state of both the local economy and the global economy. There has been talk of economic slowdown in the United States and its potential to create a spiralling effect on economies all over the world. Historically, economic indicators have provided a basis for business cycles to move on to the next stage, effectively 'boom' or 'bust' (Figure 2.2). Obviously, the impact of September 11 is a classic example of how economic indicators can be affected by world events.

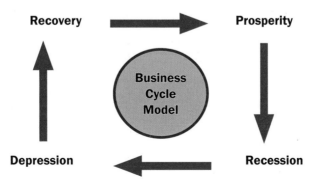

Figure 2.2: Business cycle model

Key component measures of the economy are as follows:

◆ Inflation rates

◆ Interest rates

◆ Income levels

◆ Resources

◆ Gross National Product

◆ Gross Domestic Product

◆ Employment levels

◆ Exchange rates – currency valuation

◆ Consumer spending patterns.

As a marketer, it is important to understand economic factors and indicators and also how to use the information to aid your marketing decision-making and planning process.

For example, if there is a fluctuation in interest rates, then it is likely that your organization may be involved in considering increases in costs. Essentially this is like 'cause and effect'; as the interest rate rises, there will be a cyclical effect in the marketplace. The cost of living increases, the cost of borrowing increases and, therefore, the likelihood is that availability of disposable income may drop, reducing consumer spending considerably and thereby influencing a slowdown in market activity.

From the perspective of a marketer it is important to consider closely how to manage this particular element of economic change. You will be encouraged to consider how long it might take for the impact of an interest rate rise to filter through to organizational activity, how long the anticipated rise in interest rates is likely to last, and what might be the competitive responses to this economic change. Furthermore, you need to think about what the consumer response will be to this change and ultimately what it will do to consumer spending power.

The whole area of economic pressure and power is complex, but crucial to understanding the power of buyers and suppliers in the marketplace.

Social

Understanding the social influences and implications on the marketing environment is of utmost importance, as organizations need to respond to the social infrastructure of their marketplace.

Social factors include issues such as:

◆ **Demography** – The characteristics of customers, age, sex, class, family life cycle and so on, trends in age distribution.

◆ **Society** – This reflects upon the infrastructure of society and its attitude towards many issues, that is religion, culture, families, the environment, green and ethical issues. (This will also be looked at under 'Environmental'.)

Question 2.1

The population trends for the older generation, 'the grey market', are clearly highlighting that people are living much longer. What potential opportunities could this present to you, as marketing manager for a healthcare products manufacturer?

For example, there has been a serious decline in churchgoing in the United Kingdom, which would suggest the demise of the Anglican Church by the middle of this century. There are now fewer 19-year-olds going to church than at any time previously.

In response to the 'Green Issue', vehicle manufacturers such as BMW have been stressing the suitability of their 3 series range for recycling, making them more environmentally friendly cars. This was in response to potential EU legislation that would likely have enforced the recycling of vehicles. BMW responded to this and now has 30 partner recycling plants worldwide. In doing this they have responded to the growing social and environmental awareness of their customers.

Today we find ourselves subject to lively debate and forceful demonstrations about environmental issues. There is an increasing choir of consumer voices raising the stakes in respect of environmentally friendly practices. As there is growing social concern for the environment, the impact of which could be quite major to industry practices today and ultimately upon organizational profitability in the future, organizations are being faced with change programmes as never before. The significance of understanding consumer power, customer needs and wants is critical to organizational success, and therefore failure to react to the outcomes can have a high profile and catastrophic implications in the future.

◆   **Culture** – The range of variables relating to culture is extensive, and will be covered in more depth in Unit 9, 'International marketing', but they include the following:

- ◆   Language
- ◆   Religion
- ◆   Values and attitudes
- ◆   Law
- ◆   Healthcare
- ◆   Education
- ◆   Social organization.

This is possibly the most complex area of analysis that an organization might involve itself in. Values and norms will vary greatly from country to country, and will reflect different social divides.

For an organization involved in exploiting international marketing opportunities this is important to understand, as on occasions significant mistakes have been made by large organizations as a result of their lack of appreciation of the underpinning culture of their host nation.

Technological

Technology has evolved rapidly over the past 20 years and particularly in the past 10 years. Technological developments have seen improved manufacturing techniques, new and dynamic innovations and increases in efficiency and effectiveness in a way never previously imagined.

However, marketers need to understand the drive for technological change, and the need to go with the flow, to remain competitive. Decisions to improve, change or implement new technological processes must be made in order to meet customer needs and expectations. Principally, if there is a cost-effective method or process that could improve customer service and increase efficiency and effectiveness and add to the bottom line financially, then it should be the focus of serious research and development, in order to pursue the opportunity that technological advances might present.

External or 'macro' market analysis is vitally important to the development of any marketing strategy and associated plan. As a marketer engaged in operational level marketing, you may find yourself very involved in collating much of the intelligence gathered, in order that the decision-making process may be fully informed and responsive to the challenges of the external marketing environment. It will be important to call on previous knowledge gained through Marketing Research and Information, in order that you fully understand the challenges of market scanning and intelligence gathering.

While on occasions you may collect information specifically related to developing strategies and plans, it is equally important to continue scanning the external environment, in order that change may be detected and subsequently responded to in a proactive rather than in a reactive way.

As you move on through your studies, and upwards to the Postgraduate Diploma, you will be well placed to consider the strategic implications of environmental change and how it could impact upon the strategic planning process in the future.

Environmental

The world is currently in an age where there is growing industrial wastage, discharge of effluent, emissions of fumes and acid rain, all of which have to be taken seriously by manufacturers. Due to the high level of industrialization in the modern world, the environment is under constant threat from global warming. In recent times we have experienced severe weather effects, such as heavy rain, gales and significant flooding. All of this relates to environmentalism and as such means that organizations must in the future consider their strategy in relation to these issues.

There are many organizations whose role is to dispose of atomic waste. Organizations such as Nirex are continually subject to heavy criticism by environment groups such as the Green Party and the press. Their contact with the consumer is minimal; they deal with industry, hence they are little influenced by the consumer.

However, organizations need to become increasingly aware of their environmental responsibilities and aim to ensure that inherent within their corporate mission, vision and strategy, is the need to be environmentally aware. They should position environmentalism as a principle that should be embedded within their overall CSR.

Legal

In a culture bound by regulatory bodies, legal restraints and an increasing role played by European and international legislation, organizations will clearly need to understand the legislative nature of their own marketing environment and abide by it.

Every organization is bound by controls. For example, there are regulations concerning:

◆   Monopolies and mergers

◆   Competitive activities

◆   Unfair trading

◆   Consumer legislation

◆   Trade descriptions

◆   Health and safety

◆   Professional codes of conduct (for example, the Chartered Institute of Marketing).

Sustainability

Inherent within all of the PESTEL factors is the up and coming theme of 'sustainability. Sustainability has many hundreds of definitions as organizations seek to define its meaning for them now and in the future.

Definition

Sustainability – an attempt to provide the best outcomes for the human and natural environments now and into the indefinite future. It relates to the continuity of economic, social, institutional and environmental aspects of human society, as well as the non-human environment. It is intended to be a means of configuring civilization and human activity so that society, its members and its economies are able to meet their needs and express their greatest potential in the present, while preserving biodiversity and natural ecosystems, and planning and acting for the ability to maintain these ideals in a very long term. Sustainability affects every level of organization, from the local neighborhood to the entire planet. (www.en.wikipedia.org/wiki/Sustainability)

Throughout any analysis of PESTEL in the future needs to be an awareness and indeed on the factors associated with sustainability and how organizations can develop business in a more sustainable way. If you recall in Unit 1, Marks and Spencer were introducing a major strategy designed to enhance sustainability of its business in the future.

You will notice that the definition includes references to economic, social and environmental aspects of society. It suggests that organizations should be considering the way in which they do business in the future in order that they preserve natural resources, reduce waste, be more efficient with production and ensure that eonomically the practices sustain the business and its locality.

It is a critical issue and marketers must be aware at every level within the organization how to both undertake sustainable practices, but look for ideas of introducing a more sustainable marketing mix. Again taking Marks and Spencer as an example, they intend to use more environmentally friendly resources, practices, using local produce, reducing waste and the distance all of its products have to travel. All of this contribute significantly.

Often we say of the external environment that is is uncontrollable, that we have to go and respond to the dynamics, this is a case in point. We have no choice if the world's energy and resource reserves are to be sustained, for the future of quality of life, changes must be personal and organizational.

Stage 2 – Analysis of the micro environment

Analysis of the 'micro' environment is equally important. As a marketing manager you must clearly understand the issues relating specifically to your organization.

For example, you will need to consider the following components:

◆   Sales

◆   Market share

◆   Marketing procedures

◆   Profit margins

◆   Sales/marketing controls

◆   Marketing mix

◆   Number of employees

◆   Financial resources

◆   Physical resources

◆   Production – capacity and variety.

Each of these factors will in some way affect the organization's overall achievements in terms of the key marketing objectives of meeting both the needs of customers and the organization's profit requirements. In turn this results in the undertaking of an 'internal audit'.

A more simplistic approach to this analysis will be to break it down into the following five key elements:

1   Business

2   Competitors

3   Suppliers

4   Customers

5   Stakeholders.

Business/marketing function – internal audit

When developing marketing strategies and devising marketing plans, organizations need to consider very closely the internal prerequisites for success.

In this instance, it is essential that organizations develop a strategy that primarily meets the needs, wants and expectations of their customers. They also need to have the resources and infrastructure within the organization to deliver their promises and meet their corporate and marketing objectives.

Ultimately, a culture appropriate to customer demands must be in place, that is a marketing-oriented customer-focused culture, with the customer at the centre of the business.

In doing this, serious consideration should also be given to the 'internal' customer. When a newly devised strategy indicates significant change, then the reactions, attitudes and abilities of the workforce must be considered, managed and adapted to meet the overall objectives of the organization.

To achieve this, a tightly defined strategy must be designed, which ensures that management, research and development, production, logistics, physical and financial resources are working to the same end and 'synergy' must be prevalent in the planning process. Without the appropriate mix of resources across the organizational business functions, the corporate goals may not be achieved.

Therefore analysis of each of these functions should be considered. Undertaking a company capability profile is therefore of the essence.

A full audit should be undertaken, with consideration being given to the following factors:

Managerial factors

♦ Corporate image
♦ Speed of response to changing conditions
♦ Flexibility of the organization
♦ Entrepreneurial orientation
♦ Ability to attract and retain highly creative people
♦ Aggressiveness in meeting competition.

Competitive factors

♦ Product strengths
♦ Customer loyalty and satisfaction
♦ Market share
♦ Use of the life cycle
♦ Investment in R&D
♦ High barriers to market entry
♦ Advantage taken of market potential
♦ Customer concentration
♦ Low selling and distribution costs.

Financial factors

♦ Access to capital when required
♦ Ease of exit from the market
♦ Liquidity
♦ Degree of financial leverage
♦ Ability to compete on prices
♦ Capital investment versus capacity to meet demand
♦ Stability of costs

- ♦   Ability to sustain effort in cyclic demand
- ♦   Elasticity of price.

Technical factors

- ♦   Technical and manufacturing skills
- ♦   Resource and personnel utilization
- ♦   Strength of patents and processes
- ♦   Value added to product
- ♦   Intensity of labour to produce product
- ♦   Economies of scale
- ♦   Newness of plan
- ♦   Application of new technologies
- ♦   Level of co-ordination and integration.

One way of undertaking this form of analysis is grading these areas from 1 to 5, with 1 being weak and 5 being strong. Clearly any element that falls under the level of 3 requires urgent attention, while factors above 3 demonstrate room for continuous improvement.

This type of analysis is vital to the success of organizations and will ultimately enable you to identify key strengths and weaknesses, opportunities and threats within your own environment.

It is of primary importance to undertake an 'audit' of the actual 'audit process' itself, the marketing objectives and plans and the overall marketing activity including the effective integration of the marketing mix.

Marketing managers will have some responsibility for adopting existing practices and modifying plans, in order that these factors are taken into consideration at the implementation stage.

Competitors

Definition

Competition – Those companies marketing products that are similar to, or can be substituted for, a given business's products in the same geographic area (Dibb *et al.*, 2001, p. 56).

Very few, if any, organizations exist in isolation of competition. You have already seen, earlier in this unit, some of the effects of competition in relation to the high-tech electronics industries, where as a result of intense competition, profits have declined, resulting in massive job cuts across the industry as a whole.

As a marketing manager, to truly ascertain the full force of the external environment, you must consider the influence of competitive forces upon the external marketplace and your own organization. Therefore a competitor analysis is essential.

There are many components to competitive activity, and in marketing terms, competitive strategies can be quite ferocious attack. From a strategy development perspective you will probably be familiar with terms as 'guerrilla attacks' and 'offensive attacks', which indicate some of the fighting talk that underpins competitive behaviour.

In order that your organization can respond to competitor attacks, you must be familiar with the profile of your competitors and therefore must analyse their activities and behaviour quite closely.

Ultimately, competitor attacks can provide the basis of significant threats to the successful implementation of the corporate and marketing strategy.

Typical competitor analysis should include a review of the following elements:

◆ Marketing capabilities

◆ Technical capabilities

◆ Management capabilities

◆ Production capabilities

◆ Innovation and design capabilities.

Clearly you will need to align your own strengths and weaknesses against those of your competitors in order to identify areas of improvement in your own organization.

One of the key tools for undertaking this is a Company capability profile, as previously discussed. You could do this by undertaking a SWOT analysis on your competitor. This is covered in more detail shortly, but as you will see when looking at it, there are possibilities of mapping your own capability against that of your competitors. You could potentially grade each of the components within an element and then grade your own organization against it. Not only would this provide you with a basis of understanding your competitor, but also it would highlight any opportunities to exploit their weaknesses and attack their strengths.

The main focus of most competitive attacks is on price. Competitive warfare today is most prevalent in the retail sector, with intense competition between supermarkets, making high profile headlines on a regular basis. A further example is financial services, where competition in respect of services and products offered continues to intensify on a day-to-day basis.

Porter's Five Forces – competitive analysis

It is imperative for you as a marketer to have a clear understanding not just of your competitor, but of the nature of the competitive environment, particularly if you are to succeed in developing a sustainable competitive advantage and be able to respond from a position of strength to competitor attacks. The objectives of any organization will relate closely to profit margins, increasing market share, diversification or market penetration. In order that an organization can define the future direction of its corporate and marketing strategy, it is of primary importance that it should consider the nature of the driving forces within the marketplace so as to understand exactly what is shaping the industry. Therefore when undertaking a micro analysis it is important to consider the components of Porter's forces and understand either the potential threats from within the marketplace, or the profit potential of the industry.

Porter's Five Forces model (Figure 2.3) will be particularly helpful when undertaking a competitor analysis within the existing marketing environment. It provides a framework for an analysis of a range of micro-factors, which enables industry attractiveness to be measured and helps organizations understand the complexity of the markets in which they operate.

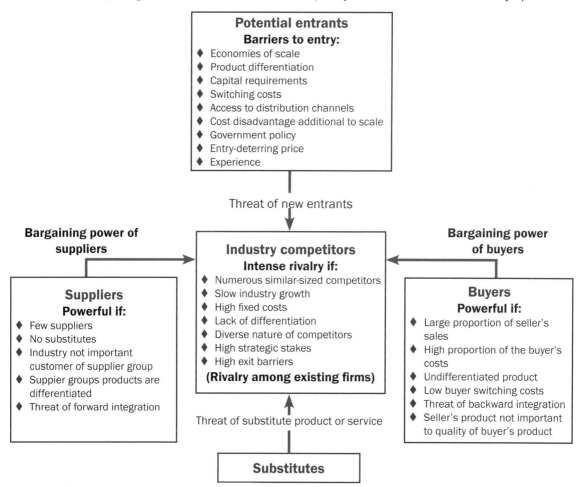

Figure 2.3: The Five Forces model. Adapted from: Porter (1980)

The threat of competitive rivalry

Competitive rivalry within the marketplace is highly intense. Intense competition has, over the years, changed the shape of a number of industries, and as a result there have been an increasing number of mergers and acquisitions to ensure that major players within the marketplace maintain market share and superior positioning. This has been particularly prevalent in the financial services sectors, with a number of mergers between key players in the banking sector, for example Royal Bank of Scotland and the Halifax.

We have already seen that competition can take various shapes. Competition can be cut-throat, with ongoing price wars, as have been experienced in recent years in the food retail industry, while at the other end of the scale, competition can appear to be non-existent. However, while rivalry might seem healthy, it can have both positive and negative effects.

Organizations who succeed in competition, possibly increasing market share, through a range of activities, potentially experience a rise in profit. However, the reverse may happen; the organization might increase market share, but at the expense of their profit margins.

Key factors influencing competitive rivalry will be identified when undertaking the competitor analysis as already suggested, but key components might be:

◆ Stage of the product life cycle (PLC) of competing products

◆ Use of specialized production techniques

◆ Liquidity of competitor

◆ Ability to achieve differentiation and brand loyalty

◆ Competitor intentions

◆ The relative size of the competitor

◆ Barrier of exit from the industry.

Understanding the balance of various forces is critical to ensuring that the organization makes the correct competitive response.

Bargaining power of suppliers

The key components of this particular element of Porter's Five Forces emphasize the following key points:

◆ **The strength of the supplier brand** – Is it a brand that all organizations will want to exploit, and will this therefore increase the price of supplies?

◆ **The source of supply spans only a small number of suppliers** – Limited sources provide the supplier with a supply and demand component in their favour: the more limited the demand, the higher the price they can charge.

◆ **Switching supplier** – The cost of switching suppliers can be quite high: negotiation of new contracts, establishing relationships and developing trust all cost time and resource. This can act as a deterrent to many organizations, who will want to retain their relationship with their supplier.

◆ **Substitute products of suppliers** – Are appropriate substitute products available?

◆ **Forward integration** – Is there a threat of suppliers establishing their own production facilities?

Bargaining power of buyers

The bargaining power of buyers is likely to be quite strong in the following instances:

◆ **Where few buyers control a large volume of the market** – A good example of this might be that larger players in the electrical goods industry can buy large volumes based on economies of scale and can pass these reductions on to their customers.

◆ **Where there are a large number of smaller suppliers fighting for a share of the market** – Again the retail industry would be a classic example of this, particularly in the food sector, that is grocery and meat products.

◆ **The cost of switching supplier is low** – The retail sector and high street are a good example of how customers who are not brand loyal will swap around to gain the best deal. This can happen where the relationship between customer and supplier is not based upon loyalty.

◆ **The supplier's product is a mass-market product and not necessarily differenti-ated** – for example where there are many variations on the same theme, such as toothpaste, soft drinks and so on.

◆ **Strong customer power** – This involves knowledge of the market and where to at-tain the best deal.

◆ **Threat of backward vertical integration** – Where the buyer goes back to the sup-plier, cutting out the middle man.

The threat for potential entrants

This issue looks at the obstacles to entering new markets:

◆ **Economies of scale** – Existing organizations often have economies of scale and therefore new entrants will struggle to achieve the same competitive economies in the short/medium term.

◆ **Access to new distribution channels** – It may be difficult to gain access to the ap-propriate distribution channels, due to competitive operations and networks in the marketplace.

◆ **Brand loyalty** – In a brand-loyal market it might be difficult to attract new customers and therefore marketing spend could be quite considerable.

◆ **Capital investment** – It can be cash intensive to enter into new markets and re-quire high levels of investment – from a competitive perspective, this would actually weaken your initial position, unless you are a cash-rich organization.

◆ **Competitor retaliation** – It is likely that competitors will follow suit quite closely behind, therefore competitive rivalry could be highly intensive.

◆ **Regulatory influence** – What is the position in respect of fair competition, monopo-lies and mergers. The case of Microsoft is a clear example of trying to prevent com-petitive rivalry.

Threat of substitutes

◆ **A new product or service equivalent** – A directly equivalent product, from a differ-ing brand, may have a competitive influence. This is typical of the evolution of 'home brands', for example supermarket brands as a substitute in soft drinks, breakfast cereals and so on.

◆ **A new product replacing an existing product** – For example, DVD players replacing VHS video players,or cassette tapes being replaced by compact discs.

◆ **Consumer substitution** – Consumer choice can be the basis of a threat, when the consumer is willing to search for substitute products; for example, when the con-sumer chooses a new kitchen over a new car.

Essentially the Porter framework is an opportunity for the organization to understand the holistic range of driving forces in the micro environment, which they can clearly link to the macro analysis, that is the SLEPT/PEST analysis.

From an audit perspective, whereby information is being collected in order that key mar-keting decisions are made and strategies developed, it will enable the organization to consider ultimately the following factors, that will in turn enable a full SWOT analysis to be developed, to inform the strategy development process.

◆ What is the likelihood of change in the marketplace, both on a macro and micro scale, and what is driving that particular change?

◆ What is the likely response that the organization can make, in order to retain sustainable competitive advantage in the marketplace – how can they develop their weaknesses and turn them into strengths and their threats into opportunity? Ultimately what is their competitive response likely to be?

◆ What is the likely response of their competitor in the marketplace – how are the driving forces affecting them, what might be their likely approach – what might it do to their competitive positioning overall?

As a marketer you must consider what the likely response of your organization might be – will it be certain retaliation – will you compete on an aggressive basis. If so what is the likely challenge that you will be presented with?

A further consideration will be what will happen if you fail to act, fail to compete aggressively. What will it do to your market share, your customer base? Will you see a loss of long-term customer relationships, will your brand loyalty be challenged, will your bottom line be challenged?

Reacting competitively does not just mean reducing prices or increasing sales promotions, it means looking at the bigger picture of increased marketing budget, diversification, new product strategies, to name but a few. The biggest failing of many organizations is to attack what is an overt competitive hit by competitors, but to continue blissfully unaware of the competitive activity that is being orchestrated behind closed doors. This will then hit the organization from behind, it will not be ready for the attack, and will then have to develop a reactive marketing approach, as opposed to a pre-emptive marketing strike.

Failure to observe competitive actions will mean inconsistency in competitor attack. Losing sight of the competitor will give them a position of strength and they will ultimately be unpredictable, preventing a continuous competitive reaction from your organization.

Finally, organizations should never be complacent, and as a marketing manager, you should not be lulled into a false sense of security by the continuous monitoring of existing competition. All organizations, without exception, should also be on the look out for new entrants to the markets, who could potentially offer a competitive proposition with the development of the same or substitute products. Competitive monitoring in line with environmental scanning are critical components of a successful marketing-oriented organization.

Suppliers

Supplier relationships are a further critical component to the success of any organization. It is of primary importance to many organizations to ensure consistent supplies flowing through in order to meet consistent demand for their products. Therefore, supplier analysis is vital.

This should include a review of the following:

◆ The basis of the supplier relationship

◆ The supply and demand components of raw materials

- ◆ Supplier innovations

- ◆ The relationship suppliers have with competitors

- ◆ Supply record – that is, ability to deliver and meet demand on an ongoing basis

- ◆ Liquidity and financial stability

- ◆ Costs

- ◆ Quality

- ◆ Warranty provision

- ◆ Supply trends

- ◆ Any potential change to the supply environment – new entrants.

There is more discussion of supplier relationships in Unit 8, 'Managing marketing relationships'.

Customers

As already indicated, customers should be at the centre of any business. Organizations should be customer-focused, meeting customer needs and managing to deal with the evolution of ever-increasing customer power.

It is essential that customers are analysed; we must know who they are, where they are, what they are, what they want, when and how they want it. The sole focus of the marketing effort should be based around meeting customer expectations, the idea being that as an organization you can provide the right product, at the right price, communicated through the right medium and distributed to the right place at the right time.

While undertaking the Professional Diploma in Marketing, your studies will cover other modules, including 'Market research and information'. Here you will look very closely at the concept of using information about your customers to support the marketing decision-making process. 'Marketing communications' will focus very much on the psychology of the customer, buyer behaviour, the necessity to understand the strategic importance of the customer, marketing segmentation and market research. Both these modules will underpin the analysis of customers and their buying behaviour.

The important aspect of understanding customers is being able to respond and react and to remain competitive for them, in order that you retain them as customers in the long term.

Ultimately, once customers have been segmented into particular market groups, then they can be targeted with a tailored marketing mix that meets their individual demands.

Once again this will require marketers to ensure that the infrastructure of human, physical and financial resources is in place to underpin the customer experience.

Stakeholders

The role of stakeholders in any organization seems to have an increasing influence on the way in which organizations can do business. For example, environmental pressure groups actually strive to influence the future direction of an organization overall. Stakeholders include:

◆ Customers

◆ Suppliers

◆ Shareholders

◆ Employees

◆ Financiers

◆ Wider social community (including pressure groups).

Stakeholder influences and expectation should be understood. In the Exxon case, it would appear that they might have underestimated the potential power of the 'wider social community' and the pressure that they may bring to bear upon the organization. It is vital that the organization understands the balance of power and influence that various stakeholders might have.

For example, in many organizations, shareholders play a vital role in the decision-making process. Mergers and takeovers can be reliant on the vote of the shareholders for the planned changes to succeed.

In order that your organization can provide the basis for strong relationships with stakeholders, it is necessary to understand the balance of power that they hold so that appropriate marketing mix strategies and indeed marketing communications strategies can be developed to keep them informed of the proposed changes. Effectively, you will need to know how influential they are and how controllable they are.

For both the 'macro' and 'micro' environments, analysis is essential, as is monitoring and reacting to changes. It is important that organizations are not just reactive, but that they are proactive, managing the components in the 'micro' environment, to provide the basic infrastructure to meet the demands of their customers and the marketing environment.

There is a key marketing tool that we can use to help us bring the main elements and components of the marketing analysis together. It is commonly known as the SWOT analysis.

SWOT analysis

A SWOT analysis draws together key strengths, weaknesses, opportunities and threats that have been highlighted as a result of the marketing audit, that is the 'macro' and 'micro' analysis and assessment.

SWOT, alternatively known as 'WOTS-UP' analysis, is an important tool in enabling organizations to distil the findings of the audit into a more cohesive and succinct model. It is essential that it is used for this purpose and that it is seen as an addition to the marketing audit, not a replacement (Figure 2.4).

Figure 2.4 highlights some of the issues that you might include within a SWOT analysis and that might have been derived from the marketing audit.

The aim of the SWOT process is to enable you to convert weaknesses into strengths and threats into opportunities, by taking remedial action to improve existing situations and plan a programme of ongoing continuous change. Where an organization is weak in respect of a skilled workforce then it is essential that training is identified as a key objective of the internal marketing strategy and that this is underpinned by financial investment and resource.

When undertaking a SWOT analysis, you should also be aware of the differences between controllable and uncontrollable. Essentially the controllable areas are those relating to internal issues. By and large your organization does have control on 'micro' issues relating to technology, skills, investment, resources, innovations, morale, motivation and so on.

External factors, however, are often uncontrollable, and while you might be able to influence their outcomes you will not be able to control them. When establishing future opportunities and how to improve upon weaknesses, you will be required to work on the controllable variables, that is that which you can change.

It is, however, essential to realize that an organization cannot aim to address all of the issues raised within the SWOT analysis and must ideally prioritize the issues appropriately. The SWOT analysis should be used to distil the critical factors that have been identified during the auditing process. Essentially it acts as a summary of the audit and not a replacement for it. Therefore the analysis should aim to identify highly critical areas, in order to focus attention on them during strategy development.

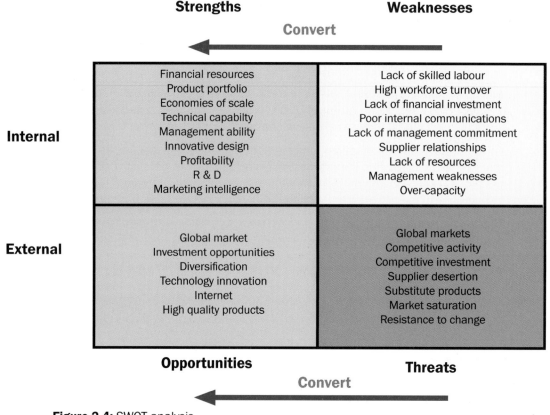

Figure 2.4: SWOT analysis

Question 2.2

Undertake a SWOT analysis for your own organization or one you know well, highlighting the key components of each element. Suggest how you might turn weaknesses into strengths and how you could potentially reduce the threats that affect your organization.

A marketer's responsibility might be to ensure that scanning and monitoring of the environment is constant and undertaken regularly. In turn, the outcomes should be used to maximize the potential of the marketing programme and adaptation of the marketing mix should be undertaken. Furthermore, remedial actions have to be taken to overcome any areas of weakness identified that may ultimately affect the bottom line of the organization.

The marketing audit should not be ad hoc, but planned, co-ordinated, structured and predetermined in nature, context and content. Without key objectives, and a planned approach taken, the marketing audit could be too extensive, too complex and ultimately meaningless, and therefore wasteful in the extreme. The marketing audit process can be costly and therefore a structured approach is essential.

Identifying key opportunities

Having undertaken the planned and objective audit process, you should now be armed with considerable information that will assist you in establishing the potential marketing strategy for the organization to pursue. A marketing opportunity provides the organization with the opening to venture into new territory, perhaps a new target market, or diversification opportunity, or indeed the opportunity to launch a new product into the marketplace.

The Ansoff matrix (Figure 2.5) provides an opportunity for an organization to think creatively about its future, about how it can take a strength and make it a key success factor or driving force for a successful outcome in the marketplace. Principally the Ansoff matrix allows you to consider a range of four strategic options:

1   Product development

2   Market development

3   Diversification

4   Market penetration.

The Easy Group started off with the core activity of providing low-cost flights into Europe. This is its core business, and with over 18 million passengers a year flying easyJet, the Easy Group needed to establish alternative options in order that the business could grow and expand.

The Easy Group has taken a threefold route. While continuing with penetrating the existing air transport market with low-cost flights, it is also developing the market potential to include greater accessibility of easyJet flights by increasing the number of airports handling easyJet passengers.

While flights are the core business of the Easy Group, a complementary diversification programme has been entered into, in order that a 'travel solutions' package is made available to meet the whole range of customer needs and expectations of both frequent and holiday travellers. The travel solutions business is aimed at both the corporate and the consumer sectors of the business.

You can see here that taking the key strengths and opportunities available to it, the Easy Group has established a further growth strategy, which includes further market penetration, market development and diversification into new, but compatible areas of the business. In addition to this, easyJet announced in 2006, the increase of is airline fleet by 2010, providing greater customer flexibility, safety, sustainable business practices, and increase travel destinations.

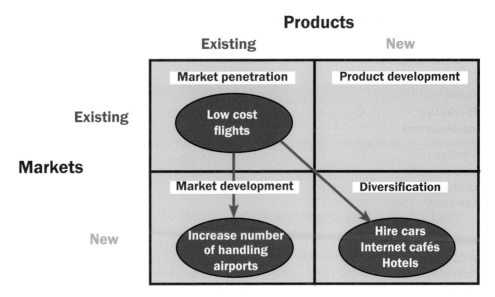

Figure 2.5: Ansoff matrix – 'easy everything' (easyJet)

It is important to consider the basis of Ansoff at this point, by way of illustrating how you can identify core strengths and opportunities and then develop them into potential strategies. However, we will return to this in Unit 3 as we consider the process of developing marketing objectives and strategies and ultimately defining the strategy and developing the plan to underpin overall achievement of objectives.

The role of marketing information in the planning process

For an organization to implement the marketing concept successfully and take a marketing- and customer-oriented approach to its decision-making, one of the first things it should be doing is to find out as much information as possible about its various customers and markets, both macro and micro. It should identify what they need, what they want, what their characteristics are, their buying power and indeed their willingness to buy. In effect, marketing research provides a useful link between the supplier and the customers.

Without information, organizations are operating in a vacuum; they are making decisions in an uninformed way and ultimately that holds a serious risk to them, that they may not meet their customers' expectations.

Furthermore, as you saw in Unit 1, the world is a volatile place, economically, socially and politically. Organizations have a duty to understand the environment in which they operate. They cannot and should not be insulated from it, but rather be able to respond to it when the time is right. Hence the necessity for scenario building and planning.

For organizations to make informed decisions about future plans, in terms of new market opportunities, international growth, new product development, change of systems and processes, new integrative communications strategies, new technologies and so on, they need information. Accurate and targeted information will enable the right decisions to be made and the right markets to be targeted in an appropriate way. In doing this it is likely that the information will serve to provide an understanding of what customer needs are and how customer needs can service the organization's needs for profit and growth.

Table 2.1 identifies the types of information you need in respect of the marketing environment, competition and indeed the marketing mix, which will in turn enable more informed decisions in relation to the planning process to be made.

Table 2.1: The task of market research – what should it determine?

Marketing environment	Competition	Product	Marketing mix	Firm-specific historical data
Political context: leaders, national goals, ideology, key institutions	Relative market shares, new product moves	Analysis of users: Who are the end-user industries?	Channels of distribution: evolution and performance	Sales trends by product and product-line, salesforce and customer
Economic growth prospects, business cycle stage	Pricing and cost structure, image and brand reputation	Industrial and consumer buyers; characteristics: size, age, sex, segment growth rates	Relative pricing, elasticities and tactics	Trends by country and region
Per capita income levels, purchasing power	Quality: its attributes and positioning relative to competitors	Purchasing power and intentions	Advertising and promotion: choices and impacts on customers	Contribution margins
End-user industry growth trends	Competitors' strengths: favourite tactics and strategies	Customer response to new products, price, promotion	Service quality: perceptions and relative positioning	Marketing mix used, marketing response functions across countries and regions
Government: legislation, regulation, standards, barriers to trade		Switching behaviour, role of credit and purchasing, future needs, impact of cultural differences	Logistics networks, configuration and change	

Adapted from: Terpstra and Sarathy (1999)

While the research needs to focus on the environment, and the customer, it also needs to focus on the necessary adaptations that might be required to the marketing mix. Therefore, it will be necessary to involve the organization in research that will ascertain the position of the product, and its appropriateness for the market, the threshold for pricing and market sensitivity and the most appropriate distribution channels.

Developing a marketing information system

A typical marketing information system (MIS) would potentially look very similar to the one in Figure 2.6, and is something that you will concentrate on in the early part of your studies in Market Research and Information.

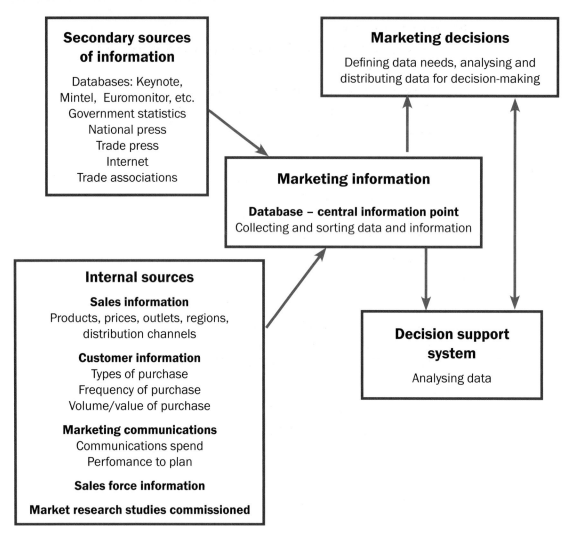

Figure 2.6: Marketing information system framework. After Brassington and Pettitt (2000)

Areas for research and information

Below is a more detailed overview of some subject areas that are researched by many organizations, as identified by Adcock *et al.*in *Marketing – Principles and Practice* (1995). This of course will feed into the grid system in the model above.

1   **Research on markets**

   a) Estimating market size

   b) Estimating/studying marketing trends

   c) Defining customer/user characteristics

   d) Defining characteristics of product markets

   e) Analysing sales potential

   f) Analysing market potentials for existing products

   g) Estimating demand for new products

   h) Sales forecasting.

2   **Research on products**

    a) Studying customer satisfaction/dissatisfaction with products

    b) Comparative studies with competitive products

    c) Determining uses for present products

    d) Customer acceptance of proposed new products

    e) Packaging and design studies.

3   **Research on promotion**

    a) Analysing advertising and selling practices

    b) Selecting advertising media

    c) Evaluating advertising effectiveness

    d) Establishing sales effectiveness

    e) Motivational studies.

4   **Research on distribution**

    a) Location and design of distribution centres

    b) Handling and packaging merchandise

    c) Cost-effectiveness of transportation

    d) Dealer supply and storage requirements.

5   **Research on pricing**

    a) Studying competitive pricing

    b) Measuring customer demand

    c) Cost analysis

    d) Pricing strategies.

6   **Research on sales**

    a) Sales per geographical area

    b) Sales per salesperson

    c) Sales per product

    d) Quarterly sales figures

    e) Repeat purchase sales figures.

Marketing research provides a useful link between the supplier and the customer by keeping up to date with customer needs and wants.

Summary

It is important to undertake a thorough, structured and objective marketing audit, in order to understand the marketing environment in which your organization operates.

Both macro and micro factors must be analysed and a clearly defined strategy developed based on sound management information. This will allow reliable forecasts to be derived that represent anticipated market share and future potential sales.

While it is essential to understand the macro environment, the micro environmental issues must be addressed so that an organization is well poised to respond to changing market conditions. An organization should analyse in depth the issues related to their internal relationships, and customer, supplier and stakeholder relationships, and ultimately must be prepared for the demands that each might place upon it.

The organization must have the capacity to respond to the driving force of change, by creating an appropriate infrastructure, based on highly skilled employees, appropriate levels of financial investment, adequate resources and technological soundness, ultimately ensuring that the customer is at the centre of the business and that the organization is marketing-oriented and customer-focused.

The marketing audit is a vital ingredient of the overall strategy and planning hierarchy and a process that organizations must successfully develop to underpin the corporate objectives and goals.

Study tip

Go to the December 2005 Examination Paper and answer Question 2(a) – this is about assessing the potential impact of the wider macro-environmental forces. Also go to June 2006 and undertake Question 1 (a) of the case study, which considers the context of an external marketing audit, including the key issues currently facing the Liverpool John Lennon Airport. Go to www.cim.co.uk to review the specimen answers.

Bibliography

Adcock,D., Bradfield,R., Halborg, A. and Ross, C. (1995) *Marketing: Principles and Practice* Prentice-Hall

Brassington. F and Pettitt. S (2000), *Principles of Marketing*, FT/Prentice Hall

Dibb, S., Simkin, L., Pride, W. and Ferrell, O. (2005) *Marketing: Concepts and Strategies*, Houghton Mifflin, 4th European edition

Drummond, G., Ensor, J. and Ashford, R. (2003) *Strategic Marketing: Planning and Control*, Oxford: Butterworth-Heinemann

Piercy, N. (2001) *Market-Led Strategic Change*, Oxford: Butterworth-Heinemann

Porter, M.E. (1980) *Competitive Strategy*, Free Press

Terpstra, V., Sarathy, R. (1999) *International Marketing*, Thomas Learning

A few helpful websites for marketing audit activities:

www.ft.com	www.tradepartners.co.uk
www.ecola.com	www.economist.com
www.asiannet.com	www.cbw.com/busbj
www.dti.com	www.mad.co.uk
www.defra.gov.uk	www.ft.com
www.euromonitor.com	www.europa.eu.int
www.oecd.org	www.un.org

Unit 3
Marketing planning, implementation and control

Learning objectives

In this unit, the focus will be on developing marketing objectives and marketing plans. The learning outcomes associated with this unit are as follows:

2.6 Evaluate the relationship between corporate objectives, business objectives and marketing objectives at an operational level.

2.7 Explain the concept of the planning gap and its impact on operational decisions.

2.8 Determine segmentation, targeting and positioning within the marketing plan.

2.9 Determine and evaluate marketing budgets for mix decisions included in the marketing plan.

2.10 Describe methods for evaluating and controlling the marketing plan.

This unit will provide you with the basics in order to understand the process of marketing planning at an operational level, and also enable you to develop marketing objectives and plans at an operational level.

Introduction

In Unit 2, the focus was on the need to undertake a planned marketing audit, so that we clearly understood the nature and context of an organization's marketing environment.

Clearly, the marketing audit plays a pivotal role in underpinning both the corporate and the marketing planning processes, effectively feeding information from the 'bottom up' in the organization to support the corporate decision-making process.

In this unit, the focus will be on Stages 4 and 5 of Figure 1.3. Next we will move on to look at the issues associated with implementation within the organization.

In any organization, there are three key questions to be asked in ascertaining the vision and direction for the future:

Where are we now? Stages 1 and 2 – Marketing audit

Where are we going? Stages 3 and 4 – Marketing strategy

How are we going to get there? Stage 5 – Marketing plan.

Planning horizons

One of the major considerations expected from strategies and plans is the time horizon. In today's marketing environment, while the ideal is to have a predetermined plan for the long term, in some environments this is becoming increasingly difficult, as we have seen, in particular, in the hi-tech industries.

Typical planning horizons

Short term	1–3 years
Medium term	3–5 years
Long term	5 years and beyond

In many organizations there is an obvious friction between long-term and short-term planning horizons. In the main, short-term planning drives marketing activities at an operational level. However, the real conflict lies in the fact that it is often difficult to establish the impact that short-term objectives might have on long-term strategies. Because marketing is subject to many changes, it is fairly typical for organizations to work on the basis of short-term objectives, short-term budgeting arrangements and short-term resource allocations. Therefore, for objectives to be strategic in nature, they should be developed within a long-term time frame. Obviously, these planning horizons will vary from writer to writer and from organization to organization (see Figure 1.3).

How to take the marketing audit to the planning process

The principal objective of the marketing audit is to provide an indication of potential opportunities and threats that might exist within the marketplace, and ultimately enable the organization to move on to develop their marketing objectives and strategies.

The most effective way of providing a more succinct approach to the audit is to produce a SWOT analysis, which highlights very specific areas that should potentially be addressed through the planning process.

Essentially, the analysis produced in Unit 2 highlighted some of the possible SWOT components that might be an outcome of the audit process, that is strengths, weaknesses, opportunities and threats.

To assist the planning process, the SWOT analysis should be substantiated with background information that underpins it and gives considerably more detail on the potential opportunities or even pitfalls that might arise in respect of developing future strategies. This might include a range of internal and external documents: for example, forecasts, company reports, secondary data, competitive information and so on.

Making assumptions can be a useful activity so that the organization can conceptualize the potential that a particular opportunity might present or indeed what the effect might be of not exploiting it. An organization might make assumptions based around competitive practices in relation to price levels and promotional activities or perhaps the introduction of a new product range or an addition to the product portfolio. For example, it is possible that launching a new product range will produce an anticipated growth at a rate of 10 per cent per year for two years and 15 per cent thereafter.

It is recommended that as few assumptions are made as possible, and that they are based on solid management information attained through the audit process.

Question 3.1

In what way does the SWOT analysis assist the planning process?

Stage 3 – The setting of objectives

As a result of the SWOT analysis and any subsequent assumptions made as a result of the marketing audit, the organization is now in the position of considering realistic marketing objectives, that is establishing 'where they are going'. It is hoped that these objectives will go a significant way to underpinning and achieving the corporate goals. One of the key issues relating to setting objectives is ensuring their relevance to achieving the corporate vision and mission.

Objectives should be widely understood by the organization and closely related to the organization's financial, physical and human resource capability.

Setting objectives within the organization is central to its overall effectiveness and its ability to achieve high level performance. In the words of Dibb *et al.* (2001):

> A marketing objective is a statement of what is to be accomplished through marketing activities.

An objective is something that you want to achieve and it should have the SMART components illustrated in the following table.

S Specific – objectives should be descriptive, succinct and provide clarity throughout the organization as to what is to be achieved.

M Measurable – objectives should clearly state tangible targets that can be measured in the future.

A Aspirational – objectives should be challenging but achievable, motivational and not demoralizing.

R Realistic – objectives should be based on sound market analysis. Financial, human and physical resources should underpin the objectives.

T Timebound – a timescale should be set against the achievement of each objective in order for performance measurement to be undertaken.

The basis of SMART objectives is that they are simple, quantifiable and therefore easier to measure, monitor and control.

Corporate objectives

In the first instance, many organizations will set corporate/primary objectives. These are expressed in financial terms. For example:

◆　　To achieve 15 per cent return on equity

◆　　To increase operating profit by 25 per cent

◆　　To achieve ROCE of 22 per cent

◆　　To achieve 10 per cent growth in earnings per share.

Profitability on its own is insufficient, as the key principle behind profit is ensuring that the original capital invested is being paid back at a percentage rate every year, so that ultimately the organization can then be more profit-oriented.

Business non-financial objectives

While financial objectives are vitally important at the corporate level, so are non-financial ones. For example, we have seen that many organizations have to adjust their strategies and plans to survive in a time of intense competition across a number of industry sectors. Therefore functional and operational objectives need to be defined so in order that survival is achievable. Functional objectives may as follows:

◆　　To increase highly skilled element of workforce by 10 per cent

◆　　To increase training provision to the organization by 10 per cent

◆　　To increase productivity by 10 per cent – operations function

◆　　To introduce new technology programme by June 2010.

As a marketer your job is to define marketing objectives to further underpin corporate objectives in order that corporate goals might be achieved.

Marketing objectives

Marketing objectives in the main are about products and markets only. Do not get confused about marketing objectives being set directly in relation to pricing and advertising. Service levels are the means by which objectives are achieved, rather than objectives in themselves.

It is likely therefore that marketing objectives will focus on:

◆　　Increasing sales of existing products into existing markets

◆　　Launching new product ranges into existing markets

◆　　Launching existing products into new markets

◆　　Launching new products into new markets.

Then transfer these concepts into objectives and you may see some of the following quantifiable and measurable objectives. Below is a list of examples highlighting some possible objectives that could be set by an organization:

◆　　To increase sales of the 'X' product range into the existing marketplace by 10 per cent by December 2009

- ◆ To launch Product 'Y' into China by October 2004, providing a sales turnover of £5 million by October 2009
- ◆ To increase market share of Product 'A' by 20 per cent by June 2010
- ◆ To increase customer retention by 30 per cent by June 2010.

Programme/subsidiary objectives

In particular, these relate to objectives specifically focused around the marketing sub-function, or marketing activities. This is most closely related to the marketing mix. You will note that in the Planning Process model (Figure 1.3), Stage 5 reflects upon the marketing mix. These are more tactical objectives. For example, in this area, you will find specific objectives relating to pricing, the promotional mix, distribution elements or product mix requirements.

Each of these subsidiary objectives is developed specifically in relation to achieving a 'higher' level marketing objective.

For example, where an objective relates to 'penetrating the existing market and increasing market share by 10 per cent', a subsidiary objective might be to drive prices down, therefore a pricing objective may then read 'to reduce prices by 10 per cent to increase marketing penetration by [date]'.

Whilst the focus on setting objectives will be based around 'marketing', it is essential that at a corporate level, objectives are balanced – that is that corporate objectives reflect across the whole organization, the idea being that the whole organization integrates, works together, consistently and with synergy, to achieve corporate goals.

Having an understanding of the 'balanced scorecard' approach to setting objectives and ensuring a balance is achieved is important.

Gap analysis

One of the most significant problems within many organizations is that they use objectives as a basis of forecasting what the levels of performance will be, and then turn the objectives into corporate goals, as opposed to setting objectives based on forecasts.

A gap analysis is used to assist the organization with its strategy development process. In simple terms it is designed to illustrate 'where are we now' and 'where do we want to be'.

The analysis undertaken as part of the marketing audit will tell the organization 'where they are now' and then a forecast can be undertaken that shows 'where the organization wants to be'. It is then possible to identify a gap between the two (see Figure 3.1). In other words, it represents the divide that the marketing strategy has to address to allow the organization to meet its objectives by crossing the gap.

The role of marketing is to try to develop attractive propositions that would allow the company to offer desirable added values superior to or not offered by competitors.

Such gaps may be closed by the clever and creative development of a competitive marketing strategy. Such strategies may include developing approaches such as the three generic strategies identified by Porter (1980): these include cost leaders, differentiation and focus.

Cost leadership could be achieved through such areas as economies of scale, linking relationships to profitability and generating costs savings and ultimately developing a cost-effective infrastructure.

Differentiation strategies could include looking at areas such as improving product performance or product perception. Here the organization may look at whether it is the performance of the product or the perception of the product which is most important.

In terms of the focus strategy, the organization will clearly concentrate on a narrower range of business activities. The aim will be to specialize in a specific market segment and derive detailed customer knowledge in relation to this segment.

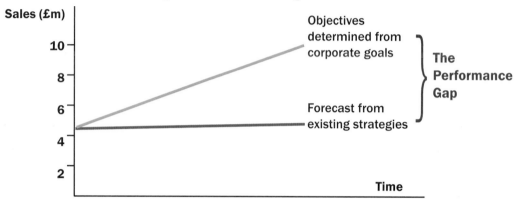

Figure 3.1: Gap analysis grid

Question 3.2

What are the key benefits of undertaking a gap analysis?

Hints and tips for the examination

In December 2004, Question 4(a) required students to explain the concept of the planning gap and the impact of this upon a marketing team.

Question 4(b) then went on to ask how the gap could be closed from an operational and strategic perspective.

Formulation of the marketing strategy

Now that the objectives have been defined and the gaps identified, it is time for the organization to define, develop and shape the direction they will take in the short-, medium- and long-term time horizons which they have planned within.

The key questions that should be asked in any organization are as follows:

◆   Where are we now?

◆   Where are we going?

◆   How are we going to get there?

Marketing strategy seeks to develop effective responses to ever-changing marketing environments. It does so by defining market segments and then developing and positioning product offerings for particular target markets.

It is of utmost importance that you have a good foundation in strategy in order to put your marketing planning into context.

Strategy or tactics?

It is important that a clear understanding of the difference between strategy and tactics is established at this early stage (see Table 3.1).

Table 3.1: Strategy versus tactics

	Strategic marketing	**Tactical marketing**
Time frame	Long term	Short term
Focus	Broad	Narrow
Key tasks	Defining marketing and competitive positioning	Daily marketing activity
Information and problem	Unstructured, external, speculative	Structured, internal, repetitive
Example	Market growth	Advertising

Adapted from: Drummond *et al.* (2003)

The constant theme of this text has been the necessity of developing a sustainable competitive advantage. This, of course, will be achieved through the development of appropriate marketing objectives and a marketing strategy, in order to achieve the corporate goals.

Two other key components of the strategy development are the need to achieve a strong market position through potential growth and to have a sound product/market strategy.

The next stage of this unit focuses on how, as an organization, you develop an appropriate mix of marketing strategies to retain the much-desired 'sustainable competitive advantage'.

Competitive marketing strategy

The marketing audit process should include a competitor analysis. It is important to develop a competitor profile, identifying likely competitive attacks, and have a full understanding of the various forces that will define the shape of the marketplace, through the analysis of Porter's Five Forces. This information, consolidated in the main within a SWOT analysis, will form the basis of your considered approach to developing a competitive strategy.

Michael Porter also defined a Competitive Advantage Grid based upon three generic strategies that enable an organization to closely identify the various competitive options open to them. Typically they would include the following:

◆   Cost leadership

◆   Differentiation

◆   Focus.

Porter himself suggested that strategy is primarily about creating and sustaining a profitable position in the marketplace. The organization needs to identify the competitive scope available to it, considering the approach to targeting and segmenting the market, and ensure that the organization is operating in a closely defined market.

Cost leadership

One of the key competitive positions to achieve in a mass market setting is that of cost leadership within your defined industry or sector. The focus of marketing and indeed over-all strategic activity at this level will relate to ensuring that a low-cost structure is implemented. In essence, the organization will be looking to achieve economies of scale, cost reduction policies, zero defects, minimum expenditure on research and development and very closely defined cost-effective marketing strategies. Therefore, the organization is likely to be process-driven and technologically focused.

The basic drivers of cost leadership, according to Drummond *et al.* (2003) are:

◆ **Economy of scale** – The single biggest influence on cost

◆ **Linkages and relationships** – Being able to link activities together and form long-lasting customer relationships, inclusive of customer retention programmes

◆ **Infrastructure** – Factors such as location, availability of skills and government support.

Differentiation

This strategy presents the opportunity to market products or services distinctive from those of its competitors. However, while it might be distinctive in nature, it is only competitive and purposefully different if it ultimately adds value to the overall customer experience.

The product/service should have unique features, characteristics and even benefits. It should enable the organization to achieve a degree of customer loyalty and should ultimately be a competitive response that cannot be challenged directly by any competitor.

The most likely scenario is that as a result of the differentiation, it will command a premium price that will essentially reflect the quality of the brand, design, product and high service levels.

Again Drummond *et al.* (2003) suggest that the common sources of differentiation will include:

◆ **Product performance** – The product's performance can enhance its perceived value from the customer perspective.

◆ **Product perception** – The perception of the product is often different from the performance.

◆ **Product augmentation** – The product can be extended and augmented in ways that will be of value to the customer (we will look at this in Unit 5, Product Operations).

Focus

Interestingly, the basis of competitive strategy is both cost leadership and differentiation, but instead of competing in a mass market environment, it is more likely to compete in a smaller or narrowly defined area of the market. In particular, the focus will be on attractive segments or niche markets. The emphasis of a focus strategy primarily implies that the organization is focusing effort on producing products for a closely defined market. Often the products will be customized, of high quality, differentiated, and potentially premium priced, for example, specialist clothing, or the high quality car market, for example Rolls-Royce, Morgan and so on.

Clearly, the more successful the organization is within the niche, the more likely it is to attract attention. Therefore, the emphasis of a focus strategy should be on:

◆ **Product and service specialism** – Producing highly differentiated, possibly exclusive products to a closely defined target market.

◆ **Geographic segmentation** – Tailoring product/service needs to geographic regions, as long as the markets are commercially viable, based upon size.

◆ **End-user focus** – The focus might be on the end-user, therefore a customer profile might be more appropriate to target than an entire marketplace.

These strategies, while studied in isolation from a student perspective, are very much part of a bigger integrated corporate and ma rketing picture.

Question 3.3

What is the significance of differentiation when establishing a sustainable competitive advantage?

Growth strategies

While Porter offers one approach to identifying competitive strategies, it is also essential to consider Ansoff's approach. The Ansoff matrix was developed to provide linkages between both products and markets. Ansoff proposes four alternative strategies to take the product to the market in order that corporate goals and related marketing objectives are achieved.

At the end of the section on 'The micro environment' in Unit 2, we looked very briefly at Ansoff to put the SWOT into context. However, now we need to consider it in the context of defining the marketing strategy, in respect of identifying options available to the organization for growth.

Ansoff's model builds on Porter's generic strategies and highlights the gap the subsidiary objectives relating to the marketing mix are used to fill.

Principally, the Ansoff matrix (Figure 3.2) allows you to consider a range of four strategic options.

Market penetration

The basis of the market penetration strategy is primarily to increase sales of existing products in existing markets. If you look at the top left-hand side of the matrix, you can see where this fits. To do this, the organization will need to demonstrate a high level of competitive force; they will need to be price-competitive, promotionally competitive and execute a hard-hitting advertising campaign.

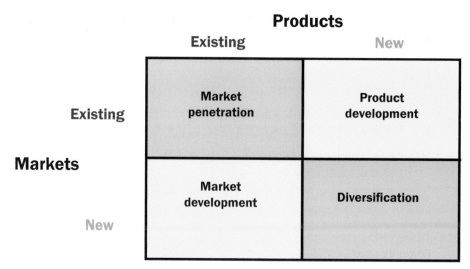

Figure 3.2: Ansoff matrix

The focus of market penetration will be on persuading existing customers to buy more of your products. A number of examples highlight this particular practice. Retailers offering store cards, with opening discounted rates of purchase, for example open a credit card account today and you will receive 10 per cent discount. The broader scope of this particular strategy is winning customers from other competitors, testing out the power of the buyers, and their willingness to change. Therefore part of your strategy might be to create easy transition between the organization and its competitors.

The main problem with market penetration is that while it is appropriate now in some industries, markets are becoming increasingly saturated, and therefore competitive intensity at this level is forcing some organizations to revisit their existing strategies. A full and comprehensive marketing audit should identify these emerging issues, and ongoing environmental scanning will enable organizations to take proactive actions in advance of market saturation, rather than waiting for it to happen.

Market development

Market development is an alternative growth strategy that focuses on the development of new markets for existing products (Figure 3.2, bottom left-hand side of the matrix). The aim will be to open up new geographical regions; target new market segments and find new uses for existing products.

Product development

Expanding and developing the product portfolio is an essential marketing activity, in order that organizations continue to move with the times and the new and more challenging expectations of their customers, that is the power of the customer/buyer. Product development is required to attract existing customers in existing markets to new products or revamped, redesigned equivalents.

In an ideal world, a product portfolio would have a range of products that should provide something for everybody. However, this is not always possible.

Product development plays an important role in attracting new customers, opening up new markets and providing many new opportunities, but clearly the main drawback can be the level of investment required. So as a growth objective, it is the one that provides the greatest strain on resources. Here the organization would need to undertake a financial analysis, including a break-even analysis, to measure how long it would take for the new product to break even, should it be launched into the market.

Related marketing activities would clearly need to reflect a strong competitive response, in order that the product is taken to the market in advance of similar competitive strikes and before the threat of substitute products arises.

The organization would clearly have to exploit the company name and brand in order that the product is given credence in the marketplace. Therefore the components of success will rely upon a good quality product, associated high service levels, and a compatible promotional and pricing strategy to give it a head start.

Diversification

Diversification potentially poses the most significant risk to the organization. This strategy is based on diversifying or moving away from the core business of the organization and looking for an alternative or complementary source of income and profit. This often results, in today's market economy, in mergers and acquisitions, as organizations seek to set up compatible business portfolios, increasing their market attractiveness and market share along the way.

This is a high-risk strategy, a move into the unknown and one that may present threats associated with 'new entrants' in the marketplace: high investment, lack of economies of scale and difficulties associated with distribution. Again, going back to the previous point, one of the benefits of mergers and acquisitions in this sense is that some of the risk is reduced. However, this is an expensive alternative option – for many organizations it is a last resort.

One of the principal benefits of using Ansoff is that in addition to contributing to identification of the potential direction to take in relation to developing the marketing strategy, it also focuses the mind of the organization on the future deployment of the marketing mix.

In linking Ansoff back to the SWOT analysis, the potential opportunities that face an organization in the future may be identified.

Market positioning strategies

When defining market positioning strategies, it is not just about product position, it is also about positioning the organization within the marketplace. Now is the time to give the organization a competitive identity. Is the organization going to be a market leader, market challenger, market follower or a market niche?

Market leaders

Market leaders are extremely dominant and high profile within their industry sector and target marketplace. This marketplace might be local, national or even global. It is likely that they possess significant market share. For example, organizations such as Coca-Cola and Pepsi are market leaders in the 'Cola' drinks industry. They possess significant market share within the soft drinks industry.

Positioning the organization as market leader immediately leaves them open for a range of competitor attacks. These attacks are likely to be aggressive in nature, and therefore constant monitoring of the competitor activities should be undertaken in order to pre-empt any potential strikes.

Typical competitor attacks might include market expansion, aggressive and offensive attacks to regain lost market share or even defensive attacks, trying to protect existing market share from a market leader contender. You should be aware that offensive attacks are not just the market leaders attacking, but in essence can be mounted by any industry player in the associated market.

Market challengers

Market challengers are particularly difficult to compete with, as they are aggressive and will very much strive to take market share. In the main, you will find that these organizations are fairly significant, cash rich and well resourced.

Their likely approach will be based around selective targeting of competitors or indeed an attack on the market leader. Armed with the competitor intelligence and competitor profile built during the marketing audit activities, the market challenger will know where to attack to cause the most pain and discomfort to the competing organization. Probably one of the best-known examples of this is the fight between British Airways and Virgin Air. The battle for clawing back market share has been particularly high profile and ongoing for a number of years. It is a battle that is continually fought in the spotlight of media attention. It is a long-term war of attrition, and it will take a long time before any change is evident.

Market followers

Quite often, being a market follower can be more favourable than being a market leader. Being second or third or even lower down the rankings within the target marketplace can have a number of advantages.

The key to success here is continually 'following the leader': whatever they do, the follower duplicates. Therefore, the strategy is somewhat reactive rather than proactive in context. If the prices go up, the follower puts them up. If the market leader approaches a new market then the follower effectively follows on behind.

It is very rare that the follower will challenge the leader in this particular market positioning area, unless they were absolutely sure of success.

Market niches

As we saw from looking at the generic strategy of 'focus' earlier, niches are known for the ability to specialize and focus on particular market segments. Their aim will be to achieve competitive advantage by differentiating their products and services, and move towards the high level, high quality markets.

When defining a marketing strategy, there are so many components that an organization and you as a marketer must consider. The essence of the message is that strategy development cannot be undertaken in isolation, and therefore the importance of the marketing audit must never be underestimated or ignored.

The basis of an earlier heading was 'How to take the marketing audit to the planning process'. Primarily you should never get to the planning process without it. You should be able to see, from the use of Porter's Five Forces, PEST and SWOT, how the information is then transferred into a decision-making pot, out of which a number of potential competitive, growth and market development strategies might be developed and defined.

While the overall basis of the strategic direction has been established, it is equally important to ensure that the specifics of the target audience are clearly understood. As a result of this, marketing segmentation is a crucial activity that must be undertaken, in order that the marketing effort is specifically focused.

Question 3.4

What are the key benefits of being a market follower?

Market segmentation and competitive positioning

At an operational level, segmentation, targeting and positioning are often linked together and the terms interchanged regularly.

For a marketer, there are three stages in the segmentation and positioning process, as can be seen in Figure 3.3.

```
┌──────────────────────────────────────────────────────────────┐
│                        Segmentation                          │
│      Consider the basis on which to segment the market       │
│    Look at the profile of people and how they break into groups │
│          Confirm the groups are valid segments               │
├──────────────────────────────────────────────────────────────┤
│                         Targeting                            │
│             Decide on a target strategy                      │
│       Decide which segments should be targeted and why      │
├──────────────────────────────────────────────────────────────┤
│                        Positioning                           │
│          Understand consumer perceptions                    │
│       Position products in the mind of the consumer         │
│  Design an appropriate marketing mix to meet customer requirements │
└──────────────────────────────────────────────────────────────┘
```

Figure 3.3: The process of segmentation

For the time being, however, the concentration of your study will be purely on the principles of segmentation.

Definition

Segmentation – The act of dividing the market into specific groups of consumers/buyers who share common needs and who might require separate products and/or marketing mixes (adapted from Kotler *et al.*, 1998).

The aim of marketing segmentation is to assist the organization to differentiate their product/service offerings to differing groups of customers. It helps describe how marketers can divide up the market into groups of like-minded customers, at the same time as understanding the different characteristics of them and the different demands that they might make.

Marketing segmentation recognizes the differing needs of buyers, and a different approach for each segment identified may subsequently be developed. This is then known as target marketing. This has grown in importance to meet the complex demands of the markets.

Therefore building on the existing stages in the segmentation process, the key steps to market segmentation may be as follows:

◆ **Identify the possible segments within the market** – This will consist of individuals or organizations with similar needs and preferences

◆ **Gather information on those market segments identified** – To do this the segments need to be accessible.

◆ **Evaluate the attractiveness of the different segments** – They need to be large enough to be viable.

◆ **Ascertain the competitive positioning** within each of the target segments.

◆ **Develop variations on product/service specifications** to meet the needs of individual segments.

◆ **Design the appropriate communications mix** to meet the target market demands.

For a market to be split into segments, specific criteria must be met. These criteria clearly relate back to the decision-making process in the previous section.

◆ Customers must want or need the associated products or services.

◆ Customers must assert their buying power, that is money, resources and so on.

◆ Customers must be willing to use their money and resources to buy products.

◆ Customers must have the authority to buy different products.

The basis for segmenting markets

Segmenting markets is a complex issue, but is often seen as a critical factor in the successful implementation of marketing strategy.

Segmentation relates to identifying customer groups and their common characteristics. Segments are often formed based upon common customer characteristics, brand preferences and customer attitudes.

Segmentation of consumer markets

It is important to understand what is often termed the 'classificatory' information and 'background' characteristics of your customer. Customers have two types of characteristics that can be measured. They have objective characteristics, which relate to:

◆ Demographics

◆ Socio-economics

◆ Consumer life cycle

◆ ACORN (see page 65)

◆ Media usage.

They also have subjective characteristics, which relate to the 'psychographics'. Psychographics look closely at various personality traits and inventories, and very importantly, particularly in the twenty-first century, lifestyles.

Geographic segmentation

Geographic segmentation is a popular form of segmentation; for example, geographic regions of television areas are used as a form of geographic segmentation. Geographic segmentation means that the market can be broken down into areas for marketing purposes – into towns, cities, regions, countries and so on. This is particularly relevant with the tourism industry, where particular regions will be promoted as holiday and leisure destinations.

Geographic segmentation is particularly important on a global basis, as there are so many different cultures, characteristics and lifestyle requirements that need to be met. Many organizations will try, where possible, to standardize their product offerings globally, while others may try to tailor global requirements. It will very much depend upon the marketing place and the competitive elements that exist within it.

Demographic segmentation

One common area of demographics is social class. This is often a contentious issue. Let us look at some of the areas developed by the JICNAR social grade definitions when looking at segmentation (see Table 3.2).

As a marketer you should be able to recognize different market segments for any major product, for example motor vehicles. There are a number of different cars available to suit the many and varied needs of customers and their lifestyles.

Table 3.2: JICNAR classification

Social grades	Social status	Characteristics of occupation
A	Upper middle class	High managerial/professional
B	Middle class	Intermediate managerial/administrative professional
C1	Lower middle class	Supervisory/clerical/junior/managerial/administrative/professional
C2	Skilled working class	Skilled manual labour
D	Working class	Semi-skilled and unskilled manual labour
E	Lowest level of subsistence	Widows, casual workers, state pensioners

Geo-demographic segmentation

Geo-demographic factors are a combination of demographic and geographic variables which suggest that certain groups of people tend to move in circles appropriate to class and occupation, while others may move together relating to lifestyles and geographic factors. There are two particular methods in this area that should be considered, ACORN and MOSAIC.

ACORN

ACORN (A Classification of Residential Neighbourhoods – Table 3.3) is a system which identifies people by geo-demographics. The current ACORN system divides the United Kingdom into 17 groups, which comprise a total of 54 different types of areas, which share common socio-economic characteristics. The basis of this type of segmentation is recognizing that different residential areas have very different profiles of people within them and therefore the products they may need may vary from area to area. In many instances, products may not even be targeted at specific groups as it is not deemed to be appropriate.

Table 3.3: ACORN consumer targeting classification

Category A Thriving	19.8%	1 – Wealthy achievers – suburban areas
		2 – Affluent greys, rural communities
		3 – Prosperous pensioners
Category B Expanding	11.5%	4 – Affluent executives
		5 – Well-off workers, family areas
Category C Rising	7.6%	6 – Affluent urbanites, town and city areas
		7 – Prosperous professionals, metropolitan areas
		8 – Better-off executives, inner city areas
Category D Settling	22.3%	9 – Comfortable middle-aged, mature home-owning areas
		10 – Skilled workers – home-owning
Category E Aspiring	13.7%	11 – New home-owners, mature communities
		12 – White-collar workers, better-off multi-ethnic areas
Category F Striving	22.6%	13 – Older people, less prosperous areas
		14 – Council estate residents – better off homes
		15 – Council estate residents, high unemployment
		16 – Council estate residents, greatest hardship
		17 – People in multi-ethnic low-income areas
Unclassified	2.4%	

Adapted from: Dibb *et al.* (2001)

From the seven overall categories, ACORN can then go on to identify issues relating to behaviour, personality, motives and lifestyle. These are what we termed the 'psychographics'. The 'objective' characteristics of ACORN versus the 'subjective' characteristics of personality, motives and lifestyle serve to move the organization much closer to understanding the basis of customer needs, wants and expectations.

MOSAIC

MOSAIC is a classification system which analyses information from a variety of sources. It analyses geo-demographic data including the census (which provides housing, socio-economic, household and age information), postcode address records (housing and special types of address information, for example non-residential addresses), the electoral role (for composition of households and population movement information) and the CCN files/ Lord Chancellor's office (to provide information on credit searches and bad-debt risks).

MOSAIC provides three types of information as follows:

◆ **Unit postcodes** – A six or seven-digit code

◆ **Census enumeration districts** – Based upon census data, containing about 180 addresses in each district

◆ **Pseudo-enumeration districts** – Areas created by MOSAIC using a combination of unit postcodes within an individual enumeration district.

Presently there are 58 individual neighbourhood types in the MOSAIC classification system.

Lifestyle segmentation

Lifestyle segmentation is a very complex area and is based upon the characteristics of psychographics. These are more subjective and less easy to measure than the typical traits of demographics.

The key areas of interest for a marketer would typically be:

◆ **Social activities** – leisure activities, sport, eating out, holidays, shopping habits

◆ **Interests** – music, reading, science, history, food, fashion, Internet

◆ **Opinions** – social and ethical issues, business, politics, culture, education, religion.

Clearly these characteristics will then be linked with demographics, to start establishing a clear customer profile, on which to base segmentation.

Behaviour segmentation

Behavioural segmentation relates to dividing customers, or indeed organizations, into groups based upon their purchase behaviour, frequency of purchase, attitudes towards the products/services, benefits sought and consumption patterns.

There are a variety of different ways that a market can be segmented. The process of market segmentation involves the following steps:

◆ Analyse and describe the market segments

◆ Validate segment choice by testing

◆ Choose an appropriate strategy for segmentation

◆ Develop the product or market positioning.

Dividing the market into smaller segments can often present a wide range of new and exciting opportunities for organizations, not only enabling them to meet more directly a wider range of customer needs, but also enabling them to remain competitive in the marketplace. Segmentation can also allow organizations to respond faster to the changing needs of the customers and also to the macro-factors of the external marketing environment.

Market segmentation is therefore essential for successful implementation of marketing strategy. It can help achieve:

◆ Lengthening of the PLC

◆ Increased sales and profits

◆ Capture of some of the competitors' share of the market

◆ Survival of a small firm operating in a competitive market consisting of large firms

◆   Effective resource allocation

◆   Strategic marketing planning.

Business-to-business and organizational segmentation

The disciplines of marketing in a business-to-business (B2B) context are often quite different, and unfortunately the segmentation techniques available to those marketing to individuals are not available to the organizational marketer. However, a particular bonus of business-to-business segmentation is perhaps the more limited size of the customer base.

For business-to-business and organizational segmentation, grouping of customers can be as follows:

◆   Using the Standard Industrial Classifications (SIC)

◆   By the industry technology, for example chemical or electrical and so on

◆   By size of organization

◆   By season purchasing trends

◆   By geographical location

◆   By the type of product needed.

Demographics, in a B2B context, assume that organizations operating in similar industries have similar needs and will exhibit similar behavioural traits.

All organizations aim to satisfy their customer needs, whether their customer is an individual or a business. As we have already identified, organizations do find it difficult to totally segment their markets for B2B buying because of the characteristics of the market they operate within.

Therefore, there are five key variables that organizations should consider:

1   The personal characteristics of the buyers

2   Situational factors

3   The organizational approach to purchasing

4   Operating variables – technologies and so on

5   Demographics.

Company demographics have a slightly different approach, and are in the main far less personal. However, they do focus on areas such as company age, location, size and the likelihood of them wanting to change their product specification in the future.

Clearly these factors are highly significant, as they will indicate the volume of purchases, the ordering procedures, accessibility for delivery and so on.

Business-to-business buying should reflect the same considerations as consumer segmentation and the same approach to developing marketing plans and strategies should apply.

Further consideration of this area is included within Unit 10.

Continuous monitoring of segmentation

As with any element of marketing, segmentation, targeting and positioning should be tightly controlled and monitored, to ensure the information provided has enabled an organization to meet its corporate and marketing objectives.

Should an organization not meet its objectives, then it should review and evaluate segments selected to ensure that the profile of customers is one that matches the benefits and characteristics of the product, or indeed that the correct medium has been selected to get the message to the customer or consumer.

If the segment that has been targeted should prove to be ineffective, then further research should be undertaken, plans revised and the marketing mix strategy redefined.

Possible examples of segmentation monitoring might include measuring the sales distribution across segments, measuring advertising effectiveness, repeat sales and responses to special sales promotions.

Achieving segmentation effectiveness

Ineffective marketing segmentation can have lasting effects and be the cause of many lost opportunities. Therefore it is essential that there is clear and perceived value in the segmenting process. It is of primary importance that the appropriate segmentation characteristics are identified, and that time is not wasted and investment is not lost in the selection of the incorrect or inappropriate segmenting variables. For example, there is little point in segmenting a homogeneous market, as it does not provide the basis for effective segmentation.

Therefore the following criteria should be adhered to:

Specific	Clearly identified, broken down into a number of meaningful groups
Measurable	Each group should be quantifiable, in order for the organization to identify opportunities and forecast the future
Achievable	The segments themselves need to achieve organizational objectives, they will therefore need to be viable groups and accessible
Realistic	What is achievable in the name of segmentation must be realistic in terms of resources, and with a clear indication that customer expectations can be met
Timebound	Appropriate segments of the market must be targeted in an appropriate and timely way and in line with the organizational objectives.

While marketing segmentation can be a very process-driven exercise, it will require a degree of common sense and perhaps even a number of related assumptions, in order that the market can be closely defined.

Ultimately the benefits of segmentation are significant and they include the following:

◆ It allows target markets to be mapped against organizational competences.

◆ It helps identify gaps within the marketplace.

◆ It enables marketers to match the product/service to their customer – a basis of competitive advantage.

◆ It provides an opportunity for mature/declining markets to identify possible growth segments.

◆ The failure to segment can reduce competitive strength.

Targeting

Targeting is the process that involves evaluating the attractiveness of a range of potential market segments that have been identified in terms of being commercially viable.

Definition

Targeting – The decision about which market segment(s) a business decides to prioritize for its sales and marketing efforts (Dibb *et al.*, 2001).

Each organization has several options when deciding which specific segment to target:

◆ Organizations could concentrate on making one product for one market and having one marketing plan or programme – this is known as undifferentiated marketing or even mass marketing.

◆ The organization could concentrate its efforts on one market but have a number of different versions of each product – This is known as differentiated marketing.

◆ Another alternative is to meet the need of each segment within the market with a specific product – this is known as target marketing.

◆ Concentrating efforts on a small and carefully chosen segment, often referred to as a niche and the basis of a 'focus' strategy.

Targeting in essence is where we identify a number of different segments within the market, whereby a sustainable competitive advantage can be built.

In ascertaining the appropriate target market strategy, the organization must take into consideration the following six components:

1 Customer needs, wants and expectations

2 Product market – size and structure

3 Brand strength and market share

4 Company capability

5 Competitive rivalry

6 Economies of scale – production and marketing.

The organization must, through market research, identify which is the most appropriate target, which they can effectively manage to meet the customer needs and wants in a cost-efficient and effective way, in order that they can meet the corporate goals of the organization.

Segmentation is not an exact science, and will require a balanced view of market conditions, clear and precise criteria for assessing segmentation attractiveness, and an understanding of the key components that will enable successful target marketing.

Question 3.5

Why is it so vital for an organization to undertake segmentation and targeting activities?

What would be the effect of failing to undertake segmentation and targeting?

Positioning

Earlier on in this unit, we looked at the concept of market positioning strategies. Here we want to look at the source of positioning, starting with the product.

Definition

Positioning – The act of designing an offer so that it occupies a distinct and valued place in the minds of the target customers (Kotler *et al.*, 1998).

Simplistically, positioning refers to how you present your product or services to the market-place, it is almost a state of mind, a perception, it is something you as a marketer have to create in the minds of your target audience.

When establishing a positioning strategy there are a number of steps that can be taken in preparing a positioning plan.

◆ Identify all of the segments within the market.

◆ Decide which segments are the most suitable to target, based upon marketing research information.

◆ Ensure that the organization clearly understands the customer requirements.

◆ Develop a product or service that specifically meets the needs of the target audience.

◆ Identify benefits, usage, user category, competitive positioning components.

◆ Evaluate how the product/service is positioned in the eyes of the target group.

◆ Identify an image that matches the requirements of the customer.

◆ Promote the product to the target audience, establish relationships, aim for customer loyalty.

Pivotal to the success of positioning is the ability to differentiate your products and services from those of your competitors.

From a competitor perspective, there needs to be a comparison of competitor positioning, which means that as a marketer you should:

◆ Determine competitive positioning

◆ Examine the competitive dimensions

◆ Determine the customer positions

◆ Understand and identify the positioning decision

◆ Track the positioning strategy.

This will ultimately enable you to monitor competitor positioning and take the necessary retaliatory action.

Perception is a vital component of positioning strategies, and therefore it is helpful for organizations to try to represent the similarities between products or services and try to ascertain what the differences are, in respect of position. The key tool to support this process is a perceptual map (see Figure 3.4).

You will see when looking at the perceptual maps that there are four perceptions to be considered:

1   High price and high quality

2   High quality and low price

3   Low price and low quality

4   High price and low quality.

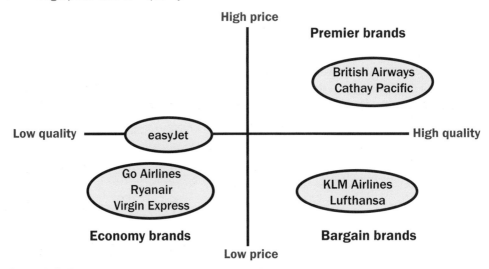

Figure 3.4: Perceptual positioning map

What effectively happens with a perceptual map is that it represents similarities and differences between products/services, and ultimately it highlights where they are similar/dissimilar.

As we can see here, the service offered by British Airways and Cathay Pacific is of a very high standard. The accommodation and service on board a British Airways flight is aimed at meeting customer expectations at a high level, which is primarily the executive market. British Airways are known for their superior service in executive, business and first-class flights. But obviously this all comes at a premium. Therefore in this instance British Airways have positioned themselves as premier quality, premium priced. Cathay Pacific seek to achieve the same positioning.

At the lower end of the scale, we have BMI Baby, Ryanair and easyJet, to name but a few. As 'no frills' brands, they are actually positioning themselves as economy brand, 'low-cost airlines'. However, in reality their positioning is somewhere between economy and high price, which is a slightly confused positioning. Other factors to consider with 'no frills' is the additional expenses customers incur while in flight, that is they add on expenses of food and drink. Of course, in terms of positioning, reliability will play a significant factor in the minds of the consumer, in respect of value for money, something for which easyJet received extremely poor publicity during the early part of 2001, through the series of television programmes that focused on a day in the life of easyJet.

Whilst positioning is a positive activity from both a customer and a competitor perspective, it is not an exact science. In positioning your organization you are raising an expectation in relation to the level of product or service quality you might offer. The important element of that is achieving the expectations that you have established in the eyes of the consumer.

Plotting on the perceptual map in Figure 3.4 is based upon the perceptions of customers, but it is also useful to consider this from a competitor perspective. Plotting competitor positioning on a perceptual map will enable you to further understand the role and positioning of your competitors, enabling the organization to have a clear understanding of the nature of the competition and, of course, where to attack. However, remember that when you attack, positioning is something that has to be sustainable, therefore in attacking a competitor it has to be more than a short-term activity and part of a longer-term strategy to compete on product and market positioning.

The positioning alternatives

Perceptual maps should be based upon marketing research, so that a factual presentation of the information can be plotted and assumptions made in relation to positioning are as accurate as possible. It is not recommended that you use either expert witnesses or expert judgements, or take the very subjective approach of establishing positions on gut feel.

There are three positioning alternatives available:

◆ **Distinctive attributes** – Identify the distinctive attributes of the product and service as a source of credible positioning.

◆ **Fill the gaps in unfilled positions** – Where there is a positional gap in the perceptional map, this may present a business opportunity to exploit.

◆ **Repositioning** – Changes in consumer behaviour (which are quite frequent) may mean that the PLC could be maturing or going into decline, therefore you might need to reposition your products to attract a different market. Clearly in the instance of the perceptual map in Figure 3.4, there is a space in the high price, low quality quadrant – but this is not one to fill. Of course, as a marketer, you would need to consider carefully why the gap might exist. It would be difficult in this instance to actually conceive what would be the benefits of selling a 'high price – economy' product, as it is unlikely that customers will pay for it. Therefore this should always be addressed and the likely gaps that you might wish to exploit are the remaining three.

Think about alcopops. They were originally aimed at the younger end of the market – 18–25 year olds. Now they are perceived as more sophisticated and are as popular with 31–40 year olds. This is a slight repositioning in order to allow for market penetration; that is, ensuring customer retention for the 18–25 year old market, but undertaking market development to target new markets, that is the 30+ more mature markets, but with the same products.

As part of the segmentation and targeting process, it is essential where possible to closely define the segmentation basis and associate it with the product/service in question. Ultimately, it is then possible to position the product clearly in a defined positioning strategy, in order to meet customer needs and expectations.

CITY COLLEGE

The role of a marketer in positioning

The role of a marketer will be to assist with the definition of positioning, in the context of the market, the brand and the product. As you move through this book, you will come across a number of different tools of the trade that will assist you with ascertaining positions in relation to the product and the brand, for example the Boston Consulting Group Matrix.

Positioning is all about differentiating your products and brands for your customers: what are the key characteristics and benefits that stand out – that differentiate your product/ brands from those of your competitors; what characteristics do your products have that your competitors may not? The purpose of positioning is to establish a position and perspective of your brands, products and services in the marketplace.

Clearly segmentation can therefore be a complex activity and should always be objective in nature, that is very clearly defined, very specific and very focused. Subjective judgements in relation to the segmentation base and target market may lead to failure to implement any marketing strategy.

Question 3.6

You have been asked by your marketing manager to develop a brief statement that clearly explains the positioning of your own company – in no more than 50 words.

The marketing plan

So far, we have looked at the essential components of developing the marketing plan, for example objectives, segmentation, targeting and position. This section now focuses upon conceptualizing the actual basis of a marketing plan. There are some components that we will only look at briefly within implementation, as they are the source of strategic planning and beyond the scope of the CIM syllabus for this module.

There is no set way in which the marketing plan must be presented. Table 3.4 shows the key headings that you should cover and also the order that is logical and appropriate.

Table 3.4: Contents of the marketing plan

1   Executive summary
    Key issues, current position, potential overview of the outcome

2   Corporate strategy
    Corporate mission/vision and corporate goals/objectives

3   Macro/micro analysis
    Market assessment
    Current state of the market
    Market trends
    Competitor analysis
    SWOT

4   Marketing objectives
    Financial objectives
    Marketing objectives

5   Marketing strategy
    Segmentation, targeting and positioning
    Marketing programme
    Product, price, place, promotion

6   Implementation
    Key tasks, resources, budgets, contingency plans

7   Monitoring and control
    Basis of the plan and the assumptions made
    Key/critical success factors
    Benchmarking
    Forecasts/costs/revenue

Planning offers you the opportunity to present the future of the organization and its marketing activity systematically, in a way that is meaningful and clearly defined. The basis of this particular plan will provide the template by which the organization will operate in the forthcoming years and will also form the basis of a planned approach to implementation. Furthermore, it will provide the basis for measurement, monitoring and control and it will act as a benchmark of what needs to be achieved, taking the organization from where it is now, to where it wants to be in the future.

Implementation of the marketing plan

There are a number of key components that you should familiarize yourself with in respect of the implementation of marketing plans. From an organizational perspective, implementation is one of the most challenging activities you will find yourself involved in.

Nigel Piercy (2001) suggests that:

> The real strategic problem in marketing is not strategy, it is managing the implementation and change.

New plans, new processes, different approaches are all components of change, and in many situations change meets with opposition and many barriers are therefore erected. You may recall these barriers from Unit 1, and here they are again as a reminder.

◆   **The existing culture** may not be amenable to marketing plans, particularly if the organization is not marketing-oriented.

◆   **Power and politics** – All organizations are subject to internal politics and often as a result of this the strategic planning process becomes a boardroom battlefield, where vested interests fight each other's proposals in order to gain resources and status.

♦ **Analysis not action** – Many organizations waste time and energy in analysing data and developing rationales for action, but ultimately fail to act. A further element of this is 'paralysis-by-analysis', too much information, not enough direction.

♦ **Resources** – This is one of the most contentious issues facing many organizations, as after years of downsizing, striving for increased efficiencies, many organizations now find themselves resource-starved. When corporate objectives are defined, it is of prime importance that organizations realistically consider the resources required, in order that they can rise to the challenge of achieving the corporate targets.

♦ **Skills** are very closely linked to the challenges of resources. One of the key components of any organization is a highly skilled workforce.

There are some key ingredients that are required and vital for the successful implementation of any marketing plan, and the driving forces of change. They are:

♦ Strong and committed leadership

♦ A marketing-oriented and customer-focused culture

♦ A supportive and effective marketing structure

♦ Financial and human resources

♦ Internal marketing – systems and processes

♦ Control and measurement mechanisms.

For a strategy to be successfully implemented, it is therefore important that these areas are managed effectively. If they are not, immediately a range of barriers to implementation will arise and then change becomes very difficult to manage.

Let us look briefly at the importance of each of these factors.

Strong and committed leadership

You might recall that, in the first unit, there was a reference to 'top-down' and 'bottom-up' planning. In a planning environment, leadership needs primarily to come from the top. A leader therefore must demonstrate commitment at the highest level to the proposed strategy and plans. Leaders need to be effective communicators, motivators and facilitators.

The process of continuous improvement will only succeed if those in influential roles demonstrate their commitment to the process and also ensure that they equally affect the commitment of their followers. Commitment is not a management function that can be delegated downwards, it has to be shown by actions.

Commitment is difficult to measure but it is likely that these key factors will be present:

♦ A vision for the future has been developed.

♦ The necessary resources have been committed.

♦ When solutions to problems are found they are promptly implemented.

♦ Barriers to change within the organization have been dismantled.

While this is a limited list, it is obvious that each relates to potential causes of conflict within the implementation process, therefore committed leadership is imperative to successful implementation of the marketing plan.

There is more to leadership than autocracy or democracy, charisma or inspiration – in the words of Sir John Harvey Jones: leadership is about making things happen.

Therefore effective leadership starts at the top, with the vision for the organization, examining closely the needs of the market, creating, exploiting and capitalizing on opportunities for the organization, at the same time as ensuring that it achieves competitive advantage.

Marketing-oriented and customer-focused culture

The 'marketing concept' in the words of Kotler *et al.* (1998):

> Holds that achieving organizational goals depends on determining the needs and wants of target markets and delivering the desired satisfactions more effectively and more efficiently than competitors do.

Reflecting on the different facets of marketing you have already examined, it is clear that marketing is increasingly dynamic, and if you and your organization are going to succeed then you need to ensure that you take into most serious consideration the expectations of your customer.

Organizations will need to be marketing-oriented, which means that there must be a clear focus throughout the whole organization on the customer needs and wants and how these needs are met constantly.

Marketing orientation consists of five key facets:

◆ Customer orientation

◆ Competitor orientation

◆ Integrated functional co-ordination

◆ Organizational culture

◆ Long-term profits.

To enable the marketing concept to continue to evolve and for marketing orientation to develop within organizations, organizations, big or small, should pay serious consideration to the following:

◆ Create customer focus throughout the business

◆ Listen to the customer

◆ Define the nature of the organization's key abilities, that is what they are good at

◆ Target customers precisely

◆ Manage profitability

◆ Make customer value the guiding star

◆ Let the customer define loyalty – how many times they may wish to repeat business

◆ Measure and manage customer expectations

◆ Build customer relationships and loyalty

◆ Commit to continuous improvement

◆ Manage the marketing culture.

For culture change to be implemented successfully, the following components must be at the forefront:

◆ Innovation must be highly valued

◆ Leadership must be an activity not just a function

◆ Shared values and rewards

◆ A learning organization

◆ Empowerment.

Ultimately, change in the context of marketing should be planned, consistent and incremental.

Strategy implementation can be a complex period full of conflict and recriminations. Cultural change must create something that did not exist before. The careful crafting of the 'internal marketing plan' may ease the situation.

Internal marketing

It is clear from everything we have seen so far that change is the one factor that is here to stay. It is also evident that the implementation of a new corporate strategy and indeed a new marketing plan may also require change within the organization.

The basis of internal marketing is focusing on the relationship that exists between the organization and its employees, often couched in terms of the 'internal customer'. It has been suggested on many occasions that the successful implementation of the marketing plan hinges upon treating internal staff like 'customers', hence the link with the internal customer.

Definition

Internal marketing – The application of marketing internally within the company, with programmes of communication and guidance targeted at internal audiences to develop responsiveness and a unified sense of purpose among employees (Dibb *et al.*, 2001, p. 731).

Nigel Piercy (2001), suggests that:

> Marketplace success is frequently largely dependent on employees who are far removed from the excitement of creating marketing strategies.

Therefore it is highly important that the internal marketing programme bridges the information gap between the strategy development team through to technical engineers, customer services staff, production and finance, to name but a few, so that essentially they are fully informed about the direction of the organization.

Internal marketing plays a pivotal role in ensuring that the organization is marketing and customer-focused, the components of which have already been discussed in the previous section. It is based upon a programme of communications externally that ultimately demands a positive response from the employees, that is buy-in and commitment to the newly formed strategy and planned changes that are due to be implemented.

One of the critical success factors of internal marketing is its ability to break down the various barriers to planning that were evident earlier in this unit. Its prime objective is to ensure that a more positive attitude is formed towards the organization and its vision and that productivity, effectiveness and efficiency will increase.

Internal marketing can go a long way to achieve the two key factors important to planning: 'synergy' and 'consistency'. These factors will come from a workforce in tune, integrated and committed to achieving the corporate vision.

Successful implementation of an integrated market plan will be based upon employees understanding the concepts and philosophy of the organization and its mission and corporate goals. It may enable them to feel part of the organization, responsible for its achievement.

One of the key components of an internal marketing programme is therefore communication. Internal marketing is, as suggested earlier, a communications programme. There are a number of steps that an organization can take in order to achieve internal synergy and employee co-operation:

◆　　Creating an internal awareness of the corporate aims, objectives and overall mission

◆　　Determining the expectations of the internal customer

◆　　Communication to internal customers

◆　　Changes in tasks and activities

◆　　Internal monitoring and control.

As with the external marketing plan, the internal plan ultimately needs the same components:

◆　　Internal vision

◆　　Aims and objectives

◆　　Internal marketing strategy

◆　　Segmentation, targeting and positioning

◆　　Marketing programme to include all elements of the marketing mix

◆　　Implementation

◆　　Monitoring and control of the success or failure of execution.

It is as important to segment your market internally as it is externally as we have seen earlier, as the basis and the focus of the message will need to be tailored to the particular audience, potentially fitting their contribution and that of their departments into the context of the proposed change.

The key aim of the marketing plan must therefore be the successful motivation and retention of the internal customer in order that the organization can meet the needs of the external market. The marketing mix will be the tools with which to achieve it.

Exam hints and tips

Refer to question 3(b) of the June 2007 examination by going to www.cim.co.uk where you can also refer to the specimen answers. This question focuses on how to develop a plan for staff (people) element of the service encounter.

Question 3.7

What is the importance of communication to the internal marketing process and why?

A supportive and effective marketing structure

For a marketing strategy to be successfully implemented, it will rely on an infrastructure to be in a place that will deliver the corporate goals in an efficient and effective way. The sign of a good leader is one who ensures that the organization is structured in a way that gets the job done.

Therefore it is essential that you are fully aware of the different ways of organizing the marketing activities.

Typically the structure of the organization might be functional, territory- or product-based.

The functional organization

The functional organization (see Figure 3.5) typically defines each of its business functions, from which each functional unit will have a management line of control established. In terms of marketing it is likely that this is headed up by the Director of Marketing, down to a range of functional specialisms including sales, product development and market research. This will allow for the marketing team to work on an integrated basis, undertaking a range of marketing activities on a day-to-day basis.

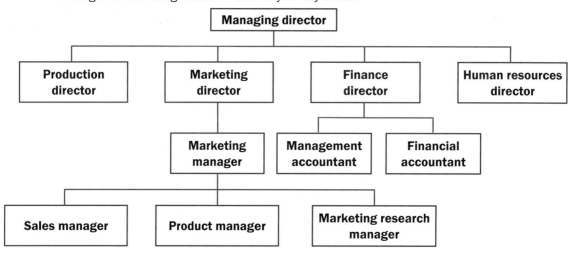

Figure 3.5: Departmentalism by function

The territory-based organization

This is quite a useful structure for organizations who trade internationally, or particularly in the retail sector, where there may be independent marketing activities undertaken in each territory (see Figure 3.6). However, this is formally known as decentralized management. This is where the business management functions are devolved to the regional centre of activity, whereby they will be responsible for their own 'territory' budget, resources and marketing activity, albeit still in line with meeting the corporate goals and objectives.

This is more typical of large organizations, and where cultural differences are significant enough to perhaps require a different approach.

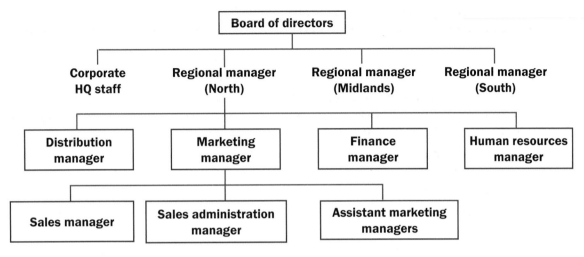

Figure 3.6: Departmentalism by territory

The product-based organization

Organizations such as Philips, Pepsi, Coca-Cola and Lever, to name but a few, work on a product-based structure (see Figure 3.7), whereby different brands and products are managed as separate business units. Each brand is individually accountable for its own performance, although it is still aligned to and responsible for meeting the overall corporate goals. In a product-based organization, product managers will have responsibility devolved down to them and be expected to ensure that their particular brand and product range delivers in line with corporate expectations.

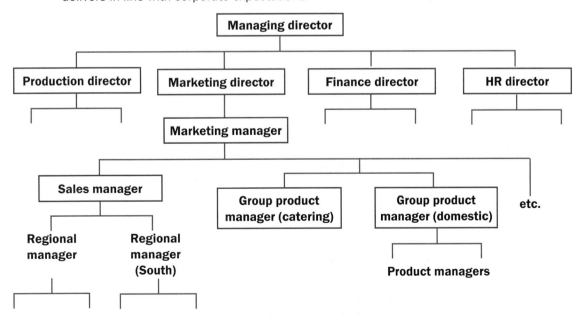

Figure 3.7: Departmentalism by product

Other organizational structures include matrix management, whereby the responsibility of the marketing manager can potentially cut across all business functions. As the role of marketing has evolved over time, it encroaches more and more on other business functions in order that an integrated and co-ordinated approach is undertaken to achieve the corporate goals.

Customer-based structures are also quite prevalent, particularly in organizations involved in financial services, whereby customers and products might be linked together and therefore the organization is run in such a way as to be able to ultimately manage and retain customers.

Whatever the structure of the organization, it is vitally important that the lines of communication are clearly defined, so that from an internal perspective, employees clearly understand the purpose and direction of the structure and ultimately their contribution overall.

Insight: Changes to Royal Mail's marketing structure

Royal Mail's Marketing Director Paul Rich is introducing a new structure to align his team more closely with the company's sales force. The move is to enable more effective and customer-driven development of products and services as the company's marketplaces become increasingly competitive.

The review of Royal Mail's marketing structure has led to five new areas covering products, sectors, brand, commercial policy plus pricing and value-added solutions. A director for each area will report directly to Rich.

The new team will be responsible for all Royal Mail branded products and services, including special stamps and philatelic products, international services and logistics, where marketing was previously carried out within separate business units.

Paul Rich said: 'The new roles provide a renewed focus for us and bring all Royal Mail branded products and services under one marketing roof. This will give us a far more cohesive, integrated and customer-focused approach. This is all part of competing effectively by making sure that we are developing and selling products and services that precisely match our customers' needs and offer best value in our marketplaces.'

Adapted from: www.royalmail.com

Financial and human resources

One of the key successes of good vision and leadership is the ability to produce the resources to get the job done. By resources we mean the money, the people and the place, in which the marketing activities can be successfully implemented.

Today resources appear to be one of the most scarce commodities in the workplace and quite often one of the key barriers to implementation. This is a result of resources actually being budget-driven. However, when strategies are being defined and planned, resource implications must be considered as part of the overall process.

For the organization to function it needs people and finance, so for the marketing strategy to be successful it is of primary importance to ensure that the whole infrastructure is in place.

Human resources

From a human resource perspective, it will be essential that the organization has the appropriate mix of management and technical skills required for implementation of the marketing plan. A team of multi-skilled marketers will be critical to successful implementation. You will learn about this within Effective Management for Marketing, where you will look at issues relating to being an effective marketing manager, appropriate recruitment, selection and teambuilding strategies.

As a marketing manager, you will have responsibility for managing the marketing team, ensuring the implementation of the process, through the successful management of tasks.

Financial resources/budgets

The processes of strategic planning and budgeting are very closely linked. In real terms, having a budget means that you are able to execute and implement a very carefully laid plan in a very controlled way, as budgeting is probably the most common control mechanism of any planning process.

When developing a plan and setting a budget, often the full picture of the situation may be unclear. This can be as a result of missing or inaccurate information. But in any case, the budget *allocation* process will ensure that an indication of the resources required to make the plan work is considered, together with the financial implications of the plan. Much of the information formulated within the budget is based on forecasts, and there is an important difference between the two.

From this a budget will be defined. The budget is a financial plan demonstrated in quantitative terms. It is likely that the budget will show volumes as well as values, over a set period of time, which in most organizations is one year. Budgets may be prepared for the various activities undertaken by the firm or they may be for products, locations and organizational functions, such as marketing, sales, administration, research and development, production and so on.

In setting a budget, you have a control mechanism, a tool to quantify plans, co-ordinate activities, highlight areas of critical importance and assign responsibilities.

According to Drummond *et al.* in their book *Strategic Marketing* (2003), budgeting seems to highlight two key points. First, they suggest that budgeting is about resource allocations, and secondly, it is a political process, hence the need for negotiation and bargaining, to secure the resources necessary to achieve the proposed plan.

Effectively what we are seeing is that a budget must be prepared to allocate resources in order to achieve marketing objectives. It should contain estimates of costs of implementing the plan; costs of each functional area of the organization and, in respect of marketing, costs of research, advertising, sales and other promotional mix activities.

A budget is effectively a financial plan of action, for an identified period of time. It is essential that the budget be developed in line with both corporate and marketing objectives. For the purpose of sales and marketing, it may include a number of project areas that have been planned for a year ahead.

It is important to understand that a plan is effectively worthless without any control element. Control will be achieved by comparing actual figures against budget figures, and the variance can then be calculated.

Budgeting can play the role of a motivational tool, when managing people who are involved in marketing activities. While organizations should be customer-driven, in many instances they are budget-driven and achieving objectives, within time and within budget, is a key motivational factor for which personnel are often rewarded.

Budgeting must not be carried out in isolation from corporate objectives or other business functions, otherwise the budget becomes ineffective, as it does not take on the realism of the situation and what can be effectively achieved corporately. This could result in lack of focus or direction.

Budgeting is critical for measuring the performance both of the organization and of individuals. Budgeting and performance can play a very significant role in personnel appraisal processes, where the budget versus the actual can be the basis of an individual achieving their employment objectives for the period. Within the organization as a whole, the same applies. It is critical that sales and production targets are met, and the only realistic way in which this can be measured effectively is by measuring actual performance against budgeted performance.

From this you will see that human and financial resources are essential to the successful implementation of the marketing plan and provide the basis of a benchmark of performance.

Typical budgetary methods include:

◆ **Bottom-up budgeting** – This is where the budgeting process is fed and developed from within the organization and where the activities happen. Here managers will prepare detailed budgets for activities that will aid the achievement of the corporate objectives. This information is then fed into the global budgeting process and considered in the round of budgetary decisions.

◆ **Negotiated budgeting** – Negotiated budgeting is, as it sounds, a process of budget *allocation* by negotiation and can often appear a little like objective and task approach budgeting (see below). Here it is likely that the marketing manager will have to negotiate expenditure based upon income forecasts in order to execute the marketing plan.

Negotiated budgeting does have a place within the organization, but more in relation to ad hoc projects, where it is possible to bid for a pot of money for extraordinary activities. However, as an overall method for budgeting, it can be arduous and also rather political as it can be open to the self-interest and self-fulfilment of individuals as opposed to the greater good of the organization.

◆ **Objective and task approach budgeting** – This is a common approach in marketing fields, where the budget is allocated specifically on the necessity to achieve output, that is to achieve objectives. The marketing team will need to clearly define the tasks that will be undertaken to achieve the objectives and specify clearly the resources required. Based upon this, budget may or may not be allocated. In some instances this can be very much like zero-based budgeting.

In relation to evaluating the effectiveness of this model, it is important to realize that much of the detail is spurious. There is no justification for the market share target or the objectives for awareness, trial or gross rating points. Different assumptions would give very different budgets and there is no criterion in the model for preferring one assumption to another.

◆ **Incremental budgeting or historical** – This type of budgeting is often based on the provision of an incremental rise in budgets year on year, in line with predicted growth in the forthcoming year, or indeed achieved growth in the previous year.

   However, this approach can be somewhat restrictive in terms of creating space for new activities, or indeed, should sales be in decline, it will be difficult to achieve the investment required to generate future growth. Some organizations are unable to increase on the previous year's expenditure and they often work on the basis of using the 'same as last time'.

◆ **Percentage of sales method** – This is a well-known method particularly relevant to the contribution from the overall budget to marketing communications. It works on the basis of a percentage of the previous year's sales being allocated to marketing communications activities for the forthcoming years. However, should sales fall the contribution from the budget falls with it, at the very time there is a greater requirement for increased expenditure to recover falling sales in order to meet targets.

   There is no rationale for the percentage chosen other than perhaps tradition, and there is no effort to consider whether or not a higher or lower amount would be more profitable.

◆ **Competitive parity** – This approach is based on spending the same percentage as competitors within the industry. This gives managers the illusion of safety in numbers – that the collective wisdom cannot be far wrong. However, there is little rationale for this approach. Clearly organizations differ in their marketing opportunities and profit margins, so that significant divergences should exist in the market. Those with better products and higher margins should spend more.

◆ **Judgement methods** – More recently, techniques have been developed to formally elicit the judgements of managers most directly involved about the future of the business. Managers are asked to judge what sales level will be attained with no advertising support, advertising at half the current level and advertising at 50 per cent more than the present level. Putting together the consensus estimate allows a projection of the optimal level of expenditure. This is a promising approach in that managers are forced to use their judgement and experience in a rational manner. The downside is that the method is only as good as the collected wisdom of those participating in the exercise.

◆ **Experiment and test** – This is particularly relevant to isolating the effects of advertising. Here the organization may run an experiment whereby one region of the country gets a higher level of spending than others. Company sales then give an estimate of the incremental effect of advertising. Whilst such approaches may give insights, they again run into a host of practical problems. How representative is the test and the test area? Is everything else similar across the regions? Has the experiment lasted long enough to judge any long-term effectiveness? Therefore this approach is limited and can be difficult to get an objective outcome for the appropriate level of advertising expenditure.

What you will find is that often organizations operate on a combined budget approach, using a hybrid of methods to suit the nature and scope of their business. It is not unusual for an organization to allocate 90 per cent of its budget specifically but to withhold 10 per cent for special, contingency projects, all of which may be negotiated or managed on the objective/task-based method.

The control process

The final component of the planning processes that is necessary to comprehend is the need to control.

In order that the goals of the organization are met, continual monitoring of the business functions within the organization must be undertaken.

Monitoring and control effectively contains four key activities:

1   Development or adjustment of marketing objectives

2   Setting of performance standards

3   Evaluation of performance

4   Corrective action.

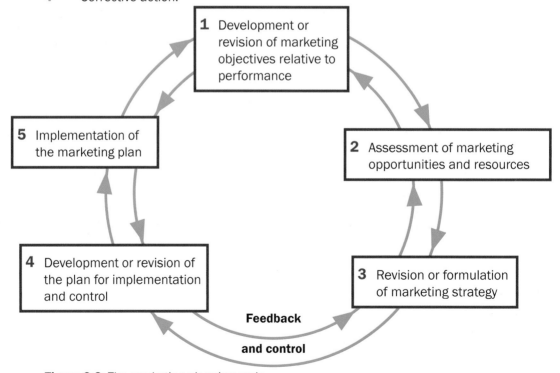

Figure 3.8: The marketing planning cycle

In Figure 3.8 you can see the planning cycle, which includes two lines of arrows, each line pointing in opposite directions. The purpose of this is to highlight the importance of planning, which is going in one direction, that is forward and onward, and control, which is continually going backwards and checking what has happened so far and essentially establishing whether the plan reached its targets step by step throughout the process. If the targets are not being met, then clearly the planning process may need to be revised.

The first stage in the process after setting the objectives, by which performance will be measured, is setting performance standards. Performance standards are principally the level of performance against which actual performance can be compared. In the main, performance standards are presented in the form of budgets. The sole purpose of this will be to ensure that the amount of money given over to expenditure is not exceeded and that the proposed targets for income and profit are actually achieved.

There are a number of techniques that can be employed in this area, but basic and generic principles apply. There are a number of organizational methods of measuring performance overall, such as performance appraisal/evaluation which includes measurement and control of staff performance. This consists of reviewing performance, giving feedback and counselling if necessary.

In addition to this there is benchmarking, which ensures that the organization develops an ongoing process of measuring processes and achievements against key performance indicators, such as competitors and best practice standards.

Monitoring and measuring performance is a critical element of business and therefore every organization must find effective ways of ensuring that plans and budget appropriations are met, or revised accordingly, and that they underpin the corporate, business and marketing objectives.

As control is an important part of the planning process, it is critical to manage it in a way that is transparent and meaningful. For the purpose of ease, it is likely that the budget will be broken down into a number of smaller areas, often termed cost centres. For each of these, planned income and expenditure are monitored and compared with the actual results.

In many organizations each function, that is marketing, personnel, production, becomes a cost centre. Splitting the budget on this basis enables an overview of how each division is performing against the plan and where the variances lie, giving an opportunity to identify each variance and potentially move towards a contingency plan if necessary, depending on the cause of the variance.

For example, typical headings on a monthly or annual budget report would be:

INCOME BUDGET – Marketing and sales division

	Actual year	Month	Budgeted amount	Variance under	Variance over
Sales					
Interest earned					
Sales commission					
Licence fees					
Royalty payments					
Property rentals					
Total income					

EXPENDITURE BUDGET – Marketing and sales division

	Actual year	Month	Budgeted amount	Variance under	Variance over
Sales					
Rent					
Advertising					
PR					
Sales promotions					
Travel					
Sales commission					
Total expenditure					

Variance analysis

One of the main things that control is likely to expose is constant variances from the planned budget. For example, when your sales are planned for £300K for the first quarter and they are only £200K in this session, then this is a variance from the actual budget.

Variance analysis is commonly used along with budgetary control. What it seeks to do is to compare the planned budget, and then the variance is examined in order for the difference between the two to be established. It is a little like looking for a cause and effect. It is not confined to price or volume, but can include variance on profit achieved, budgeted costs and change in potential market size.

The key to this control tool is to be fully aware that very often variance in budgets is inevitable and can mean that changes to the existing plan, be they contingency or fully fledged changes, are for the duration of the plan.

Budgetary control

In essence, budgetary control involves financial control of the whole business through a system of budgets. It consists of:

◆ Preparation of budgets

◆ Measuring actual performance

◆ Comparing actual results with budget results

◆ Taking corrective action if necessary.

Other methods of measurement and control might relate to customer satisfaction surveys. These may be carried out at peak points during the control process or monitored on an ongoing basis. It is essential that the organization identifies whether or not they are meeting customer expectations, needs and wants, and if not what remedial action is required.

Brand awareness is a further example of measuring marketing effectiveness.

Both these measures are vital to the measurement of the organization's performance. High levels of customer satisfaction and brand awareness are vital to the achievement of corporate goals. Should there be a decline in either of these key areas, then the organization may have to take remedial action, particularly at the marketing mix level.

Benchmarking

In the words of Drummond *et al.* (2003), benchmarking is defined as:

> A systematic and ongoing process of measuring and comparing an organisation's business processes and achievements against acknowledged process leaders and/ or key competitors, to facilitate improved performance.

Benchmarking is about demonstrating a commitment to continuous improvement and showing that the organization is a learning organization, willing to learn from mistakes and successes, and develop an approach to best business practice. It falls into three categories:

1   **Competitive analysis** – Reviewing on an ongoing basis, competitor activities to learn from their success.

2   **Best practice** – Here the organization should involve itself in reviewing the best way of undertaking activities across the whole of the organization.

3   **Performance standards** – Ensuring that targets are either met or surpassed.

Effectiveness of the marketing mix

Understanding key components of measuring the marketing mix will be essential in the long term. Some of the potential performance standards might be based upon price, whereby the effects of a particular pricing policy will be measured.

Organizations such as easyJet, now combined with Go, will frequently undertake promotional activity to generate interest and awareness in the brand. It will be vital, therefore, to monitor the response to the promotional campaign, in order that future successes or failures are identified in relation to the marketing mix.

Competitor performance

Many of these factors are internal analysis components. It is therefore essential that while monitoring your own performance you also continually monitor that of your competitors. This can be done not only through scanning the press, but also from obtaining financial information in relation to their performance.

Typical competitor comparisons will be based upon the original financial factors relating to their organization, such as the objectives in Table 3.1. Going back to the capability profile will allow you to monitor the performance of your own organization against your competitor quite effectively, and again will also highlight the need for pre-emptive or reactive strikes.

For an effective control process to be implemented, the marketing manager should consider ways of developing and maintaining effective marketing control processes. Information is the key to monitoring and measuring marketing success effectively. The quality, quantity and speed of information will be critical.

The control process should be designed to enable a flow of information that will allow a marketing manager to quickly identify the difference between the planned and the actual performance, that is the variance, and therefore be able to make informed decisions about any possible remedial changes. Should control procedures trigger a change in the overall plan, or even part of the plan, the full implications of the change must be carefully considered and, ultimately, carefully communicated.

Effective marketing control therefore hinges on quality, quantity and speed of information. The biggest single factor that inhibits the control process is that areas such as environmental changes, time lags between marketing activities and their outcomes and, more seriously, the cost of marketing activities are often difficult to determine. This means that careful budget monitoring and control is essential.

Corrective action

Implementation of marketing strategy very rarely goes directly to the plan, as external driving forces, time lags, competition and economic downturn may all change the pace at which the organization's growth can be achieved.

As a result of this, many organizations will have to take varying forms of corrective action. In the main, this is required when a performance standard falls below what is termed a 'tolerable' level. For example, if sales are in decline at an unsustainable rate, then corrective action may have to be taken.

Corrective actions can take the form of:

◆   Revised forecasts

◆   Revised sales targets

◆   Increased advertising

◆   Competitive responses

◆   Price reductions or increases

◆   Repositioning of products

◆   Marketing development strategies.

These are only a few, but it gives you an insight into the potential for change, in extenuating circumstances, when the organization can effectively no longer 'tolerate' the market conditions.

This probably brings us back to a key learning point in respect of setting objectives, developing strategies and plans. Objectives always need to be achievable, and it may be that in many instances the reason for the failure to meet performance standards is the lack of realism in the original objectives set, and perhaps failure to resource the implementation programme satisfactorily.

Summary

This has been a particularly extensive unit, focusing on the broad range of issues associated with planning. However, you are reminded that while you have been provided with an insight into the notion of marketing planning, the basis of Marketing Planning is to look at marketing at an 'operational' level. In the text, we have looked closely at:

◆   Taking the marketing audit to the planning process

◆   Setting different types of objectives

◆   Segmentation, targeting and positioning

◆ Strategy development

◆ Implementation of the marketing plan.

The influence and importance of marketing planning must never be underestimated; it is vital to the success of the organization. There is endless academic writing in relation to this subject area, but while many are a slight variation on a theme, there is a core at the heart of planning that never actually changes. It is very important to read around the subject wherever possible and gain a real insight into the major driving forces behind the planning processes and what makes planning such a vital activity.

Study tip

Operational level marketing will focus quite clearly on involvement in the marketing audit, preparing the audit for strategy development and thereinafter providing information to support the decision-making process that ultimately culminates in the development of the marketing mix programme.

At an operational level, you will be expected to define, based upon the key strategic marketing objectives presented to you, a marketing strategy and tactical marketing plan, that is define a marketing programme based upon the marketing mix.

To answer Question 1 in June 2007 and Question 1 in the December 2007 exam paper – go to www.cim.co.uk to collect the specimen answers.

Bibliography

Dibb, S., Simkin, L., Pride, W. and Ferrell, O. (2005) *Marketing: Concepts and Strategies*, Houghton Mifflin, 4th European edition

Drummond, G., Ensor, J. and Ashford, R. (2003) *Strategic Marketing: Planning and Control*, Oxford: Butterworth-Heinemann

Kotler, P., Armstrong, G., Saunders, J. and Wong, V. (1998) *Principles of Marketing*, FT Prentice Hall

Piercy, N. (2001) *Market Led Strategic Change*, Oxford: Butterworth-Heinemann

Piercy, N. (1999) *Tales from the Marketplace*, Oxford: Butterworth-Heinemann

Porter, M. (1980) *Competitive Strategy*, Free Press

Useful websites include:

www.cim.co.uk

www.cimvirtualinstitute.com

www.revolution.haynet.com

www.marketing.haynet.com

www.ft.com

www.acnielson.com

Unit 4 Marketing decisions and the communications mix

Learning objectives

This unit has two purposes, one is to consider the role of branding and its impact upon marketing decisions and the second is to examine how the marketing communications mix is co-ordinated as part of the marketing plan.

The syllabus elements directly relating to this unit are as follows:

3.3 Explain the role of branding and its impact on the marketing mix decisions.

3.4 Describe methods for maintaining and managing the brand.

3.10 Explain how the marketing communications mix is co-ordinated with the marketing mix as part of a marketing plan.

The marketing mix in the context of marketing planning

The marketing mix is a set of tools that provides the basis of implementation of the marketing plan. The promotional tools provide the means by which an organization communicates with potential and existing customers about their products, services, distribution outlets and overall prices.

For many organizations, the marketing mix provides a basis for developing their marketing strategies, plans and tactics. They will take the marketing mix and develop a marketing strategy that will enable them to meet customer needs, be highly competitive in terms of both proactive and reactive competition, and allow them to differentiate on brand, products and services and position themselves successfully against competitive equivalents.

The principal approach to marketing should be based around three key ingredients, that is integration, co-ordination and communication. This applies to the design and development of the marketing mix as well as every aspect of the planning process, with synergy and consistency as critical success factors to the overall implementation of the plan.

The marketing mix cannot be developed in a vacuum or in isolation of the other elements. For example, an organization cannot develop a quality, value-added product/service without due consideration to the cost of the product and how they can charge that to the customer. Organizations will then have to give due consideration to how they will distribute it. Then, of course, how do they communicate with their customers to inform them of the existence of the new product or service?

For a truly marketing-oriented, customer-focused organization it is of primary importance to understand the impact of each element of the marketing mix upon customers and their perspectives of the organization.

For a clearer understanding of customer responses and reactions to the marketing mix, it is useful to consider the key components of the 7Cs model as shown in Figure 4.1.

Organizational perspective of the marketing mix		Customer perspective of the marketing mix
Produce	=	Customer value
Price	=	Cost
Place	=	Convenience
Promotion	=	Communication
Physical evidence	=	Confirmation
People	=	Consideration
Process	=	Co-ordination and concern

Figure 4.1: The 7Cs of the marketing mix

This model provides you with a framework of reference when identifying customer expectations of the organization's marketing mix. For example:

◆ The customer does not buy the product/service, but the value that the product/service provides.

◆ The price of the product/service is not the customer issue, but how much it will cost them.

◆ What is important to the customer is not the method of distribution, but the convenience of the product for purchase.

◆ The customer perspective is not the promotion but how the messages are communicated to them.

◆ The customer is not concerned with the surroundings or physical evidence, but wants confirmation of their assumptions.

◆ Customers are not concerned with people involved in providing services, but that consideration is provided when purchasing.

◆ Customers are not concerned with the process, but that efforts are co-ordinated to meet their requirements.

It might appear that the main focus of the 7Ps is very much on the services aspect of marketing; however, it is becoming extremely clear that more and more products and services are integral and reliant on one another. What is important is the 'customer experience' – this will require a co-ordinated approach to some or all of the marketing mix elements simultaneously and not in isolation.

Profiling marketing segments for promotional activities

It has already been suggested that segmenting markets in relation to promotional activities can be a complex process. However, whatever the range of variables that the organization uses in order to establish target groups of customers, it is essential that they establish a clear understanding of the characteristics of the individuals within the group before ultimately defining their make-up.

Definition

Profiling – the task of building up a fuller picture of the target segments (Dibb *et al.*, 2005).

Profiling is achieved by taking a group of what are commonly known as descriptors, based around traditional segmentation criteria, that is demographics, geographics and socio-economics of the target group, and seeking to understand how these descriptors match against the variables established to identify customer needs and wants. The idea is that while some of the customer base might have matching demographics, their socio-economics might differ and result in differing customer needs. It is essential that you profile customers in this way, to highlight as many similarities as possible, in order to maximize the potential impact of a fully co-ordinated marketing mix.

A good example of this would be the motor vehicle market. While most 30–45 year olds possess a car, the needs associated with the car will differ significantly. So, in the context of promotional needs, the targeting of cars in the upper range, such as high-specification Mercedes or BMWs, might require a different promotional mix to those who are looking for a low-cost family saloon. Typical profiling strategies will ensure that the differences between target groups are identified to maximize the potential of the promotional mix.

This then allows for very specific targeting in promotional terms, and allows the organization to define its approach on either a mass media basis, or indeed a concentration strategy or even a focus strategy approach to promotional activities.

Push and pull strategy

Prior to moving on to look at the intricate detail of the promotional mix, and how the promotional tools are used to implement the marketing strategy, it is essential that you understand the nature of 'push and pull' strategies.

Push strategy

This is where the manufacturer effectively takes the decision to concentrate their communications effort on the members of the distribution channel, that is the wholesaler and retailers. This means that the wholesalers may possess a significant amount of stock that they need to move on from a particular manufacturer, and therefore they in turn promote the products to the end-user and customer.

The basis of this strategy is that the manufacturer is promoting directly to the suppliers, and the products are, therefore, pushed down the line by the different members of the channel. By the same token, the promotional activity is also pushed down the line in parallel with the product. In this instance it is highly unlikely that the manufacturer will therefore have any direct contact with the customer.

Pull strategy

This strategy operates in contrast to the push strategy in that it requires the manufacturer to create demand for the product through direct communication with the customers. From here it is likely that the retailers might identify and perceive the demand for this product and that it is essential in the interest of serving their customers. They might then demand the product from their supplier/wholesaler. This effectively sees the product being pulled up the line by consumer demand, that is the consumer is pulling it to the market and being pulled by the manufacturer.

However, on this occasion it is likely that the promotion and communications activity will be working in the opposite direction from the product, and therefore the communication relates to pulling the product to the market, effectively developing a strong consumer demand.

Of course, in reality, manufacturers will involve themselves in both push and pull situations, in order to assert as much influence as possible on the supply chain and the customer.

Promotional operations and the planning framework

Figure 4.2: Promotions and the planning framework

It is important to understand the role of promotional operations and the role it plays in terms of the implementation of the overall marketing strategy. Figure 4.2 provides an insight into where promotional operations will fit into the planning hierarchy.

Aims and objectives of the promotional communications process

You will probably by now realize that the process of product adoption is a high level objective – for any component of the promotional activity and the promotional mix. Therefore it is essential that you translate this into five key communication effects:

Category needs	The perception and understanding of the actual customer needs
Brand awareness	The ability of the consumer to identify and associate with a particular brand and differentiate from another brand
Brand attitude	This relates to the consumer's particular observations, view and perceptions of the brand – cognitive beliefs
Brand purchase intention	Once the category needs have been identified, the brand purchase intention follows
Purchase facilitation	The purchase activity needs to be facilitated by the organization, by ensuring that the product is available at the right price and the right place – this in essence is the manifestation of the co-ordinated marketing mix.

These aims break down into a number of more specific promotional objectives that the promotional operations activity will seek to achieve to meet the corporate goals and marketing objectives and also to ensure successful implementation of the marketing strategy.

Possible communications objectives will therefore include:

◆ Clarification of customer needs

◆ Increasing brand awareness

◆ Increasing product knowledge

◆ Improving brand image

◆ Improving company image

◆ Increasing brand preference

◆ Stimulating search behaviour

◆ Increasing trial purchases

◆ Increasing repeat purchases

◆ Increasing word-of-mouth recommendation

◆ Improving financial position

◆ Increasing flexibility of the corporate image

◆ Increasing co-operation from the trade

◆ Enhancing the reputation with key stakeholders

◆ Building up management ego.

Source: Based on Delozier (1976)

Ultimately, any activities that you undertake as part of the promotional process will therefore be aiming to achieve one or more of the above promotional objectives, reflecting very much the nature of the key marketing objectives and strategy.

The critical success factors associated with achieving the aims of the promotional communications process relate to targeting specific customer groups through a clearly defined profiling process.

In the same way that short-term and long-term objectives are an issue within the marketing strategy framework, so are they in terms of promotional activity, as the promotional strategy will be shaped and determined by those objectives. However, it is likely that much of the promotional activity will be based on short-term activity, but in the context of the broader picture of the long-term achievement of goals.

You will realize from the above considerations that branding is an essential part of the strategy development process, both from a generic perspective and also from a promotional operations perspective, therefore understanding the strategic implications of branding and how to manage the brand is an essential component of your learning.

Branding

> A successful brand is an identifiable product, service, person or place, augmented in such a way that the buyer or user perceives relevant, unique, sustainable added values, which match their needs most closely. (De Chernatony and McDonald, 1998)

A brand is a highly powerful tool, because it provides a balance of functional benefits and performance values. The term 'brand' is used to describe the 'personality' of a particular company's products. The brand concerns use of design, colour, typography, the quality that brand portrays and the actual identity of a product or service as the customer sees it. The brand is not just a name, the brand is a multifunctional concept.

There are many well-known brands throughout the various segments that have built up reputations as providers of good quality produce or services. For example, Nokia, Coca-Cola, Nike, Reebok, BMW are all well-known brands of reputable quality.

Branding is of primary importance to the organization, as it provides the organization and its product portfolio with an identity, something that people can associate with. It is essentially the key to successfully differentiating the organization and its products from the competition. However, to develop a successful brand will require a considerable investment in both time and money, an investment, which if properly planned and managed, should reap significant rewards.

The brand plays a number of roles from an input, output and time perspective.

Brands are complex, but ultimately they rest in the minds of customers as a basis on which to identify with a product, quality and image that is portrayed (Table 4.1).

These points realistically need little explanation. However, it is essential that you are aware that the input perspective relates to everything that is put into the brand to actually make it a brand and, from the perspective of the organization, what the inputs are that make the brand successful. This means the way in which the brand is managed, that is the resources required to ensure that the brand is of significant value, both rationally and emotionally, to the customer.

Table 4.1: Different brand interpretations		
Input perspective	**Output perspective**	**Time perspective**
Logo	Image	Evolving entity
Legal instrument	Relationship	
Company		
Risk reducer		
Positioning		
Personality		
Cluster of values		
Vision		
Value added		
Identity		

Adapted from: De Chernatony (2001)

From an external perspective, the brand will be perceived and interpreted by the customer: how it motivates and fulfils them and actually achieves some purpose for them.

'Time-based' is something of a radical component in branding. How long is a piece of string, some might say, but it is indeed an important factor. It may appear that some brands, such as Ford for example, might go on into perpetuity. However, this would be a complacent and dangerous strategy to follow; one with likely catastrophic results.

Brand values

Brand values are often difficult to define. However, they represent KSF of the organization and its products. Rokeach (1973), in *The Nature of Human Values*, suggested that:

> A value is an enduring belief that a specific mode of conduct or end-state of existence is personally or socially preferable to an opposite or converse mode of conduct or end-state existence.

Values are essential in any organization, not only from the internal perspective, where values will define the basis on which the organization does business, but also from the external perspective, where values essentially become meaningful and often the source of 'added value'. For example, where quality is a value, quality is a perceived benefit to the customer.

Brand values, therefore, become the basis of an organization being perceived as different. However, while they might form the basis of differentiation, the organization must be clear as to why they arrived at these values in the first place, and what they might mean to the future vision of the business.

As a customer it is likely that you will be drawn to brands that hold values compatible to your own personal ones, and by the same token employees are often drawn to organizations that are associated with core principle values very much in line with their own.

Where are values formed? Values are formed as a result of a range of influences on each individual from childhood through to adulthood. Key influencers in our lives – parents, peers and colleagues – form them. A value is a belief, something we believe in, see as important, and allow to shape and form our behaviour.

As a result of the key components that define values, organizations therefore are challenged to specifically develop values that are akin to their customer groups, their target markets, which makes the segmentation process all the more complex. However, not only is the segmentation process complex, but the expectations of the organization in the minds of the customers as a result of their brand values are highly demanding and need careful planning.

An excellent example of brand values is that of the Virgin brand. Richard Branson declared that the qualities associated with Virgin are as follows:

◆ Quality

◆ Innovation

◆ Value for money

◆ Fun

◆ A sense of challenge.

These are more formally known as a cluster of values. These core values will, therefore, be at the core or heart of whatever Virgin do in the future. If they continue to extend the brand, as they have done on many occasions before, these values should continue to be the core of all of the businesses, not exclusive to one.

Branson used five values to demonstrate the ethos of his organization, five being an appropriate number and sufficiently challenging to deliver.

Many organizations develop brands for an external perspective and with the 'external' customer in mind. However, more and more organizations are moving towards making the brand values the focus point of the whole business, for both internal customers and external customers, actually making them a core rather than peripheral activity.

Core and peripheral values

While developing and defining corporate values is an essential activity, there are two levels of values which a company can focus on.

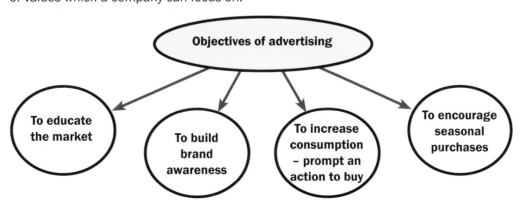

Core values are those values that the brand will always uphold, regardless of the external drivers of change, which are here to stay. On the other hand, peripheral values are those that are of secondary importance to the brand, and those that might change with market forces and conditions. Therefore, while quality might always be a core value, a peripheral value might be related to an activity or service level that the organization changes in line with market forces.

In essence, establishing brand values provides a robust basis for appropriate behaviour on the part of the organization. Values contribute in part to the vision and mission of the organization and ultimately establish a culture based upon which the organization can do business, meet customer needs and actually make a difference to customer experiences and customer achievements.

Case study: Cadbury's brand values

We are all consciously and unconsciously affected by brands in our daily lives. When we go to purchase a pair of training shoes we rarely make a purely practical decision. There are numerous branded and non-branded options available. For many people, a pair of trainers must sport a brand logo because that will communicate certain values to other people.

The confectionery market elicits similar conscious and unconscious feelings of passion, loyalty and enthusiasm. For many people, chocolate is Cadbury, and no other brand will do. This consumer loyalty is critical because of the value of the chocolate confectionery market and because, in all markets, a small number of consumers account for a large proportion of sales. Loyal customers are the most valuable customers to have because they will buy your product over and over again.

Branded products command premium prices. Consumers will happily pay that premium if they believe that the brand offers levels of quality and satisfaction that competing products do not. The most enduring brands have become associated with both tangible and intangible properties over time. The most successful provoke a series of emotional or aspirational associations and values that go way beyond the physical product.

Cadburys has identified these brand values and adjusts its advertising strategies to reflect these values in different markets. Its strategy can vary from increasing brand awareness, educating potential customers about a new product, increasing seasonal purchases, or as is currently the case in the 'Choose Cadbury' campaign to highlight the positive emotional value of the brand.

After identifying brand values, the marketing manager must match these to the specific market. For this reason it is important to identify possible segments that have specific needs, and to highlight appropriate brand values that will promote the brand in that market.

Brand loyalty

One of the benefits of defining corporate values is that there can be a brand association between the customer and the organization. This can often be the basis of a long and loyal relationship. Brand loyalty is a hot topic in today's competitive environment, with significant pressure on brand switching to gain market share from competing organizations.

In achieving brand association the brand should be tightly targeted and assist customer achievement, so that brand loyalty and customer retention can be achieved.

Brand loyalty, brand preference and brand recognition are objectives of branding and form the structure and basis upon which brands are developed. However, in this context there is a significant difference between brand recognition and brand preference. Brand recognition is a measurement of customer awareness.

The more important measures of success will indeed be brand loyalty and brand preference – they will form a very vital part of the brand planning process.

Question 4.1

What are the long-term benefits of building brand loyalty?

Brand planning

Planning in relation to brands is an essential activity, as it determines the future behaviour of the organization and provides a SMART basis on which it is to operate. Planning ensures delivery of brand values and the whole brand experience to the marketplace.

Typically there are long-term and short-term objectives relating to the brand, as with any other marketing activity. Long-term objectives are often perceived as being particularly stretching on the part of the organization, where they form part of the greater vision for the future. For example, back in the 1960s, IBM set themselves a brand objective of 're-shaping the computer industry' while Boeing set a long-term brand objective of launching a commercial jet aircraft, which they ultimately achieved through the launch of the Boeing 707, bringing jet travel to the commercial market.

Short-term objectives, however, relate to the more immediate future, whereby sub-sets of objectives need to be defined to underpin the longer-term vision. Therefore, they will relate to ways of achieving the long-term goals. For example, Boeing determined that they would:

- Be the airlines' first choice
- Show strong profitability and meet investors' expectations
- Have a global network and a global outlook
- Delight customers.

In many ways, brand planning will be quite a strategic role. However, it is useful for you to be aware of the implications of brand planning, as in a product management role or marketing management role, responsibility will lie with you in terms of the overall implementation of the plan and the tactical activities involved.

Brand strategies

It is important at this early stage to examine closely the importance of brand naming strategies for naming products and services across the organization. The focal point for decision-making in relation to brands is on the emphasis an organization wishes to place on creating a 'distinctive' offering in the market against the weight it wishes to place on the origin of the product or service. There are several options open to the organization, which we will now explore.

Corporate brands

This is where organizations would use one corporate name across all products, for example, organizations such as Heinz do this. Individual products carry a descriptive name under the corporate umbrella of the Heinz brand, for example Heinz Tomato Ketchup, Heinz Soups and, of course, Heinz Baked Beans. The linking of these products by the use of the name Heinz enables the organization to create a strong overall image, whilst at the same time potentially creating economies of scale in marketing communications and distribution. Clearly this is an advantage to organizations such as Heinz.

However, in their book *Strategic Marketing: Planning and Control*, Drummond et al. (2003) suggest that there is a clear danger, and on some occasions, a disadvantage in this approach in that if there is a problem with an individual product the reputation of all of these products may suffer. A clear example of this would be the Mercedes A Class, where back at the early stage of its launch it became known for a variety of problems relating to its stability on the road.

Other brand naming strategies include:

- **Multi-branding** – Manufacturers introduce a number of brands that all satisfy very similar product characteristics. For example, in the detergents market, Procter & Gamble have several brands all fulfilling the same purpose. It also means that anyone trying to enter the market for the first time would have to launch several brands at once to compete. Again there are many advantages and disadvantages associated with this approach. For example, an advantage is that this approach allows for individual differentiation of the brand and also allows products to occupy different positions in the same market, that is premium and discount brands from the same company. However, this is countered by disadvantages. Disadvantages for multi-branding include factors such as each brand requiring a separate promotional budget in order to promote it and sell it effectively. However, a side point here is that, of course, these products are therefore dependent on the market containing enough potential to support more than one brand.

- **Company and individual brand** – Unilever used to practise a multi-brand approach with its washing powders, but has been moving closer to the strategy of linking a company name to an individual brand name. Their products now have Lever Bros as a high profile endorsement on individual brands such as Persil and Surf. The main advantage of this approach is that the product can clearly be supported by the reputation of an existing corporate brand while at the same time the individual characteristics of the specific offering can be emphasized. However, this is countered by two clear disadvantages. First, the product failure has the potential to cause some damage to the company brand, and secondly, the positioning of the company brand constrains decisions on quality and pricing of individual products.

- **Range brand** – Some organizations use different brand names for different ranges of products, in effect creating a family of products. Ford has done this to an extent, using Ford for its mass-market car range and Jaguar for the upmarket executive car range. Volvo, Ford's latest acquisition, has its own distinct brand values to appeal to a particular market segment and therefore will become another brand family for the Ford Group. Of course there are some advantages and disadvantages of this approach. For example, an advantage would be that the strength of the brand would be conveyed across all of the products in the range and that promotional costs are spread across all of the products in the range also. However, this is countered by any new product failure damaging not just the discrete brand, but rather the range and also positioning the brand constrains decisions on quality and pricing for individual products.

◆ **Private brand** – This is better known as the distributor's own brand. An organization may decide to supply private brands, in particular retail brands. In this case the private brand is owned and controlled by the distributor who will make decisions regarding the product's position in the market. The distributor is likely to use company or individual brands for its products. The advantages of this are that the promotional spend by the producer is quite small and this therefore enables them to concentrate on gaining cost efficiency through volume production. However, the downside is that marketing decisions then tend to be controlled by the distributor which can then remove the producer from direct contact with the market.

Insight: Product brands

The Cadbury brand has a profound impact on individual product brands. Brands have individual personalities aimed at specific target markets for specific needs. TimeOut, for example, is sold as an ideal snack to have with a cup of tea. It derives benefit from the Cadbury parentage, including quality and taste credentials. To ensure the success of product brands every aspect of the parent brand is focused on. Flake, Crunchie and TimeOut are clearly different and are manufactured to appeal to a variety of consumer segments. However, the strength of the umbrella brand supports the brand value of each chocolate bar. Consumers know they can trust a chocolate bar that carries Cadbury branding. The relationship between Cadbury and individual brands is symbiotic, with pure chocolate brands such as Dairy Milk benefiting more from the Cadbury relationship. Other brands have a more distant relationship, as the consumer motivation is to purchase ingredients other than chocolate, for example Crunchie.

Similarly issues such as specific advertising or product quality of a packet of Cadbury biscuits or a single Creme Egg will, in turn, impact on the perception of the parent brand. Similarly the umbrella brand has a strong brand value and a reputation that must be supported by its individual brands.

Brand threats

Brands are no exception when it comes to threats from external forces, as attacking a brand, particularly a well-known brand, can reap rewards in terms of high levels of publicity, as in the case of British Airways and Virgin and indeed Camelot and Virgin. But it can also actually impact upon marketing share.

Typical threats therefore include:

◆ **Competition** – This component has just been covered. Brands do need to protect themselves against high levels of competitor threat. The key to success in overcoming brand threats is to ensure that the branding strategy relates to uniqueness, differentiation, robust corporate identity and strong core brand values.

◆ **Brand names** – The key threat here is the potential misuse or copying of brand names. Some organizations use brand names in order to heighten awareness of their brand, or to give it a comparable position with another brand. For example, Kleenex is a brand of paper handkerchiefs (i.e. paper tissues) in the United Kingdom; while in Iran, if you wish to purchase a box of tissues, it does not matter what the brand name is, tissues are known synonymously as 'Kleenex'. Therefore, in Iran, this has diluted the power of the actual Kleenex brand and its associated product.

◆   **Copyright** – A major infringement of intellectual property rights is the use of trademarks, designs and logos that have been legally protected against misuse and copy. If they are not legally protected, then other organizations can use them and benefit from them.

Managing the brand

Branding is an absolute minefield, and is a subject in its own right. We have only touched upon some of the generic issues associated with branding. Branding is a core activity, a differentiating activity and one that enables the organization to establish a corporate identity and a vision based around clearly defined brand values.

To ensure that the brand is successful and there is synergy between the branding strategy and the remainder of the product, and the marketing mix, it is essential that the brand be carefully managed.

Successful brands

Key points

To create a successful brand a company must:

◆   Make quality a priority

◆   Offer superior service

◆   Get there first

◆   Differentiate its brands

◆   Develop a unique positioning concept

◆   Support the brand

◆   Deliver consistency.

Adapted from: Dibb *et al.* (2005).

These key points set the tone of the role of brand management, which is essentially based around building an effective brand that will ultimately support the corporate goals and marketing objectives.

The focus of any marketer's role is based upon creating an awareness of the brand and its associated values to the customer, monitoring consumer reactions and meeting their needs.

The marketing communications mix

You may wonder why we are now moving from branding to the marketing communications mix. Branding and marketing communications are essential to one another, and the way in which the brand is communicated can often determine the outcome of the success of the brand strategy. If the message is wrong then the outcome is that the brand will potentially fail. In past years we have seen organizations aim for a brand name change or a brand image change and they have failed because the messages were not right. A perfect example of this is the change of the UK Post Office to Cosignia, only for it to change back to Royal Mail several years later, because the name Cosignia failed. The change from Anderson and Anderson to Accenture was also slow to be received, although several years on from this change Accenture is now well established.

Tools of the marketing communications mix

The tools of the marketing communications mix are deliberately selected for their ability to attract customers, fulfil their desire for information and ultimately persuade them to adopt the products. In this unit, we will be looking specifically at advertising, sales promotions, public relations, direct and interactive marketing communications, sponsorship and personal selling.

Choosing the ultimate promotional mix is a complex task that requires skill in creatively matching the profile of the customer and the target group with a promotional mix that will essentially attract them to the product. Of course the complexity of the exercise will differ based upon the market. Certainly from a B2B perspective, it is highly complex given the number of people involved in the decision-making process.

It has been suggested on a number of occasions that the key to success in implementing the ultimate promotional mix is understanding customers and their characteristics, something that is a consistent theme to implementation of communications and promotional objectives.

However, the success of any promotional campaign will impinge upon the co-ordinated approach to using the promotional mix.

Co-ordinated marketing communications

Co-ordinated marketing communications is growing in impetus and importance in marketing today as more and more organizations realize the importance of taking a more structured, ordered and integrative approach to their marketing communications activities.

In the simplest form, it involves the integration and cohesion of all elements of the marketing mix. A campaign that is co-ordinated is planned, it is uniform in terms of its design, and it shares a unique selling proposition (USP) and communicates the same message in a co-ordinated way. By combining more than one element of promotion, the message that is communicated is more powerful.

For example, Walkers Crisps have been involved in implementing a co-ordinated campaign. This has been on both TV and poster advertising. In addition to that, they are developing a consistent approach to advertising, using key personalities to identify with their products. As a result of this, Walker's market grew by 21 per cent, while the crisp market generally rose by only 11 per cent.

Customers require a variety of different communication and promotional activities to fulfil their need to know about products and services and then to purchase them. So, while we are predominantly talking about advertising, you must consider the need to integrate and co-ordinate all of your marketing and communications/promotional activities.

Communications plans can only be successfully developed if the key factors within the marketing plan are clearly defined, identified and developed.

According to Chris Fill, in his book *Integrated Marketing Communications* (1999):

> Co-ordinated marketing communications cannot be achieved just by saying the same message through a variety of tools; the marketing mix is also a strong communicator.

Co-ordinated communications are mostly likely to occur when organizations attempt to enter into a co-ordinated dialogue with their various internal and external audiences. The communications tools used in the dialogue and the message sent should be consistent with the organization's objectives and strategies.

Co-ordinated marketing communications often mean different things to different people, but in the main the view is that the subject should embrace the marketing mix, the promotional mix, internal communications and all those who contribute to the overall marketing communications process. This means that PR, advertising, direct mail, trade promotions, consumer promotions, packaging, point-of-sale signage, brochures, literature, merchandize, websites and sponsorship all have their own individual role, but all achieve the corporate and marketing objectives for the brand.

There are a number of driving forces at work encouraging the growth in co-ordinated marketing communications. From the organizational perspective, there is the need for improved efficiency, rapid growth in global marketing, co-ordinated brand development and competitive advantage and the organization's drive to provide direction and purpose for the brand.

From the market-based perspective, drivers include better-educated audiences, cost of media and greater amounts of information – 'message clutter', competitor activities, growth in relationship marketing and the growth of networks, collaborations and alliances.

Communication-based drivers include technological advances such as the Internet, databases, new segmentation techniques, message effectiveness, more consistent brand images and the need to build brand reputations to provide clear identities.

As we move on, it is essential that while you look at each element of the promotional mix in isolation, to understand its role in the promotional operations process, you should also look at ways of maximizing the mix potential by integrating it and aligning it with other promotional tools in order to optimize the marketing effort.

Advertising

Advertising is one of the most influential forms of communication within the promotional mix, and the one that perhaps has the most impact upon our everyday lives. It does not matter where we go during a day, it is likely that we are bombarded either by radio, hoardings, TV, cinema or by banner advertising on a regular basis.

Definition

Advertising – a paid form of non-formal communication that is transmitted through mass media such as television, radio, newspapers, magazines, direct mail, public transport vehicles, outdoor displays and the Internet.

It is likely that advertising will serve a number of purposes in terms of communicating with both individual and organizational customers. It is used to meet a number of specific marketing and promotional objectives as you have already seen, but its main emphasis is to inform, persuade and remind customers to purchase products and services.

Ideally, advertising is used to promote products and services, but it is also a source that creates long-term images and perspectives of the organization. It is likely that there have been a number of adverts that stick in your mind that have impacted upon you in a direct way, created an image and perception in your mind.

Take for example 'Orange Tango' – being 'Tangoed' became a way of life for young people for a long time as a result of the orange coloured man running around and slapping an unsuspecting person in the face. It is probably one of the most successful advertisements in achieving 'recall'.

Advertising objectives

You will see later in this unit where advertising objectives actually come into play, and how they break down into different categories. Advertising objectives should be SMART in the same way that marketing objectives are SMART and they should relate directly to achieving the marketing objectives overall. It is therefore likely that advertising objectives will reflect some of the following components:

◆ Promoting product, organizations and services

◆ Stimulating demand for products

◆ Competing – offensive/defensive advertising

◆ Increasing sales – growth

◆ Educating the market – brand and product awareness

◆ Increasing the use of product and services – market development

◆ Reminding and reinforcing – market penetration

◆ Reducing fluctuations.

However, there is a fine line between advertising to create sales and advertising to create awareness and each of these will require a different approach in order to achieve the long-term goals of the organization.

It is quite clear that one of the key tools of the marketing communications mix to support the sale of products is advertising. This is particularly so for consumer-based products, where advertising serves to create an awareness of the product, its characteristics, its image and buying habits.

A good example to demonstrate how consumer-based products interact with advertising is chocolate. A low involvement, low unit-price bar of chocolate would not, of course, warrant an investment in personal selling to the millions of consumers who purchase it on a day-to-day basis. In this situation it is much more likely that the emphasis would be through some form of advertising or even sponsorship through advertising. Sponsorship-based advertising is becoming increasingly common, with organizations such as Cadbury sponsoring the UK soap opera *Coronation Street*, for example.

It is critical that you understand the impact of advertising and the role it plays on the product, and the link between the advertising campaign and the different stages of the PLC. However, it is also important that first you understand the appropriate media and their characteristics and how they can be used.

Question 4.2

Why is it important to define advertising objectives?

Advertising and the marketing mix

Advertising is used to support many elements of the marketing mix, but in most instances the product and brand are the key focus to advertising activities.

Advertising for both distribution and retailing is very much related to the 'push' and 'pull' strategies that we discussed earlier. In essence an organization at this stage may be developing a strategy related to increasing the number of outlets it has, for example a marketing objective may have been set to increase the number of retail outlets by 15 per cent within a 12-month period.

Advertising will be focused on encouraging retailers to stock their products. In this situation, advertising will be very closely linked to a high level of promotional activity to support the advertising and give an incentive for distribution outlets to stock their products.

A good example of this is electrical wholesalers, who are encouraged by organizations such as MK, Mitre and Crabtree to sell their products on to electrical retailers. They will therefore advertise in trade media and quite possibly offer incentives for wholesalers to carry stock.

A push strategy would often include a range of personal selling, trade (sales) promotions, advertising and direct marketing, in addition to public relations.

For a retail outlet, a pull strategy would be developed. The key to developing this is to create an awareness of the brand and its associated product and encourage customers to purchase it from them.

Advertising on this occasion will take several forms, such as TV, radio, press advertising and possibly a big poster campaign. Clearly the level of advertising will be based on the budget available both through the manufacturer and through the retailer.

Quite often in retailing situations some promotional support will be available from the manufacturer, such as various brochures, point-of-sale display materials and merchandizing support. Again this is very relevant with the sale of electrical goods. Organizations such as Philips or Electrolux offer keen incentives to their retail outlets and distributors to sell their products.

As a marketing communications planner, you will need to undertake the following activities in this area:

◆ Liaise with channel members to ensure that stock is available.

◆ Be aware of the needs of the channel and how and when they need communications support.

◆ Provide consistency for all communications.

◆ Ensure that all members of the channel support and are empowered by the message the advertisement seeks to deliver.

Case study: Porsche 04 Cayenne advertising campaign

Below is an example of how Porsche, through the use of advertising Agency Carmichael Lynch, invested some $15–25 million dollars on advertising.

Objective	Raise awareness and sales.
Target audience	Thrill seekers who want room for the family: Adults 48-years-old and married with children; manager, supervisor, or self-employed. Beyond demographics, the Cayenne target enjoys life to the fullest and likes to have fun. Passionate people with a competitive nature. Outer-directed; feels success and keeps up with fashion and technology. The Cayenne target believes their automobile is an expression of who they are; they need a vehicle that works with their life and activities.
How magazines were used:	• Magazines were used to create personal connections with prospects in high involvement editorial environments for auto enthusiasts. • Additional titles were used for the financial-minded • Special interest sporting titles were used which reflect the target's lifestyle and leisure interests.
Results:	Became the highest-selling 2003 SUV in its category.

Repositioning through advertising

Taking a more strategic perspective, advertising can also be used to reposition a product and redefine it in the mind of the customer. Quite often this happens in response to competitive pressures and therefore both aggressive and defensive advertising is likely to be used in order to improve or at least sustain a competitive position.

Positioning is the definition of how and where the brand is going to compete: what particular virtues does the product possess, what are the benefits it offers and when can it best be used?

The most likely approach to this would be opening up new segments of the market to operate within, based on either a benefit usage or possibly geographical or demographic segments.

Ultimately, the brand repositioning will need to provide an even stronger point of differentiation for consumers. Advertising must represent how the brand is meant to fit into its market. It must represent the truth about the brand and offer benefits that are strong enough to encourage customers to buy.

Advertising and its influence on price

The role of marketing communications is informing the target market about the price of a product or service offering. This can be undertaken through advertising in addition to the other elements of the promotional mix, for example personal selling, promotions and so on.

There will be many instances when buyers will be concerned with the price of their purchase. However, they may not consider the price in isolation, indeed it will most likely be considered in respect of the product, its size, shape, smell, colour and overall benefits.

Organizations must be aware that price can in fact inhibit purchase of products and services for many people and therefore a pricing strategy needs to be reflected in the communications undertaken by an organization. The customer/consumer has thus a clear understanding of the cost impact upon them.

Price issues will vary from product to product and from target group to target group, but the prominence that price receives will depend upon a number of factors:

◆ Target group

◆ Level of involvement

◆ Attitude to risk

◆ Complexity and technical nature of the product/service

◆ The importance of price to the decision-making process.

Therefore with this in mind, the design of an advertisement and its emphasis on price will be based on the target audience, positioning of the product and the competitive position the product has in the marketplace.

Question 4.3

In what way does advertising support the other elements of the promotional mix?

Sales promotions

Sales promotions traditionally are complementary to advertising. They are used to reinforce and encourage customers to trial the product and then to purchase. Sales promotion provides a range of short-term tactical measures to induce sales of particular products or services. Its aim is to provide extra value to the product or service, creating the extra impetus to purchase products that we might not normally buy.

Definition

Sales promotions – A range of tactical marketing techniques designed within a strategic marketing framework to add value to a product or service in order to achieve specific sales and marketing objectives.

Sales promotion should be part of a planned approach and very much an integral part of the marketing communications planning framework. It should be planned and executed in parallel with associated advertising and possible public relations campaigns.

Marketers will therefore rely upon sales promotions to enhance the performance of other components of the promotional mix. Again this reinforces the nature of a 'co-ordinated marketing communications' approach to promotional activity.

The main aims and associated objectives of sales promotions are usually:

- To increase brand and product awareness – attracting new customers
- To increase trial and adoption of new and existing products
- To induce customers to switch brands and products from competing organizations
- To level out fluctuations in supply and demand
- To increase brand usage
- To increase customer loyalty
- To disseminate information
- To encourage trading up to the next size or the next range – particularly pertinent to the car market.

If you were to align this in respect of the hierarchy of objectives, it might look like this:

Marketing objective	To increase market penetration by 20 per cent
Advertising objective	To reinforce product and brand to existing customers
Sales promotion objective	To encourage repeat purchase of products and brand loyalty

To achieve sales promotion objectives a number of techniques must be considered.

Sales promotion techniques

There are a range of sales promotion techniques that can be used to achieve each of the above aims and objectives. Typical techniques in both sectors will include the following:

- Money-off vouchers/coupons
- Buy one get one free
- Customer loyalty bonus schemes
- Twin packs
- Bulk buying
- Discounts
- Try before you buy

- Cash rebates
- Trial-sized products
- Prize draws
- Competition codes
- Point-of-sale displays.

Trade promotions

Earlier on we looked at the nature of the 'push and pull' promotional strategies, whereby manufacturers are looking to encourage their wholesalers and retailers to take their products and effectively 'take them to market'.

As a result of this process, trade promotions are often based around ensuring that product penetration is achieved. However, in order to achieve product penetration the incentive levels often have to be quite high, as product penetration is likely to be contrary to the typical 'volume stock traffic' aims of the wholesalers.

It is likely that manufacturers will encourage organizations to increase their stock levels in order to gain some level of commitment to increase sales potential in the marketplace, but also perhaps with the view of gaining some kind of supply chain relationship, with priority given to one particular supplier.

Alternatively, there is intensive competition for increased shelf space within retail outlets. The greater the incentive provided by the manufacturer, the more potential there is for greater shelf-space in the retail outlet. 'White goods' products are often at the heart of this scheme, with particular brands securing more floor space or shelf space than some of the lesser brands. There is the potential in this situation for a joint promotional activity between the manufacturer and perhaps the retailer to give incentives for a greater number of sales, from which both organizations will clearly benefit.

Good trade promotions, that is a good 'push strategy' highly incentivized, backed up by appropriate merchandizing and appropriate advertising, may be advantageous. Policies such as sale or return are also good incentives and ultimately reduce the financial risk involved.

Seasonal fluctuations are often problematic to both manufacturers and suppliers, and therefore it might be that through a range of sales promotion activities, incentives to buy the products outside the typical season could be achieved. The likely nature of these would be to involve the manufacturer in both the push and the pull strategy context, in line with both consumer and trade promotions.

Competitor response sees sales promotion being used as a tactical weapon to dilute the impact of competitor activities. Therefore during the launch of a new competitor product, it might be that the focus of trade activity relates to creating high barriers to entry for the trade in order to sustain your market share in the wholesale community.

Specific methods might include the following:

- Allowances and discounts.
- Volume allowances.
- Discount overriders – based upon retrospective performance, for example on a quarterly or annual basis.

- Free merchandise.

- Selling and marketing assistance – co-operative advertising, merchandising allowances, market information, product training.

- Sales contests.

- Bonus payments.

Retailer to consumer sales promotions

The key aims and objectives of this process will be to increase sales through a range of promotional techniques, as you can see below:

- **Increase in-store trade and customer traffic** – the use of coupons and money-off vouchers.

- **Increase frequency of purchase** – discounted promotions for next purchase.

- **Increase in-store loyalty** – through the use of scorecards and rewards systems.

- **Increase own brand sales** – encourage customers to purchase own brand products through a range of sale promotion incentives such as trial packs, in-store demonstrations and so on.

- **Achieve consistent demand** – reduce fluctuations and provide sales promotions in particular time bands to encourage a more consistent approach to shopping.

Manufacturer to consumer sales promotions

This relates to the 'pull' strategy, whereby the manufacturers take responsibility for creating awareness and demand in order to pull products up through the supply chain to the customers.

Typical sales promotion activities might include the following:

- Encouraging trial – samples, gifts, trial drives of vehicles, allowing customers to decide for themselves.

- Disseminating information – information packs on a door-to-door basis, perhaps closely linked with a direct marketing campaign (again utilizing the co-ordinated marketing communications approach).

- Trading up – encouraging customers to trade up from their existing models, a typical activity of car manufacturers and white goods manufacturers.

The list of promotional activities is endless, but the important issue from a promotional operations point of view is to ensure that demand for the products is continuously stimulated and is consistent with the marketing plan.

We will look at the impact of sales promotions on a B2B basis later in the text.

Customer loyalty schemes

Achieving that customer loyalty is a major focus of promotional activity (Table 4.2).

Table 4.2: The 11Ps of loyalty marketing		
1	**Pricing**	Be customer-specific
2	**Purchases**	Make product-specific offers
3	**Point flexibility**	Occasionally offer double points
4	**Partners**	Develop alliances with retailers
5	**Prizes**	Weekly draw for cardholders
6	**Pro-bono**	Allow customers to convert points to charity donations
7	**Personalization**	Direct mail, specifically targeted at the customer
8	**Privileges**	Invite cardholders to special events
9	**Participation**	Invite best customers to take part in new schemes
10	**Pronto**	Generate offers at point of sale
11	**Proactive**	Use information to predict/pre-empt customer behaviour

As with advertising, a planned approach must be undertaken and programmes tightly managed. Therefore, the typical planning process will include the following:

◆ Identification of the target market.

◆ Sales promotion objectives versus budget appropriation.

◆ Identification of both cost of communication for the sales promotion campaign and also the actual cost of the campaign, that is the 'fulfilment cost' – the cost of actually hosting the campaign in terms of postage, free gifts and so on – effectively the cost of the promotion to the organization. Obviously, this should be looked at in association with the ultimate benefits in the longer term.

◆ Implementation – the same applies here as to the advertising programme, but clearly the promotion will probably run in parallel with the advertising programme, therefore issues relating to timescales, drip and burst style promotions and so on will apply.

It is essential that whatever your promotional objectives are, the appropriate sales promotional activity is applied in the right context. Figure 4.3 highlights possible solutions to meeting PR objectives that might enable you to select the most appropriate method to meet your organizational needs.

Question 4.4

What are the most likely sales promotion alternatives open to a manufacturer when trying to attract consumer attention?

Question 4.5

How do you perceive that sales promotions add value to the process of advertising?

Objectives / Mechanics	Immediate free offers	Delayed free offers	Immediate price offers	Delayed price offers	Finance offers	Competitors	Games and draws	Charitable offers	Self-liquidators	Profit-making promotions
Increasing volume	9	7	9	7	5	1	3	5	2	1
Increasing trial	9	7	9	2	9	2	7	7	2	1
Increasing repeat purchase	2	9	2	9	5	3	2	7	3	3
Increasing loyalty	1	9	0	7	3	3	1	7	3	3
Widening usage	9	5	5	2	3	1	5	5	1	1
Creating interest	3	3	3	2	2	5	9	8	8	8
Creating awareness	3	3	3	1	1	5	9	8	8	8
Deflecting attention from price	9	7	0	7	7	3	5	5	2	2
Gaining intermediary support	9	5	9	5	9	3	7	5	1	1
Gaining display	9	5	9	5	9	3	7	5	1	1

Each square is filled with a ranking from 0 (not well matched) to 10 (very well matched).

Use it as a ready reckoner for linking your objectives to the mechanics available.

Figure 4.3: Matching mechanics to objectives

Public relations

Publicity and public relations are often interrelated and seen as companions within the promotional mix. Indeed publicity is often deemed to be part of public relations activities and certainly seems to happen as a result of PR. However, let us be clear on the differences:

◆ **Publicity** – is information, news, communications in relation to the organization, transmitted through a range of different media.

◆ **Public relations** – is a planned and sustained effort to establish and maintain good-will and mutual understanding between an organization and its target public.

The role of public relations is to look after the nature and basis of the external relationships between the organization and its stakeholders. It is aimed at creating a sustainable corporate brand and an overall company image within the marketplace. 'Public' is defined as:

Any group with some common characteristics, with which an organization needs to communicate. Each public poses a different communication problem, as each has different information needs and requires a different kind of relationship with the organization, and may start with perceptions of what the organization stands for. (Marston, 1979 as quoted in Brassington and Pettitt, 2000)

Public in the main consist of the following:

◆ Customer groups

◆ Local and central government

◆ The general public

◆ Financial institutions – investors/shareholders/borrowers

◆ The media – TV, press, radio (locally and nationally)

◆ Opinion leaders/formers

◆ Internal marketplace – employees, trade unions, employee relations bodies

◆ Potential employees.

Aims and objectives of public relations

Typically, PR aims and objectives will closely link to the following:

◆ To create and maintain the corporate and indeed brand image

◆ To enhance the position and standing of the organization in the eyes of the public

◆ To communicate the organization's ethos and philosophy, and corporate values

◆ To disseminate information to the public

◆ To undertake damage limitation activities to overcome poor publicity for the organization

◆ To raise the company profile and forge stronger, lasting, customer and supply chain relationships.

Public relations, as with all other elements of the marketing mix, requires a planned approach and plays an important role at a strategic level. It is also subject to strategic level objectives. For example, the launch of a new model by Mercedes Benz will be subject to a significant PR campaign running in parallel with significant advertising and direct marketing, perhaps on a local level by the local dealerships. Therefore PR becomes a high-level communications objective and it is critical that it is subject to the same intensity in respect of targeting specific groups of the public.

Marketing versus corporate public relations

While publicity is a sub-set of PR, public relations is not a sub-set of marketing – although that is how it is often portrayed. Public relations is very important to marketing, but its role is far broader and of primary importance to corporate level activities in terms of marketing communications.

The public relations practitioner will often report directly to the board, probably to the chief executive officer and/or the chairman. He or she will be very concerned with corporate identity and will be establishing a corporate communications policy, which will include the equivalent of a positioning statement.

If this is the case, it must follow that the marketing communications strategy is determined to a great degree by the public relations strategy. Here again is the influence of co-ordinated marketing communications. PR is a companion to virtually all elements of the marketing mix, and without the level of publicity raised through PR activities, many of the other promotional mix strategies may not be as successful.

From a marketing perspective, it will be used to meet marketing objectives and will support them by continually raising awareness, raising the profile and enhancing other marketing activities.

At a corporate level, PR is part of the long-term relationship-building strategy implemented by the organization to remain close to all components of the public. However, it does have a contingency use, with a short-term tactical benefit, in that it is used to respond to certain unpredictable or unexpected events, such as fatal accidents, disasters and so on. We will look at this a little later in the unit under 'crisis management'.

Public relations and attitude change?

The whole basis of PR is to continually reinforce a positive attitude towards the organization in the minds of the public, and therefore for PR to be successful it has to change a range of negative attitudes into positive ones (see Figure 4.4).

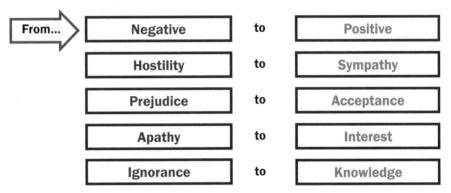

Figure 4.4: Attitudinal change

In order to undertake this level of attitudinal change you will require a clear and specific understanding of the nature and breakdown of the market in which you operate, both from a customer perspective and from a media perspective.

Public relations techniques

It has already been identified that PR has two roles, a long-term developmental role and another that reflects the need to have contingency activities in place. From a marketing operations perspective, you need to understand when to use which particular public relations technique to optimize the level of 'positive publicity' the organization can deliver.

Typical techniques include the following:

◆ Press releases

◆ Press conferences

◆ Publications

◆ Advertising

◆   Media relations

◆   Events

◆   Annual reports

◆   Lobbying

◆   Internal PR.

During your studies for Marketing Communications, you will find that you learn much more about how these sources of information are used effectively in a co-ordinated communications mix.

Internal PR

We looked at the importance of internal marketing in Unit 3, which highlighted the importance of developing a structured and meaningful communications process in order to win over the confidence of the workforce and gain support for strategy implementation and the associated change. Internal PR plays a vital role in respect of this communication and while they are part and parcel of the overall public, the workforce requires a more tailored and organizational approach.

The likely emphasis of internal PR will be based around keeping people informed, avoiding cloak-and-dagger style internal politics. Should a successful PR campaign be implemented internally, then motivation and attitude levels might appear to be more positive within the organization.

Particular techniques included in this area will relate to journals, newsletters and internal briefings.

It is likely that on some occasions internal PR will be based around 'crisis' style PR, perhaps announcing redundancies, changes in management structure, disaster and so on.

When selecting the appropriate public relations technique it is essential to ensure that you undertake an assessment of three criteria:

1   **Suitability** – It is vital to ensure that the techniques chosen are targeted and therefore appropriate to the target market, in respect of tone, content and style; that the appropriate medium is chosen, which again meets the profile requirements of the customer base; of primary importance will be the necessity to establish the level of influence and impact the actual technique will achieve.

2   **Feasibility** – As with any other promotional activity, PR will be restricted by a budget – therefore any activity or programme of activities will need to come within the required budget. Particular considerations will relate to resourcing the programme physically, financially and from a human resource perspective. Ultimately it is important to establish whether the programme is considered achievable and realistic.

3   **Acceptability** – Are the activities chosen acceptable to the organization as a whole, are they appropriate in keeping with the corporate identity? An assessment of alternative sources of PR should also be undertaken to ascertain which is the most acceptable approach to achieving the desired level of publicity.

Question 4.6

In what ways do public relations complement other elements of the promotional mix?

Direct and interactive marketing

Direct and interactive marketing must be one of the most rapidly evolving and changing areas of marketing communications and promotional activities. Key driving forces of change relate to:

◆ Changing dynamics in demographics and lifestyles

◆ Increasing competition

◆ Customer power

◆ Fragmentation of the media

◆ Increasing costs of media

◆ Emerging distribution channels

◆ Changes in market information (EPOS, smart cards etc.)

◆ New technologies.

One of the key drivers of growth is the massive movement in technologies, including the rise of databases, improving analytical systems, developments in phone technologies and the information superhighway.

Added to these, it would appear that in today's marketing environment, organizations know more and more about their customers. Their profiling and research techniques are far more sophisticated, making direct marketing an excellent tool for very specifically targeted communication campaigns.

These drivers are the common denominator in almost all change strategies; therefore direct marketing is not an exception to the rule.

The use of direct marketing by an organization effectively demonstrates that the organization has taken a decision to avoid dependence on marketing channel intermediaries and has also decided to deal with customers in a highly targeted way. This of course has implications for the level of marketing and management information that a company may need to obtain and retain in the future.

Direct marketing has in the past been viewed as a very tactical approach to meeting marketing objectives, and like sales promotions and PR, has been used as part of both an ongoing programme of marketing communications and promotional activities. However, in cases of emergency, that is in crisis or indeed in competitive response, direct marketing has proved to be a useful tool.

As a marketing tool, direct marketing evolved from the mail order business and now it is seen as another compatible element of the promotional mix that supports and underpins the marketing communications activity and can often be found conveying the good news of sales promotions.

However, over the years, direct marketing has come under fire as 'junk mail' and has also been found to be the source of 'confusion marketing'. In addition to this, direct marketing has been subject to considerable change due to the Data Protection Act and therefore the introduction of issues such as permission-based marketing has had a tremendous impact upon the future shape of direct marketing.

Definition

Direct marketing – An interactive system of marketing which uses one or more advertising media to effect a measurable response at any location (Institute of Direct Marketing).

While this is quite a broad definition, it does however identify some of the key component characteristics of direct marketing. For example, it provides the basis of the relationship, which is defined as interactive, being a two-way relationship between the organization and the customer. At the customer's location this could be via phone, fax, e-mail, Internet, post, to name but a few. However, whatever the nature of the communications and wherever and whoever they go to, it is essential that as with every other form of the promotional mix, there is an underpinning and SMART set of quantifiable objectives.

Objectives of direct marketing

Direct marketing performs a number of tasks, depending upon which element of the promotional mix it might work in parallel with and support.

The aims and objectives of direct marketing might include the following:

◆ Increasing direct mail order levels from new and existing customers.

◆ Dissemination of information – provision of information to aid customer enquiries and support the adoption process.

◆ Generation of sales leads – to increase the number of sales leads and ultimately influence a rise in sales income.

◆ Generation of trial leads – to increase the number of customers willing to trial the product, to influence the process of adoption and influence a rise in sales income.

The aims and objectives of direct marketing can be achieved in a number of ways, and can often play a pivotal role in enhancing the selling process, by way of providing sales leads, that might directly result in a sale.

Furthermore, direct marketing objectives can be achieved through techniques such as direct mail, direct response advertising, telemarketing and the Internet, all of which are aimed at increasing sales leads and increasing sales turnover.

Database marketing

For an organization to really optimize its effectiveness in relation to building and developing long-term customer relationships, it is essential that it secures as much relevant information as possible about its customers and retain it in a database system. This in turn provides an opportunity to create closely defined profiles, in order that a tightly defined targeting exercise can take place.

> Database marketing is the application of digital information collected about current and/or potential customers and their buying behaviour to improve marketing performance by formulating a strategy and building personalized relationships with customers. (Chaffey *et al.*, 2002)

As information technology plays such a tremendous role in day-to-day business operations, it is increasingly likely that databases will be built to collect information from customers accessing websites. Databases are essentially known as the 'brains' behind the website, which enables a high level of customer profiling and personalization to take place.

Typical consumer information for database building might include the following:

◆ Name

◆ Address

◆ Occupation

◆ Geo-demographic profile

◆ Psychographics profile

◆ Previous contacts

◆ Previous responses

◆ Frequency of purchase

◆ Purchases made

◆ Value of purchases

◆ Type of purchases

◆ Media responsiveness

◆ Promotional responsiveness.

Source: Dibb *et al.* (2005)

However, many underpinning database systems have failed as yet to achieve the level of sophistication required in developing appropriate data-mining opportunities. In addition, unless the site is a transaction-based website, that is where customers actually carry out a transaction online, it can be difficult to glean sufficient information about the customers to develop the typical profile basis you might prefer.

A further consideration in database marketing currently is that where databases are highly sophisticated, organizations do not understand how to use the information and put it through the data-mining process.

One of the key benefits of a good database, whether it be based on information gleaned from websites or through other sources, is that it forms the basis of the relationship and how it might be maintained in the future. While databases aid relationship management, database marketing does not constitute relationship marketing, in fact it only provides the means by which the relationship might be maintained.

Direct marketing techniques

Direct marketing provides significant scope for communicating directly with customers, and can cut across just about any promotional activity as part of the co-ordinated marketing communications activity, and is not used exclusively for the consumer (B2C) market. It is also used very much in the business (B2B) market. However, it has been a central component of marketing strategies in the consumer market for years.

Direct mail

Direct mail has probably been the most used form of direct marketing over the years, but it is probably the one subject to the most abuse.

It is widely used in both consumer and business/organizational markets to target customer groups directly. The financial services sector is a classic example of its use. Even with the Data Protection Act, it is likely that some households receive as much as one piece of direct mail per day, in relation to mortgages, pensions, insurance, credit cards, to name but a few.

There are many advantages associated with using direct mail, such as targeting. Targeted campaigns can include working on a basis of either geographic or geo-demographic segmentation. This level of segmentation combined with the level of knowledge that exists in relation to market segments means that targeting can become a very exact science.

Other advantages include:

◆ **Personalization** – Being able to personalize direct mail where appropriate.

◆ **Response rates** – If targeting is exact and appropriate to customer needs, response rates can be quite high. However, if targeting is not tight, the response can be as little as 5 per cent.

◆ **Flexibility** – Levels of flexibility available in direct marketing can provide much scope for an interesting and creative campaign. It allows for phased postage, delayed mailing, inserts, different size and frequency, to name but a few benefits associated with flexibility.

However, when developing a direct mailing, you must ensure that the information you have is accurate, that customer groups are profiled and then targeted specifically and that the content matches the needs, wants and expectations of the group. This process will be assisted through the database marketing process, and ultimately the information collected will provide a greater insight into the customers and their buying behaviour. The mailing will only be as good as the marketing research information that underpins it.

When purchasing a list externally, it is essential that you ensure the list provides you with relevant and up-to-date information, and is inside the data protection limits, defined in the Data Protection Act.

There are a number of organizations now that specialize in the development of appropriate automated mailing lists:

◆ Dun and Bradstreet – they offer 48 list options

◆ Wyvern Direct Response – based around occupational groups such as accountancy, medical practitioners, hospital contacts

◆ Wise and Lovey – website address www.mailing-labels.com

It is expected that more and more online automated mailing lists will become available to keep abreast of the changes in technology and the direct marketing sector.

On a less positive note, when looking at the effectiveness of direct mail, consider these facts. In 1997 over 3.7 billion pieces of mail were sent out, and over 100 million were marked 'return to sender', with another 80 million so badly addressed that they were unable to be delivered.

It is essential that, for any list you are purchasing, very clear criteria have been developed in relation to:

◆ Relevance of the list in relation to the target market

◆ The source and ownership of the list

◆ The level of detail in the list

◆ Frequency of updates

◆ Whether the list is of enquirers, purchasers or respondents

◆ Frequency of purchase

◆ Level of accuracy.

Direct response advertising

This is another form of direct marketing and appears in the standard broadcast and standard print media.

Principally it is different from other forms of advertising, as it actually demands a response, by giving a website address, telephone number or a coupon for a personal visit. This is becoming a popular approach in direct marketing and is growing continually as advertisers try to gain greater value from their advertising experience.

The targeting for direct response advertising is probably a little less scientific than direct mail, and relies much more on an assessment of the average reader or viewer profile than a prepared mailing list. However, the information collected can be used as a database for other forms of direct marketing in the future.

More and more organizations are involving themselves in direct response advertising in order to optimize their expenditure in advertising.

Telemarketing

We have touched upon the issue of personalization, and how through the use of database marketing we can glean enough information to personalize organizational approaches to customers. However, the difference between telemarketing and other methods of direct marketing is that it is truly a personal approach, whereby there is a direct personal contact, which provides the basis for an interactive relationship between the organization and the customer.

While the personal approach is preferred and is seen as a way of getting closer to the customer, customers can find this approach rather intrusive and are somewhat resistant to embracing deeper and more meaningful relationships with organizations that they might purchase from.

Telemarketing, like other components of direct marketing, should be a planned, highly targeted and controlled activity that will both create and exploit a direct relationship between the customer and the seller using the telephone.

Telemarketing provides the organization with significant scope as telephone rental and ownership is very high, with over 80 per cent of households possessing them across the European Union. The telephone is a particularly powerful communications tool, which gives you direct access to new and existing customers in a flexible environment, that is wherever they are. There are now some 16,000 call centres alone run out of the United Kingdom so the business potential is very extensive.

Telemarketing also provides the scope for customer service initiatives and customer satisfaction surveys, as well as the basis for developing the existing customer relationship overall.

The scope of telemarketing

- To generate sales leads
- To screen leads prior to following-up
- To arrange appointments for sales representatives
- To direct sales
- To encourage cross/upward selling
- To provide dealer support
- To manage and service accounts
- To undertake market research
- To undertake test marketing.

As regards promotional and marketing operations, it is clear that telemarketing plays a pivotal role in:

- Increasing sales levels
- Supporting customers
- Increasing levels of customer service
- Providing technical support
- Information gathering
- Credit control.

One of the key disadvantages of telemarketing is the cost. It is a costly exercise, where few economies of scale can be charged. However, the management in many financial services organizations sets very tough limits so that economies are achieved, but unfortunately this can be to the detriment of the long-term relationship with the customer.

A key factor of telemarketing as a direct marketing tool is that volume is rather limited in comparison with other direct marketing techniques. While a typical telemarketing representative might make between 30 and 60 calls per day, an equivalent piece of direct mail could actually achieve a significantly greater proportion of contacts.

Telemarketing, while having many qualities, is probably one of the least effective direct marketing mechanisms. It is certainly one of the least cost-effective; it is personally intrusive and does not achieve the necessary volume of hits on a day-to-day basis.

Question 4.7

How can direct marketing complement advertising and sales promotions?

Sponsorship

Sponsorship is the provision of financial or material support by a company for some independent activity ... not usually directly linked to the company's normal business, but support from which the sponsoring company would hope to benefit. (Wilmhurst, 1999)

Sponsorship is a two-way mutually beneficial partnership between an activity being sponsored and the sponsoring organization. It works on the premise that association largely affects image and that the sponsor may exchange money and/or goods or services in kind in return for the association that sponsorship provides.

Sponsorship objectives

Typical sponsorship objectives may include:

◆ Increasing brand awareness

◆ Building and enhancing corporate image

◆ Raising awareness of brands related to products restricted in advertising through various legislation, such as alcohol and cigarettes.

There are two perspectives to consider in sponsorship, the perspective of the organization being sponsored and that of the sponsor. Both parties will need to consider if the alliance created as a sponsorship arrangement is one that is required by the existing image of the organization and will enhance overall organizational credibility. They will also need to consider how relevant the association would be between the two parties and how both will benefit. The sponsor will need to consider what exposure will be gained as a result of the sponsorship and how similar or dissimilar the target audiences are to their own.

Types of sponsorship

The main types of sponsorship include the following:

◆ **Programme sponsorship** – for example, *Morse*, sponsored by Beamish Stout. Typically this is used at the start of a TV programme, during the interval and at the end. The cinema and major films often form the basis of sponsorship alliances. There has been a massive boom in TV sponsorship and the opportunity is providing broadcasters with a valuable new revenue stream as money from spot advertisers is no longer as plentiful.

A decade ago broadcast sponsorship was worth £1 million in the United Kingdom. In 2001 it was worth in the region of £85 million, with TV sponsorship increasing by as much as 25 per cent in the first quarter of 2001 (*source*: lexis.nexis.com).

◆ **Arts/sports sponsorship** – for example, the Carling Premiership. Carling sponsor the Premier Football League in England. Events sponsorship is expensive but can be very high profile and potentially the most cost-effective way of getting increased brand awareness.

◆ **Sponsorship of other events** – for example exhibitions, festivals and opening ceremonies. These are again high profile, and are sometimes very useful forms of sponsorship for smaller businesses that wish to raise their profile locally.

◆ **Sponsorship of individuals or teams** – Mercedes Benz sponsor the British tennis player Tim Henman and Siemens sponsor Formula One motor racing.

Role of sponsorship

Sponsorship can provide a more cost-effective means of reaching your target audience, but the design, content and message are much more controlled. From a corporate perspective and PR perspective, sponsorship raises the profile of the organization and its corporate values, and in some instances can really bring the brand name and corporate image to centre stage.

Advertisers are being drawn in by the opportunity to convey their brand values by clever association with programming, that is in keeping with their product and the desired company image.

Many organizations succeed in ensuring that as part of the sponsorship deal their name is an integral part of the overall event, for example the 'Benson and Hedges Cup'.

However, while sponsorship may appear to be a good idea, it is essential that, like all other elements of the promotional mix, it clearly fits a need and will enhance the possibilities of directly achieving predetermined marketing objectives.

Sponsorship offers vast opportunities for the organization in terms of the value-added perspective of merchandising, public relations activities, improved stakeholder relationships and highlighted ethical and social values. The benefits are quite considerable.

However, a number of key factors should be considered prior to taking the decision to proceed with sponsorship arrangements:

◆ What **relevance** does the particular sponsorship arrangement have in terms of the match between the two organizations and the potential target audience? For example, it is clear that when Carling Black Label sponsor sports events it will bring in additional sales of both drinks and cigarettes, both during and after the event, as support for sport is effectively linked to both of these habits.

◆ **The period of impact** – How long before and after the event will the sponsorship profile last for? Is the event a one-off or a sequence of events?

◆ **The uniqueness of the sponsorship agreement** – From a competitive perspective it is essential that the agreement with the sponsored individual or organization allows the brand, market and competitive position to be differentiated in a unique way. In some situations this level of expectation is not achievable, but if the fit of the organization and the deal is good, then high profile sponsorship might be achieved.

◆ **The level of spin-off promotions is also essential** – For example, the importance of a co-ordinated approach between other elements of the promotional mix will be essential to maximize and optimize cost-effectiveness of particular high profile events.

Here advertising, merchandising and promotional incentives may be a particular match for the promotional mix.

Therefore, for successful implementation of a sponsorship strategy, it is necessary to clearly define the position of sponsorship and ensure that it is fully representative of corporate and marketing communications goals and effectively integrates sponsorship with other elements of the promotional and marketing mix.

Insight: Marketing through sport

The European Sponsorship Association (ESA) is the voice of the sponsorship industry across Europe. It is made up of the leading sponsors, consultants, rights holders, suppliers and professional bodies working within the sponsorship industry. ESA provides information and expertise on all types of sponsorship activity including sport, broadcast, the arts, music, environmental and charity.

European Sponsorship Association is committed to developing all aspects of the sponsorship industry. The ESA advises the European Union in Brussels on matters relating to sponsorship and works very closely with the European Union on a number of legislative issues. Training and education programmes, sponsorship seminars and conferences are all key areas which have been developed over the years. The ESA Annual Congress is attended by the leading practitioners and professionals within the industry and is recognized as the leading Congress in its field.

Social and networking opportunities are also key elements of ESA's work. The association also works closely with educational establishments developing career programmes and professional qualifications. If you would like to find out more about ESA and the opportunities to join the association, please turn to the 'Membership' section. Cussons Imperial Leather won the 3rd ESA European Sponsorship Award, which recognizes the outstanding sponsorship programmes in Europe by inviting the winners of leading national sponsorship awards to compete at a European level. This year's award was endorsed by MEP Viviane Reding, European Commissioner for Education and Culture.

The 130 delegates at the ESA Congress heard presentations from the four award finalists from Ireland (AIB Grassroots sponsorship), Netherlands (Eiffel Basketball Programme), Sweden (Assa Abloy in the Volvo Ocean Race) and the United Kingdom (Imperial Leather).

Imperial Leather's Commonwealth Games sponsorship campaign qualified for the finals by winning the Hollis Sponsorship Awards for Outstanding Sponsorship of the Year and the UK Sports Industry Sponsorship Award.

The decision was made by Congress delegates voting and a panel of sponsorship experts, headed by the ESA Vice Chairman, Helen Day who commented: 'Cussons Imperial Leather's campaign showed excellent use of different marketing disciplines to fully exploit a sponsorship opportunity. The planning and execution which went into the campaign was outstanding as indeed it needed to be in order to dominate in the way they did in a multi sponsored event such as the Commonwealth Games.'

http://www.europeansponsorship.org.

Case study: Powergen

Powergen is part of E.ON UK, which is part of E.ON – the world's largest private-sector energy services company. Powergen is one of the largest energy suppliers in the United Kingdom, and also offers a range of additional home energy services including boiler and central heating installation, maintenance and insurance.

Powergen has three main sponsorships along with three community initiatives. They help raise our brand awareness and brand engagement in our key customer heartlands therefore increasing brand warmth. We also run specific internal communications around each of our sponsorships enabling our colleagues to benefit from exclusive 'money can't buy' opportunities.

Powergen's sponsorship portfolio includes Rugby League's Powergen Challenge Cup and the Powergen Champion Schools Tournament for children; Ipswich Town Football Club and Ipswich Town Community Trust; Rugby Union's Powergen Cup and Powergen National Rugby Community Programme.

(*Source:* www.powergen.com, 2005)

Personal selling

In the context of promotional operations it is important that you have a clear overview of how the personal selling process can be both compatible with other elements of the marketing mix and also enhance the effectiveness of the marketing mix.

Personal selling is one of the biggest sectors of business within the United Kingdom, with UK organizations employing some 766,000 sales professionals, yet it can appear to be one of the most disorganized and disjointed components of the marketing mix.

Definition

Personal selling – An interpersonal communication tool which involves face-to-face activities undertaken by individuals, often representing an organization, in order to inform, persuade or remind an individual or group to take appropriate action, as required by the sponsor's representative.

When preparing a marketing communications plan, the role of the sales department will usually include some form of personal selling objectives. Particular emphasis will include an analysis of the specific responsibilities associated with personal selling, the role of personal selling overall and how it will influence and enhance other elements of the marketing mix.

It is a known fact that personal selling is the most expensive element of the marketing mix. It is resource-intensive, time-ineffective, contributing little or no economies of scale, with high contact costs and customer maintenance costs. However, it is probably one of the most effective methods of influencing decision-makers to the stage of adoption. At a strategic level the balance of personal selling versus other more cost-effective methods of the marketing mix must be considered in order that the target market receives the most relevant approach to meet its information-based needs.

Sales force activity will be subject to a number of associated sales objectives that will directly relate back to the marketing objectives, and will be predetermined in order that the organization can optimize and maximize the potential impact of the personal selling team in association with other promotional activities.

Sales force objectives

Sales force objectives will not all relate directly to increasing income. They may also relate to cost saving, customer relationship management and developing new leads.

Therefore typical sales objectives could be:

◆   To increase sales turnover by 20 per cent within a 12-month period

◆   To reduce the number of clients with minimum viable order levels at the end of a 12-month period

◆   To reduce the cost of sales by 10 per cent within a six-month period

◆   To increase the number of distribution outlets by 15 per cent in a 12-month period.

Often personal selling goals are misunderstood and are assumed to be about an increase in sales, where actually personal selling goals will be about increases in overall revenue and profitability. Profitability might be improved by an increase in minimum order levels in order to achieve economies of scale.

Personal selling is a vital role within the organization, but it underpins a range of other promotional activities that it can only achieve through the appropriate level of sales and marketing support and with the appropriate tools of the trade.

It is essential from a marketing and promotional operations perspective that the sales team is kept briefed of any changes to the product portfolio, services mix or any essential information that might either enhance or inhibit sales team performance. As a marketer you therefore have a responsibility to support the sales team in a range of ways in order that they can open and close a sale effectively and efficiently.

◆   Provision of market information to support the selling process – customer and competitor intelligence

◆   Provision of potential leads from the market scanning process

◆   Client history – database information about purchasing behaviour, purchasing trends, frequency and value of orders

◆   Financial reports – Dun and Bradstreet reports, annual reports and so on

◆   Provision of a range of appropriate promotional materials that include company history, product portfolio, services mix, financial package, support packages and so on

◆   Sales aids – product samples, service packages, demonstration equipment

◆   Provision of promotional plans in order that sales staff can co-ordinate their call plans in line with particular promotional initiatives

◆   The provision of promotional incentives, merchandising and so on.

Summary

One of the key objectives of any promotional programme will be to ensure that potential customers adopt the product offering and are converted to the brand, in a way that can establish long and loyal relationships. One of the critical success factors of implementing the programme will be the degree of synergy and integration between the elements. It is clear that they are complementary. Some are more effective for targeting volumes, while others have a strength in developing long term customer relationships. The key success factor for any promotional mix will be its ability to meet the marketing objectives and bridge the successful implementation of the marketing strategy. Promotional planning in isolation of the marketing plan could be untargeted and a waste of valuable resources.

You are likely to be involved in the development and implementation of promotional plans, so you will need to clearly identify the direct objectives, relate them back at all times to the plan and undertake a co-ordinated approach to promotional mix tools. This is covere in more detail in the Marketing Communications unit, which will focus you on the finer details of developing a co-ordinated marketing communications mix.

Further study

For this unit a more in-depth approach is found in Chapters 15–17 of Dibb et al. (2005). In addition to this, you should be looking at Mad.com or purchasing *Marketing* and *Marketing Week* in order to keep abreast of various promotional mix activities.

Bibliography

Brassington, F. and Pettitt, S. (2000) *Principles of Marketing*, Thomson Higher Education

Chaffey. D., Mayer. R., Johnston. K. and Ellis-Chadwick. F, (2000), *Internet Marketing*, FT/Prentice Hall

De Chernatony, L. (2001) *From Brand Vision to Brand Evaluation*, Oxford: Butterworth-Heinemann

De Chernatony, L., and McDonald, M. (1998) *Creating Powerful Brands*, Oxford: Butterworth-Heinemann

Delozier, M.W. (1976) *The Marketing Communications Process*, McGraw-Hill

Dibb, S., Simkin, L., Pride, W. and Ferrell, O. (2005) *Marketing: Concepts and Strategies*, Houghton Mifflin, 5th European edition

Drummond, G., Ensor, J. and Ashford, R. (2003) *Strategic Marketing: Planning and Control*, Oxford: Butterworth-Heinemann

Fill, C. (1999) *Integrated Marketing Communications*, Oxford: Butterworth-Heinemann

Fill, C. (2003) *Marketing Communications*, Oxford: Butterworth-Heinemann

Rokeach, M. (1973) *The Nature of Human Values*, Macmillan

Wilmhurst, J. (1999) *The Fundamentals of Advertising*, Oxford: Butterworth-Heinemann, 2nd edition

Unit 5
Product operations

Product operations

While the basis of this unit will reflect product operations, it is in line with the syllabus that you are reminded of the nature and purpose of the product, its components and the PLC. You may have already studied this for Marketing Fundamentals, where you will have covered some of the basics of the product; however, this is a useful form of revision and will also look at some additional elements of the product.

The product is the core of the marketing mix and is the basis of meeting customer needs and wants with the benefits and features that the product might offer them. From an operational perspective, should the product fail to live up to expectations then ultimately its failure will impact upon the achievement of the marketing objectives and will likely weaken any competitive strength that the organization might possess.

The product poses enormous challenges to many organizations and in turn the marketing function. The product is at the centre of the decision-making process and ultimately the adoption and exchange process that essentially links the organization and its customers together. The product is the component that gives the customer the benefits and possibly the experience they have been looking for.

A product is a tangible item purchased by a customer and designed to meet their needs and wants. However, while the customer does purchase a product, what they are actually purchasing is the benefits that the product has on offer.

Primarily, the product is the acid test of whether or not the organization fully understands the nature and disposition of the customer and their actual needs and wants.

At this point it is advisable to ensure that the differences between products and services are clearly understood, as services will form the subject of another unit in this book.

As marketers, what we need to do is to market these benefits to the customer, as the purchase of benefits is critical to the customer experience. Products are described as having three characteristics:

1   Physical

2   Functional

3   Psychological.

Physical characteristics such as shape, size, colour and so on can change according to the function of the product. For example, a hairdryer could be black with a curved handle, which is difficult to hold. A functional characteristic could be the speed at which the dryer works and the number of varying heat settings it has.

The psychological characteristics are unique. This is concerned with the customers' values and expectations relating to the product or service. If the hairdryer provides a professional finish to your hair and you feel good about yourself then you are likely to be pleased with all of the three key features. If it gives you a good style from drying but it is difficult to hold, then it might have a psychological effect in that you may not wish to purchase another one.

Benefits are key to the success or failure of a product and to assist you in understanding how the product evolves, you need to realize that the product can be broken down into smaller elements (see Figure 5.1).

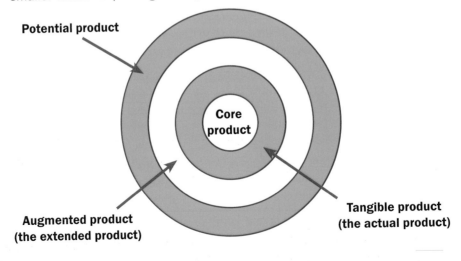

Figure 5.1: The anatomy of the product

The core is as it sounds, the centre or heart of the product. The core product provides a very basic function. It is usually seen as the no-frills version of the product; it should deliver the desired benefits effectively. The core product then provides the basis for the next level.

The tangible/actual product relates to making the product a reality. The product becomes a real product, with real characteristics and benefits that can then be communicated to the customer to encourage purchase.

The augmented product is the core/tangible product with a number of add-on extras which makes the product more marketable and enables organizations to be competitive. These extras do not directly affect the workings of the product as it can exist without them, but they add value to the product in the long term. For example, a car with leather seats: it does not matter whether or not the seats are fabric or leather, what is important is that you can sit on them to drive. The third level is the potential product. This means that the company must be responsive to the marketplace and to the change that continues to take place within it, and therefore the organization and the marketer will need to consider what the potential product will be like in the future. The car market is a classic example of this. No sooner have they launched a new model than they are working on the launch of the replacement product. The continuing future development of the product is a strategic issue and will be reflected in the overall strategic direction of the organization.

Question 5.1

Using the concept of the model in Figure 5.1, explain how BMW might build from the core product through to the augmented products.

Product classifications

Part of your role as a marketing manager at an operational level will be to categorize the products manufactured by your organization so that you can ascertain issues relating to features, benefits and functions. Then you can contribute to the development of an appropriate integrated promotional mix.

There are three categories:

1 Durable

2 Non-durable

3 Service products.

Durable

Products that are durable last for a period of time, for example a car, stereo system, washing machine and so on. Eventually they will have to be replaced, but they do have a steady life cycle appropriate to the product.

Non-durable

Non-durable products are different in that they can be used only a few times, or even only once. They do not have a durable lifespan, for example food, drinks, printing paper, disposable contact lenses or disposable nappies. Many of these products are known as FMCGs – fast-moving consumer goods.

Service products

Services are intangible – you have nothing physical at the end of the service experience, for example holidays, hairdressing, personal banking/financial services.

These three classifications then break down into smaller groups as follows:

◆ **Convenience products** – These are frequently purchased products such as food, drinks, petrol and so on.

◆ **Shopping goods** – These goods are those that customers will shop around for, comparing and contrasting value in terms of benefits versus brand and price.

◆ **Speciality products** – These possess unique characteristics that customer/consumers will look for. The likelihood is that they will have very specific ideas and expectations of the products and alternatives would not be considered as appropriate. There will also be much emphasis on the brand, for example, cars – Porsche, clothes – Calvin Klein.

◆ **Unsought goods** – This area is particularly interesting and relates to customers not really wanting this product, but who ultimately could be persuaded to purchase through strong marketing and effective promotions and communications – for example, air circulation systems in the home, air conditioning units.

◆ **Business products** – This is quite a substantial area as it really relates to any products that support and enable the business function to take place.

◆ **Process products** – These ultimately become part of the producer's own products.

◆ **Plant and equipment** – These products are exactly as they sound: they are the fabric of the organization, the equipment and machinery that are needed to enable manufacturing and productivity to take place. Clearly in today's technical age there will be a huge amount of computer-aided technology that will enable a higher level of competitive design with more technical detail and capability than ever before.

◆ **Supplies and services** – Here you are looking at the things that make the world go round and make business happen. All of the supplies and support that service organizations need come under this heading – maintenance and repair, financial services, cleaning services and so on.

Being a product manager in a marketing context will be a very challenging and complex role. Your aim will be to develop a product that is compatible with the existing product portfolio, meets customer needs and wants and forms part of the overall strategy in line with both corporate and marketing objectives.

Product management

Creating a product range

One of the key functions that you will undertake in a marketing role is assisting in the creation of an appropriate portfolio of products, that is a product range. This means that an organization will have a range of products that they sell, either similar or even diverse products. The better and more appropriate the range of products the more likely they are to sell them. Take, for example, many 'white goods' organizations which sell a range of products from TV and washing machines to kettles.

Within the product range there is a product mix, which is the portfolio of products an organization sells. This can be broken down into three areas. This really relates back to the circular diagram, the anatomy of the product, earlier in this unit. In simple terms it means that a manufacturer will start off with a core product and will then build on that product, or the idea of it, to build a product range.

The product line is a group of closely related products. For example, Colgate offer a number of various toothpastes, but they are all marketed as Colgate-Palmolive in terms of TV advertising and overall marketing.

The product mix is the total portfolio of products that a company has on offer. For example, Canon manufacture a variety of photographic products; this would then be their total product mix. Procter & Gamble also have a very broad range of products from medically related products through to soaps, soap powders and so on – this would be their product mix.

When considering the product mix, organizations must establish the breadth and depth of the product mix, the depth being how many products are within a product line, for example how many different types of toothpaste are under the Colgate–Palmolive brand, as opposed to the breadth of the product, relating to how many product lines Colgate–Palmolive make, for example toothpaste, soaps and so on.

As part of the strategic planning process, the organization should reflect on their existing product range to ensure that their products fit with one another, are compatible and continue to meet the needs of increasingly powerful and vocal customers. Therefore, a decision will be made at a strategic level whether or not to launch new products, withdraw existing products and to extend or decrease the life cycle of a product.

As the product is at the heart of the organization and the reason for its overall existence, this is a serious decision that must be undertaken in an informed way, with a structured analytical approach, understanding customers, market forces, key drivers and factors influencing change. Much of this information will be provided through the marketing audit process, where both the macro and micro audit will likely identify critical issues associated with the product mix.

The product life cycle

The PLC (see Figure 5.2) is probably one of the best-known concepts in the whole theory and practice of marketing as a business function.

Every product has a life cycle. It does not matter what the product is, it has an existence, sometimes a planned existence – sometimes even planned obsolescence.

The PLC is an invaluable tool in providing an insight into a common pattern of industry sales, one that might be helpful in ascertaining the expected life of products within the product portfolio. One of the big failures of many businesses has been the failure to recognize a product's ability to exist and to operate at a competitive level.

The marketing mix will vary at each stage of the PLC. As you saw in Unit 4, different types of promotional activities are required to underpin particular points in the cycle. A PLC can effectively be extended or decreased according to particular marketing activities that are undertaken. This could be achieved by product modifications, product repositioning, rebranding and market development, to name but a few possibilities.

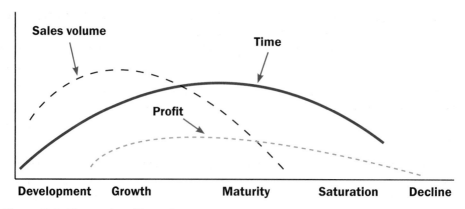

Figure 5.2: The product life cycle

New markets can often mean that new uses for the product have been identified. This can extend the product for a considerable period of time.

One common factor across all industries in relation to the PLC is that different products have different time horizons: some extend forever and others will decline and become obsolete very quickly.

Development

Figure 5.2 illustrates the various stages involved in a product's life cycle existence. A product is in the development stage when market research, product development and marketing testing activities are undertaken. Development costs are high and sales volume will be low, income levels will be non-existent.

Growth

The product then passes through a growth stage when it is received positively and sales volume increases rapidly. Development costs start to be recovered and costs per unit decrease as production quantities improve. Some profit may appear to be emerging – this will of course vary between organizations based upon the nature of the products and the level of investment required.

Maturity/saturation

The product becomes fully developed and the initial needs are satisfied. Its success will be dependent on repeat purchase. It is likely that competitors will appear in the market. As the market becomes saturated, sales will slow down and profits will start to decrease.

Decline

It is very likely that during the decline stage of the life cycle, sales will eventually decline and it will be too expensive to maintain the product.

Figure 5.2 illustrates a typical PLC curve. However, in practice, PLCs can be short, long and of various shapes, depending on the curves. For example, fashion products come into play very quickly and drop out of the market very quickly as the next fashion comes on board.

At each stage of the PLC, the marketing activities and communication activities will change. For a new product launch, the message will be creating awareness, introducing the product to the market. The saturation stage will probably include incentives and promotional activities to encourage customers/consumers to keep purchasing the product.

By the time you get to decline the organization should be ready to launch a new product and therefore the message will be to complete the cycle of the existing product in preparation for the new product. A good example of this would be the car market. Often car prices are decreased significantly to clear existing stock, to make way for the latest model.

However, the PLC does have some limitations. There is a significant danger that organizations might have an over-dependence on the life cycle, meaning that a temporary drop in sales might actually indicate the need for early withdrawal from the market, and be wrongly interpreted as an early decline.

One of the most inhibiting factors of the PLC is that in the real world, the PLC is flexible and will change rapidly depending on demand and the activity within the external marketing environment. The change in demand could be based around government policy, competitive activity, technological advances and so on. The changes can be quite sudden and then be misunderstood.

The PLC is a very difficult area to manage, but organizations should understand that:

◆ It is dangerous to rely too heavily on one product for too long.

◆ PLCs must be tightly managed and continually monitored.

◆ While there might be a predetermined cycle that defines the direction that a product might follow, it does not always take into account the unexpected and the unforeseen external driving forces, technological changes or competitor activity, and can therefore be seen as a little inflexible.

◆ A product portfolio should undergo ongoing review and identify products that should be discontinued or products that should be modified.

On a more positive note, it does aid planning and enables organizations to set key objectives relating to new product development, when to launch products and when it may redesign products or even make them obsolete. The PLC has several advantages when used as a planning tool.

◆ It is a very valuable tool as it helps demonstrate the various stages in the product's development.

◆ It helps forecast potential future demand.

◆ It reminds us of the fact that all products have a limited life.

◆ Profit levels are not constant but change throughout a product's life cycle in a way that is, to some extent, predictable.

◆ Products require different marketing programmes at different stages of their life cycle.

It is important to understand that not all products go through the stages as described above. For example, a product may be developed and launched and may not be successful and therefore declines before it has the opportunity to grow or mature.

Later in the unit you will be spending some time looking at the management of the PLC to provide you with an insight into some of the marketing challenges, both at strategic and at operational levels. It is essential that the PLC is examined in this context in order to highlight potential tactical level activities that a product or marketing manager might be involved in.

Managing the product life cycle

Product operational planning in the context of Marketing Planning is concerned with the tactical activities that underpin any particular product-based objectives, such as product development, product line extension, product differentiation and product positioning.

This level of operational planning should without exception underpin the strategic marketing process, exploiting marketing opportunities and growth strategies in an ever-changing environment.

One of the challenges of product management is that a massive growth in innovative products, competitive activity and market saturation will find organizations presented with fewer and fewer opportunities. Therefore, the management of the PLC is an essential activity, in order that every opportunity available can be exploited and the life cycle is extended. Sales will thus be optimized and profit potential maximized.

Marketing strategy for growth

With new and innovative products it is very likely that product sales could grow at an unprecedented rate. At this stage in the PLC, the competition may see and anticipate the rapid rate of growth and enter the market with their version of the product. It is likely that the competition will be highly aggressive, with high levels of advertising and sales promotion activity as they strive to gain their market share by incentivizing customers to switch brands.

As a product or marketing manager, it will be necessary for you to monitor these reactions very carefully and feed back into the strategic marketing process, in order that remedial action can be taken. It is more likely that the actions taken will be of a more tactical nature, principally striking back at the competition. However, in many instances, a strategic decision may have been made much earlier on the product offering, either by extending the product line or by differentiating the product offering.

Targeting of customers may need to be much more tightly defined as each of the competitors strives for market share. Increasing variations on a theme may be required in order to fully differentiate the product offering from that of the competitors.

Typical strategies at this stage will include an increase in push strategy activities by the manufacturer in order to gain preference with suppliers and retailers and command a higher proportion of supplier preference, and pull strategies, targeting more and more distributors, effectively saturating the market where appropriate with your own products.

As indicated in Unit 4, advertising activities will change to include brand awareness and brand benefits, aiming to position the products suitably in the minds of the customer.

In respect of the pricing element of the marketing mix, if growth is rapid then it might be expected that return on investments (ROIs) will also be achieved at an early stage, or that there is significant payback to reduce the price of the products. However, it might be that an increase in sales and volume might also generate economies of scale that could also enhance the possibilities of price reduction.

Price sensitivity may be an issue at this stage depending upon the products, but with more and more substitute products entering the market, it is likely that price will be a critical issue that will need careful management. Pricing will be positioned to sustain market share, and continue the life cycle as long as appropriate.

Marketing strategy for maturity

Managing the PLC through maturity throws up some interesting dynamics. It is likely that once a product has reached maturity, new products and modified products are running closely behind. It is probable that in this instance enough modifications will be made to differentiate the product suitably in order to reverse its position in the cycle, back towards a growth trend. This is a common policy of car manufacturers who are known historically for changing the light settings, bumper shapes and perhaps superficial features to enhance the look of the car, in line with customer expectations. In doing this, it is likely that the life cycle of the car will be extended. Modifications will reflect three particular categories: quality, functional and style modifications.

Segmentation and positioning become an issue, as customers' expectations change and become more diverse. It is a possibility that marketing development and market penetration strategies could be pursued simultaneously, maximizing profit potential.

Other typical activities might include cost cutting, intensive promotional opportunities and repositioning or even re-branding.

Marketing strategy for declining products

It is likely that the product has declined to such a stage that profitability has been significantly reduced and is probably non-existent. More innovative products and more up-to-date versions of the same will have replaced the product. The fall may have been predicted, or it might have been forced. However, where possible the decline of the product in the life cycle should be carefully managed.

The organization has a number of potential choices available at this stage:

◆   **Obsolescence** – Remove the product from the portfolio altogether and replace it

◆   **Repositioning** – Identify new uses for the product and new markets; position it differently in the minds of the existing and potential customers.

Obsolescence is increasingly common as a result of new technologies. In the last 20 years we have seen the demise of the record player for the CD player and the video player will ultimately be replaced by the DVD player.

In respect of distribution, high levels of promotional activity might encourage customers to continue to purchase and assist distribution channels in moving the stock over for replacements or new products. It is likely that a number of distributors will remove themselves from the channel for a period, or even be removed, in order to maintain profitability.

Depending upon the product, again price sensitivity may be an issue. In the car market it is usual that the price of cars that are in decline is ultimately reduced to clear them once the new replacement models are launched.

Advertising at this stage will be limited, but as already indicated, some level of promotional incentive may still be offered to speed up the decline and obsolescence process in order to release the stock.

Making a product obsolete and actually deleting it from the portfolio also requires some careful management. It is suggested that there are three key ways of deleting a product from the market:

1. **Phase it out** – A natural process, whereby the product strategy does not change until the product has sold out. It is expected that no attempt will be made to revive the product or change it. The Ford Escort was phased out in favour of the Ford Focus.

2. **Run it out** – Increase and intensify the marketing effort in order to effectively clear out stock.

3. **Drop it** – If retaining the product is eating into company profits, and it is being retained at a cost, it is likely that the organization will drop the product immediately and end its PLC.

As already suggested, a lot will depend on the product itself, the circumstances – that is, is it a natural deletion, a forced deletion, is there loss of face and an effect on competitive positioning? These factors will all impact upon the approach to product deletion.

Question 5.2

You are one of a team of product managers for a large motor vehicle manufacturer. You have been asked to prepare a briefing paper on the possible marketing activities that might be involved in sustaining a mid-range vehicle at the maturity stage of the PLC for a further three years.

Product portfolio planning tools

You should now understand that while the PLC has its own set of limitations, it is still a critical planning tool which helps focus the organization on the future of its product portfolio.

It is of primary importance that organizations continually monitor and control how their products are doing in the marketplace, what products are in growth and what products are in decline. To assist with this process many organizations use what are formally known as portfolio matrices.

Probably the best-known and most established matrix is the Boston Consulting Group matrix, known as the BCG (see Figure 5.3). Its main purpose is to provide a framework for considering future market growth for both products and services.

The BCG matrix

The BCG matrix has two key dimensions associated with it, namely the level of growth in the product's market and the product's market share in comparison to that of its competitors.

Market growth is an imperative to many organizations, as it presents an opportunity in the marketplace for extension, expansion and innovation. However, in low growth markets, it is more about survival of the fittest, as competition is highly intensive as each competitor strives for its own portion of a much smaller market potential.

Each of the four quartiles of the BCG offers an indication of potential opportunities or even potential decline in market share.

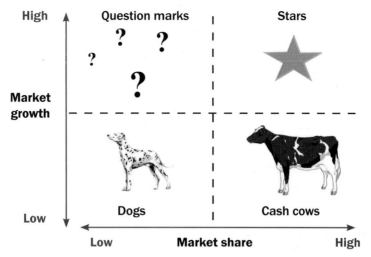

Figure 5.3: The BCG matrix. Adapted from: Boston Consulting Group, (1970) 'The product profolio', *Perspectives*, August

Stars

Principally, stars are products that command high levels of market share, with good potential for growth in the future. Key components are as follows:

◆ The product has moved to a position of leadership in a high growth market.

◆ Income needs are high to maintain market growth and keep competitors at bay.

◆ The product generates a large amount of income.

◆ As long as the market share is maintained, the product should become a cash cow.

Cash cows

Cash cows are essentially products that have a dominant share of the market, but with little potential for growth, effectively having reached a level of maturity. Key components are as follows:

◆ The product has a high market share and a low level of market growth. Stars become cash cows when the market rate begins to fall.

◆ The term 'cash cow' comes from the principle that products generate considerable money but use little cash.

◆ Economies of scale are strong.

Question marks

Question marks, alternatively known as problem children, are very much as they sound. They are principally products that have a small market share of a growing market. However, they are often subject to high levels of investment in order for them to achieve any significant growth in market share overall. Key components are as follows:

◆ The product has a low market share in a high growth market.

◆ Considerable investment is required to keep up with market developments.

◆ If trying to improve competitive position, levels of investment required are high.

◆ The 'question mark' arises over whether one needs to invest or divest in a market.

Dogs

The position of 'dogs' in the BCG is typically one of low market share, with no real potential for growth. This can often be an indication that the product is nearing the end of its current life, and should be potentially considered for repositioning or deletion from the product line. Key components of dogs are as follows:

◆   The product has a weak market share in a low growth market.

◆   A low level of profit or a loss would be typical in return.

◆   Very often dogs take up more time in terms of management than can be justified, so phasing out of the product is likely to be considered.

◆   Strategically, the issue is whether or not to hold on to the business.

From a marketing perspective, the BCG enables the organization to classify the company's products into four clear categories that will, in the main, shape their place in the future marketing strategy. While principally this is a planning tool, which should be used in the strategy development stages, it is important that it is clearly linked with the product in the context of product operations. This is because it will be part of the marketing manager's role to continually evaluate the performance of the product within the marketplace, and to contribute to inform the planning process of the potential growth and market share of the existing product portfolio. Both the PLC, which we looked at in the previous section, and the BCG matrix have a number of attributes (see Table 5.1) that will be tremendously helpful in planning for product involvement in the marketing strategy.

Typical outcomes from analysis undertaken through the BCG matrix will be the identification of new opportunities for product development potential, the need for repositioning or for deletion of products. In terms of potential marketing strategy, the BCG will assist in defining how growth objectives might be achieved through product-based activities.

Table 5.1: Strengths and weaknesses of the PLC and BCG

	PLC	BCG
Planning strengths	Five-stage view Easy to understand	Focus on SBU or products Allows variety of planning approaches Can be quantified Allows prediction
Planning weakness	Historical only No predictive capability Not quantifiable	Circle sizes may not reflect true benefits Likely to distort true picture as visuals are simplistic Quadrant position dependent on management decision, not objective data
Control strengths	Can suggest possibility of need for action Provides a useful visual shorthand	Relative market share shown Can be current or future based Encourage forward planning
Control weaknesses	Totally useless Imprecise and inaccurate Not quantifiable	Little value in stable markets, but has been developed into models which are useful

The General Electric matrix (GE matrix)

There are a range of alternative models, such as the GE matrix, or market attractiveness business position model (Figure 5.4); however, this is more of a strategic level model. This model indicates levels of market share on the same basis and will ultimately be able to indicate high, medium or low levels of market attractiveness. In using this, organizations will be able to potentially establish market attractiveness and different levels of growth, which will indicate the need either to invest and grow or to divest and harvest.

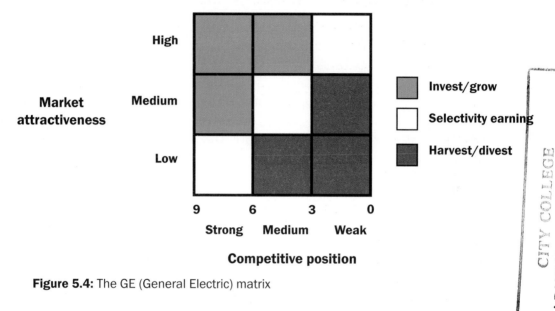

Figure 5.4: The GE (General Electric) matrix

Shell Directional Policy matrix

This model takes a similar approach to the GE matrix in that both have cells that contain policy recommendations for their business, for example invest, divest or grow. However, the Shell Directional Policy Matrix (see Figure 5.5) does focus on ascertaining the potential suitability of market segments versus the capabilities of the organization, so identifying all levels of market attractiveness.

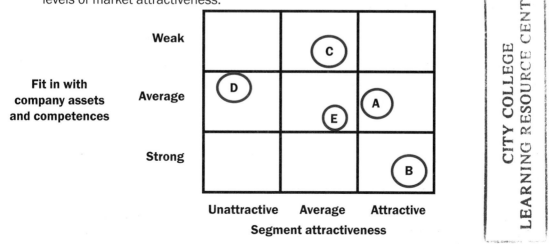

Figure 5.5: Shell Directional Policy Matrix. The letter s A-E indicate potential market segments and show how different segments may be positioned.

141

The organization must establish whether entering a particular segment is consistent with their long-term aims and objectives, and if not, it does not matter how tempting or attractive the segment looks, it should be resisted. Otherwise the organization wastes both management and time resources and is diverted away from the core goals of the enterprise.

An organization should enter segments that allow it to exploit current assets and competences, or will allow capabilities to develop into strengths. Therefore the Shell Direction Policy Matrix can be adapted to enable it to analyse market segment opportunities against corporate strengths.

This provides the basis for products/services to be analysed and their overall position with respect to the PLC determined. It shows whether there is scope for growth and expansion, or whether phased withdrawal is required.

As you move forwards onto the Postgraduate Diploma in Marketing, the technicalities of how to use the GE and Shell Directional Policy Matrix become more evident.

Question 5.3

As a marketing manager using the BCG matrix, what information would you expect it to provide you with, and how might you use it?

New product development

Product development is one of the possible outcomes of the marketing strategy development process, determined by the outcomes of the marketing audit and the use of the BCG and the Ansoff matrix.

It is a known fact that new products and new ideas are far more appealing to some customers than others.

Number of new product ideas

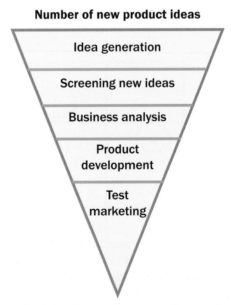

Figure 5.6: The new product development process. *Source:* Lancaster *et al.* (2001)

New product development is a highly expensive process that requires massive amounts of time and investment and thus a clear understanding of the rationale for product development is needed (Figure 5.6). Therefore a number of critical questions should be answered:

◆ Has a customer need been identified?

◆ Has the analysis from the BCG shown that the potential market is large enough to generate sufficient revenue, ROI and profitability?

◆ What is the level of resource required – does the company have the R&D expertise, technological ability and innovation required for new product development in the twenty-first century?

The basis of the answers to these questions will come from producing a formal method for assessing new product ideas – the 'new product development process' – where the feasibility and viability of future development is likely to take place.

Before moving forwards to look at the new product development process, it is important to consider the type of product that you are going to develop.

Type of product development	Nature of product development
New world/innovative	The focus of this model of NPD is on technical development and often incurs a high-risk return which can often revolutionize or create markets
New product lines or additions	Such products can be (1) new to the provider as opposed to the marketplace or (2) be additions to the product ranges already on offer
Product revisions/replacements	Replacements and upgrades of existing products. Changes may be aimed at generating cost reductions – no perceived change in performance but more economic production of the product
Reposition	Aim to diversify away from existing markets by uncovering new applications, uses or market segments for current products
Imitative products	Copycat products produced by others, but where there is a market for many alternative and competing versions

Adapted from: Drummond et al. (2003)

The new product development process

Idea generation

The formal process begins with the generation of new ideas. These can come from a variety of sources. A company's own R&D department will be working on new ideas all the time. Innovations can also come from the customer service department, where staff and customers can be encouraged to come forward with ideas. The sales and production departments are another important source. All ideas are listed and submitted to the new product team, where they will be considered. Effectively, a number of people can be involved in this process, both internally and externally to the organization.

Screening new ideas

Once the ideas have been assessed for their initial viability, it is necessary to devise a method of screening these so as to reduce them to a manageable number that are considered to have real prospects. A series of potential KSF, which research has shown are desirable to the consumer and to the company, will have been identified. In the twenty-first century, with the continuing rapid growth of ICT, and substantial databases, it is possible to closely match the characteristics of your products to consumer needs.

By clearly identifying the characteristics of your customers, it is possible to identify relevant market segments and niches to which marketing activities can be targeted.

Having identified the different segments, it is likely that they will have different needs. As a marketer, you need to establish the difference or differential between your products and services and those provided by your competitors.

The new ideas can then be compared so as to establish a short list of those that fit most closely to these criteria. Some of the factors that will come under consideration are raw material availability, production, distribution and the effect on sales of other products. Robust research programmes should inform the product design and development process. The characteristics identified against the potential benefits on offer should provide a basis of designing the perfect product solution.

Product development

At this stage in the process it is likely that the first prototype will be developed in order that the product is taken from conception to reality. The costs involved in this particular element are phenomenal. One of the key issues of product development will be to ensure that the investment in product design will create a new, innovative product that will achieve sustainable competitive advantage in the future. Therefore good sound design principles will provide the basis for competitive advantage in the marketplace.

From a technical perspective, it is likely that the key activities will relate to fine tuning both from a performance point of view and also in relation to ensuring that customer expectations will be delivered.

The product will have been technically designed and specifications drawn up in preparation for the manufacturer in advance of any full-scale production. However, the decision to launch is a critical factor and will require high levels of business and analytical skills, in order that full-scale production can be implemented.

Concept testing

The next stage, known as concept testing, is to determine whether the new product is likely to appeal to customers. A sample is often made up with varying forms of packaging and often company employees are asked for their opinions. Focus groups are frequently recruited at this stage. The beauty of concept testing is that it makes it possible to gauge consumers' reactions before the company has incurred heavy costs in production runs.

Packaging is also part of the concept testing, and with revolutionary technology a range of packaging options can be designed and form part of a virtual concept test. This is an evolving process.

Packaging, like the product, will provide a basis for differentiation and competitive advantage, therefore it is equally important to concept test the packaging in line with the product.

Business analysis

At this stage, the company has to consider the financial viability of the new idea. Research and forecasting techniques are used to determine the likely level of demand. A cost analysis will examine not only direct production costs but also capital investment and marketing costs and even new personnel. Profitability can then be established in terms of 'break-even' and rate of return analysis.

Test marketing

The purpose of test marketing is to gain consumers' reactions in an area that has been selected for the test. These are often television areas, such as Tyne Tees, which are considered to be representative of the total market. The test allows the company to evaluate sales and distribution prior to a full-blown launch. Any problems or flaws in the product or its promotion can be identified and made good before the continued rollout.

Launch

Assuming the test market operation has proved successful, then the product can be launched nationally. Production capacity will have to be increased to cope with the anticipated demand. The promotional campaign can be extended to national media and further distribution channels enlisted. Having an existing distribution network will improve the chances of success.

Case study: EarthShell's biodegradable hot beverage cups

EarthShell® Corporation is a technology company and innovator of a revolutionary development in food service packaging. Their business model is to license technology to manufacturers of food service disposables who will manufacture, market and distribute EarthShell Packaging® to quick-serve restaurants, food management companies, the U.S. government, universities, leading retailers and more. It is specifically designed with the environment in mind, from the beginning to the end of its PLC – and beyond.

Patented, innovative technology allows us to combine simple, abundant, renewable materials, such as limestone and starch, into a material that, like leaves and grass, is 100 per cent biodegradable and recyclable through composting. The result is a line of high quality, new-to-the-world food service packaging that is environmentally preferable and price-competitive to paper and plastic alternatives.

EarthShell have developed cups that are designed to meet or exceed the performance of other disposable hot-cup products currently available while offering the unique environmental attributes associated with other EarthShell products.

EarthShell's initial product development focused on plates, bowls, hinged containers, the recently announced new sandwich wraps and now, cups for hot beverages. Following product testing, the company will provide more details regarding product availability and other significant characteristics of its first entry into the cup market.

In keeping with the company's mission, hot cups from EarthShell are designed to have unique environmental advantages when compared to traditional hot cups made from polystyrene foam and paper.

EarthShell packaging, made from a composite material consisting primarily of natural limestone and renewable starch, is environmentally preferable from start to finish. When compared to traditional packaging, it uses less total energy and results in low greenhouse gas emissions.

EarthShell packaging is strong and provides good insulation, biodegrades when exposed to moisture in nature and is recyclable through composting.

EarthShell packaging is designed to be cost and performance competitive, compared to other foodservice packaging materials, and also to provide environmental advantages.

www.EarthShell.com

Source: Lexis-Nexis

Study tip

In June 2007 the Marketing Planning Examination, Question 3 focused upon the New Product Development Process and methods of product development. This was an optional question which constituted 25 marks, and thus is a very important area.

In the December 2007 Marketing Planning paper, Question 3 focused upon product positioning, standardization and the consideration of using the marketing mix to achieve a new positioning.

The product adoption process

The product adoption process identifies categories of customers who adopt products at different stages of the PLC. For instance, some people will adopt a product immediately after it is launched, whilst others will wait for a long time for the product to settle down. For instance, the most recent wave of LCD television screens are being slowly adopted in the market, whilst prices remain high. As prices start to fall it is expected that sales will increase.

Everett Rogers identified several different categories of people, based on the ease with which they adopted new products.

Innovators

These are people who will buy simply because the product is new. This is not a good indicator of a product's future potential.

Early adopters

This group are those who are willing to try new products before they have achieved widespread acceptance. They are often regarded as opinion leaders in their own circle. Acceptance by this group is essential for any new product.

Early majority

The early majority are a cautious group and will only adopt the new product once it becomes socially acceptable. Acceptance by this group will determine whether the product will gain widespread acceptance and succeed as a mass-market product.

Late majority

This group are even more risk-averse than the early majority. They will only consider adopting the product after they are sure that they are going to like it. At this stage, the product is well established.

Laggards

The laggards are those who resist the new product and may never adopt it. They are generally timid and cautious by nature.

The categories of adopters will vary according to the product. For instance, innovators are not always the same people in each market. Some people may be early adopters in the telecommunications market but laggards in new organic food. Having knowledge of adopters is very important and careful targeting of this group with launch promotional material such as direct mail will help the launch to be a greater success.

Despite all this effort, it is reckoned that only 10 per cent of new products are successful.

Targeting decision-makers

We looked at market segmentation and targeting within Unit 3, 'Marketing planning, implementation and control'. To remain competitive and cost-effective for both marketing and promotional operations, it is critical to profile and target your audiences and hence communicate with them very specifically, ensuring that all messages are relevant at that particular point in the decision-making process. It is also important to ensure that the messages are meaningful in a way that will pull decision-makers towards the product and a long-term loyal relationship.

However, targeting decision-makers at the right time can be a very complex process, particularly in a B2B setting. It is therefore of primary importance that you ensure that all communications, at each stage of the decision-making, and for meeting each element of the overall marketing strategy, are specifically targeted and provide the basis of synergy and consistency in terms of the overall implementation.

Summary

The product is the very core of what the organization is about – the product is the purpose. The product on its own is worthless, but carefully managed, branded and packaged; the benefits it provides and the satisfaction it will achieve are the key factors to its overall success.

The main aim of any organization should be to create products that customers need, want and expect, always ensuring quality, innovation, customer delight and value are at the core of their strategy development and business activity.

It is of primary importance that the organizations create a differential between themselves and their competitors, through the successful planning implementation of a brand and product strategy that places them in a uniquely differentiated and competitive position.

However, the critical success factor in establishing product and brand success is ensuring that an integrated approach is taken towards the utilization of the marketing mix. This will be a marketing imperative.

Marketers are becoming increasingly aware of the speed of change, resulting in shorter life cycles, faster levels of innovation, rapid speed of products to market, accelerated diffusion and excessive competition.

With the added impetus of global marketing and new technologies, product development, product innovation and robust product planning are providing the most significant challenge of the twenty-first century – where do we go from here?

Study tip

Product-based questions are highly likely within every exam. Questions will be framed on the basis of being part of the overall marketing mix, or on an individual basis. You will be expected to take an integrated approach to the managing of the marketing mix, and while being able to understand key marketing elements in isolation, it is essential to look at them as integrated also.

You will be expected to have some understanding of branding applications, product development, product portfolio matrix models and of course the PLC. The questions will put you in the position of a marketing manager, product manager or even brand manager, therefore you will need to look at these subjects in an applied way.

Further study

As with all other units, the purpose of this text is to consolidate your more extensive learning, providing you with an overview of the key elements. Therefore additional reading is recommended in order that you supplement your learning significantly.

Chapters 8, 9 and 10 of Dibb *et al.*(2005).

Bibliography

Drummond, G., Ensor, J. and Ashford, R. (2003) *Strategic Marketing: Planning and Control*, Oxford: Elsevier Butterworth-Heinemann

Unit 6 Price operations

Learning objectives

In this unit you will be focusing on the importance of pricing operations, and the implications and impact of pricing.

The syllabus elements for this unit are as follows:

3.7 Explain pricing frameworks available to, and used by, organizations for decision-making.

3.8 Describe how pricing is developed as an integrated part of the marketing mix.

Introduction

The focus of this unit on pricing operations is to allow you to consider the role of pricing within the marketing mix, the importance of price and its overall influence, and the considerations when setting pricing objectives. Furthermore, it is essential that you consider how flexibility in the role of pricing must be delivered in order to develop a marketing mix designed for sustained competitive advantage.

One of the key differences about price is that it is the only element as such that generates income rather than having a cost base to it. It is the determinant that focuses on maximizing revenue in order to meet profitability objectives and goals determined by the organization. Price is not just about generating revenue for the organization, it is about creating a better environment and a more effective long-term relationship with the customer. It is about placing a value on something, be it a product or service.

Value has to be perceived by the customer in order that the required revenue is generated. Customers do not just want products to be cheap or reasonably priced, they expect a certain level of value for money. That means that the product needs to have a certain level of quality, demonstrating that value in a clear and transparent way.

A marketer's involvement in pricing is necessary to ensure that price does reflect the product offering, that is the quality, the benefits and the functionality. Furthermore, the pricing strategy being implemented must match the expectations of the customer. Setting a high price is only acceptable if offering high value.

While price is seen to be possibly the most flexible element of the marketing mix, it is probably the most difficult to manage and it has to reflect the state of the market on a continuous basis.

Due to the intensively competitive nature of the marketplace today, price is the most changeable element of the mix. It has to respond to economic changes, competitive activity, customer demand and cost of materials, costs of distribution and a number of other key market drivers.

The role of the marketing manager in relation to pricing is sometimes rather ambiguous in many organizations and the waters become muddied between marketing and the accounting/financial arm of the organization in trying to maximize profitability. Sadly, in a less market-oriented organization, price setting will often be undertaken in a vacuum without considering the influences and implications of pricing and without realizing that considering price alone is not enough.

In many instances, setting prices is a thankless task. If it is too cheap, the customer thinks it is too good to be true and asks the question 'What's wrong with it?'. If the price is too high, customers may not want to buy it. If organizations do not get the price right the rest of the marketing mix could potentially be wasted; therefore the mix depends on the right product at the right price!

It doesn't matter who the organization is or what it does, what matters is to understand that price does not stand alone, it interacts with the whole organization and the other 6Ps. Price is very visible; therefore it has to present 'value' to the customer.

Price perception and the customer

In the introduction it was stated that price is the value placed upon either a product or a service. For the marketer, developing a marketing mix that is appropriate to customer needs and understanding the implications of it will be critical.

Having developed and communicated the nature of the marketing strategy, the organization is effectively signalling a whole range of information, perceptions and values about the product, its characteristics, benefits and performance. Ultimately, putting a price on a product raises expectations. It is then up to the customer to decide if it meets their needs or matches their perception.

Understanding the implications of price means understanding customer behaviour, motivations, culture, attitudes, values and perception. Of course, market segmentation does offer some answers to these questions, but it does, needless to say, leave price as the hot potato of the marketing mix.

Price is often perceived as being constant, but unfortunately it will change, both in reality and in the minds of buyers depending upon how their circumstances change. Constancy is one thing that price does not necessarily present. With supply and demand indicators changing, as demands of raw materials and components vary, competitive intensity and product rarity, price can change drastically.

Perspective of price and the organization

Price is the only element of the marketing mix that generates revenue for the organization. Everything else about the organization relates to a cost. Therefore pricing is the opportunity to gain some ROI or return on capital employed, meeting profit objectives and looking at growth opportunities from profits year on year.

It is, however, essential that the organization always considers the price from the perspective of the customer and then relates it to demand. The price that is charged is very much based upon the supply and demand factor of the market, the supply being the availability of the product and the demand based around how many people in the market actually want it. This is often a good starting point for the organization in establishing its potential pricing strategy.

Pricing in relation to demand

You should now be aware of the link between product quality and price and how price can be sensitive to the perception of the customer and how they see value for money. However, pricing is more complex than this. Pricing has to reflect a number of influences, demands and key drivers, and therefore pricing is subject to the following:

◆   The subjective beliefs of customers with regard to different pricing

◆   Competitors

◆   Quality.

It is necessary to predict the impact of price changes on consumers, distribution and on your competitors. Prices need to mirror the degree of demand for a product in a given market.

Different pricing strategies are relevant at different stages of the PLC in line with the relative costs involved. Generally speaking, price decreases in time in line with the decrease in costs involved.

This concept is known as price elasticity. This is a term used to explain that, generally speaking, demand will decrease as prices increase and that supply will increase as prices go up. 'Elasticity in demand' is the term used to explain that price changes in line with the volume sold.

Influences on price

One key activity of the marketer through both marketing research and the audit process is to understand the key influences upon pricing.

Pricing is a complex area to manage, if only taking on board the internal considerations such as the running costs of the organization, development costs, overhead costs, the organization's objectives and its corporate mission. But to add to the internal complexities, there are a significant number of external considerations an organization must be aware of.

Organizations have to be very responsive to the state of the market environment, and responsive to the range of factors already discussed, such as competition and demand.

While an organization has to be responsive, it also needs to manage the uncertainty. The twenty-first century seems to have given the market higher levels of uncertainty than previously experienced. To this end, organizations need to endeavour to understand a range of factors relating to the external environment. Figure 6.1 highlights the factors affecting the pricing decisions of the organization.

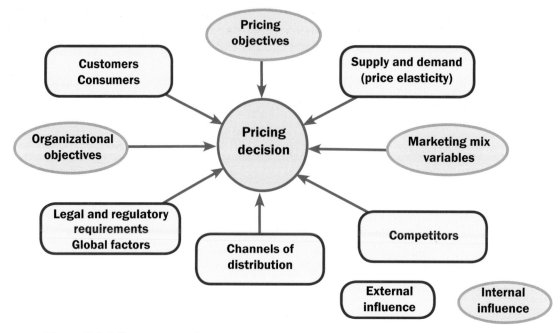

Figure 6.1: Influences on price

Question 6.1

On what basis do external market forces influence the price charged for a hotel room?

One of the most prominent headlines from autumn 2000, and an issue still going strong, has been the significantly high fuel prices and vehicle taxation in the United Kingdom and indeed some parts of Europe. Consumers, it would appear, have been subject to ever-increasing fuel prices and are continually threatened with the £5 gallon of petrol and the £1 per litre.

In addition to this, the increasing demand for gas has pushed up prices as reserves of gas reduce. It is suggested that in 20 years' time the United Kingdom and other countries could start to run out of gas completely.

However, there is still much concern in relation to fuel prices, and in 2008 the price of petrol and diesel was nearing £1.09 per litre, thus the £5.00 gallon is fast approaching. As a result, consumers and businesses alike are continually angered by the threat of high fuel prices, particularly as some of the big oil producers, such as Shell, BP and Esso, have been announcing considerable annual profits. However, while profits are being made on a global scale through other business opportunities, the influence of supply and demand factors in the oil production markets is eroding profits made in the United Kingdom. This coupled with the high levels of taxation invoked by the government finds the UK oil market subject to high costs and high demands, a balance that appears very difficult to manage.

Recently, legislation in respect of transportation has also had a significant impact upon costs, not least because of the vehicle emissions ruling. The higher the emissions, the higher the tax burden. The higher the tax burden the higher the cost of purchase is to the consumer.

The issue of high priced fuel is continually pertinent to many organizations, impacting on external influences such as customer dissatisfaction, government intervention and the actions of the World Trade Organization.

Marketers should continually be alert to the power of the various driving forces in the marketplace and how they can ultimately, through asserting their power, command changes in pricing structures and overall prices charged.

The process of globalization is also having an effect on price, and later in the text we will look at the implications of price from an international and global perspective.

Correlating price with value

Having looked at a number of influential factors in relation to pricing, it is clear that perceived value has a major impact upon the customer's decision to adopt.

Some of the typical factors that affect perceived value are as follows:

- Life cycle of the product
- Product benefits and functionality
- Quality
- Prestige and status of the brand
- Ease of use
- Value-added measures
- Differentiation
- Packaging
- Service and technical support
- Competitive alternatives (substitutes).

While these are just some of the factors affecting value, clearly it is a prominent issue. Principally the customer will be paying a price in exchange for 'perceived value and benefits', and therefore the price has to be representative of the overall deal. Essentially these factors start to form the basis of strategic price determinants.

There is a basic rule in pricing, that you price your product or service at the level that your customers expect to pay for the quality you are delivering. This does not just mean that high quality justifies high price, nor does it mean that high price means high quality. What it does mean, however, is that the organization has to justify the price that it charges.

Question 6.2

The value proposition, that is perceived value, is of vital importance when determining a price. How might you use other tools within the marketing mix, such as product and promotion, to justify the value proposition?

Strategic pricing determinants

Before setting pricing objectives, it is important to consider the determining factor of pricing, that is the key influences in relation to ascertaining the correct pricing positioning and pricing objectives for the organization.

Demand as a determinant

As a marketing manager, you will most likely be responsible for collecting various data that, through analysis, will identify the forecast levels of demand for products within the marketplace.

Demand relates to customers actually wanting to purchase or even needing to purchase particular goods or services. The likely scenario is that the higher the demand for the product the lower the price, and the lower the demand for the product the higher the price.

The basis of this scenario is that the higher the demand, the more likely the organization is to invoke economies of scale, and from there it can pass on its cost savings to the customer, thus lowering the price. However, whilst it is likely that reduced costs can be passed on to the customer, organizations must be aware of the impact this move will have on the supply and demand scenario.

It is important to realize that this strategy may not always be appropriate as in many markets demand needs to be controlled in order to avoid a situation of its spiralling out of control, which in turn could cause a great deal of instability within both the organization and the industry. Therefore, whilst organizations aim to pass on cost savings to customers, there may be a limit to how much they are likely to do this, in order to avoid an unmanageable and uncontrollable increase in demand. This approach would of course avoid early saturation of the market, and enable organizations to exploit future opportunities relating to supply of further similar or associated products.

The lower the demand, the less likely it is that economies of scale will be achieved; therefore likely costs of raw materials and related products will be higher, therefore the cost of the product will be higher.

Forecasting demand can be quite a difficult process, but once potential demand has been established, the price can be set accordingly. Forecasting demand will provide an insight into potential for growth; high levels of growth would potentially mean high levels of demand.

While demand is important, issues relating to elasticity in demand need to be answered. As a marketer it will be part of your role to undertake a range of exercises relating to ascertaining the level of demand and how fluctuations in price might increase or decrease the demand.

The likely findings of this exercise will probably highlight that marginal increases in price are unlikely to affect demand and therefore if they do not affect demand, demand is inelastic. However, if a significant increase in price is implemented, demand could potentially drop dramatically, therefore highlighting elasticity in demand and probably a fickle market.

As an example, if an organization reduced prices by 25 per cent, but as a result only saw a 5 per cent increase in sales, demand would be deemed inelastic. On the other hand, should the 25 per cent price reduction invoke a 50 per cent increase in sales, then price would be elastic. This highlights a degree of market sensitivity at a certain level in respect of price (Figure 6.2 and 6.3).

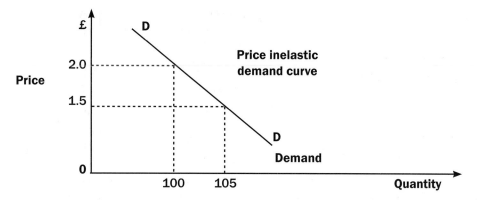

Figure 6.2: Inelasticity of demand

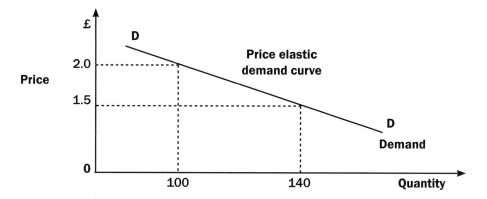

Figure 6.3: Elasticity of demand

Price-sensitive markets as a determinant

One of the most frequently asked questions in marketing today is 'Is the market price sensitive?' or 'How price sensitive is the market?'. The volatility of the marketing environment currently dictates that organizations should maintain an awareness of the price sensitivity issues within the market.

In order to be able to balance price sensitive issues and address them fully, it is essential that the organization defines some key indicators that will ultimately signal to them the level of sensitivity that exists.

Some of the key indicators to observe are as follows:

◆ How frequently is the product purchased?

◆ How essential is the product?

◆ How much does the product cost?

◆ What are the competitor alternatives within the market?

◆ What else can the customer's money be spent on?

◆ What is the effect of quality on price?

◆ What are the issues relating to stock/inventory?

Drawing anything conclusive from an analysis of the above points may prove to be rather difficult and will be the result of some quite complex analysis. However, the flexibility that surrounds pricing strategies will ultimately provide a basis for a well-balanced pricing strategy that will possibly provide perceived value, a robust competitive response and the level of profitability required.

A word of caution however: while price sensitivity is an issue, customers do not always make their purchasing decision based upon price, and on occasions it will be quite the contrary.

Understanding levels of price sensitivity in association with demand will help the organization ascertain the most appropriate pricing strategy in order to retain some form of consistency in demand, to avoid significant fluctuations.

Competitors as a determinant

On a number of occasions, the significance of the levels of intense competition has been mentioned. Competitive response profiles for each competitor are essential in managing price competition.

It has already been established that competitor activity also plays a leading role in the price of products for the customer. In the 21st century, price wars are commonplace. Price cutting is used to increase demand, improve market share and beat off the competition. Supermarket wars are a prime example of this. Cost cutting, special offers and reward cards are all part of the war to gain market share. However, Nigel Piercy (2001) suggests in his book *Market-Led Strategic Change* that price wars are both dangerous and contagious.

Customers are responsive to price cutting, as long as the perception of brand and product value remains unchanged. However, all organizations are forced to consider feasibility and viability of their marketing activities and corporate goals. Should the competition continue to intensify and profit margins continue to narrow, the infrastructure of the organization may have to change radically to remain competitive.

The pressure on organizations to be involved in competitor price war is significant. Some of the key influences on price wars are as follows:

◆ Customers no longer equate low price with low quality.

◆ Saturation of some markets.

◆ Price is a good tool to attack competitor weaknesses.

◆ Undercutting the competition is the only way to compete successfully and make an impact.

◆ The perception of reduced price and increased value is attractive to customers.

◆ Part of the retail sector culture is to implement ongoing sales promotions.

Price wars create a vicious circle. For example, over the past two years or so there have been significant supermarket wars. As ASDA (Wal-Mart) has reduced its prices on the 'roll-back system', Sainsbury and Tesco have followed suit with alternative promotions and have come up with appropriate strategies to detract from the cost cutting in the competitor organization. The mobile communications and personal computer market is another very visible example of this type of behaviour.

In order to manage the demands of competitive intensity and its impact upon price, there are a number of options open to organizations to pursue, they include the following:

◆ Matching the price of the competitor.

◆ Reducing the price below that of the competitor.

◆ Implementation of further price changes. This may include additional reductions in further product lines.

◆ Introduce new promotional incentives – 2 for the price of 1, get 25 per cent free, free delivery and so on. However, you must be aware that promotional incentives are often only a quick fix to what is a long-term problem.

Case study: Pharmacies price war

When the Restrictive Practices Court ruled in favour of lifting price controls on over-the-counter drugs, the UK's leading supermarkets quickly moved to slash prices on a range of branded medicines like headache tablets, vitamins and flu remedies by up to 50 per cent. As a result of the knock-on effect on independent pharmacies, it is widely believed that many will go out of business.

Even some of the larger operations say they will feel the pinch. Shares in Boots fell 6 per cent on the news of the ruling and the company said the decision would knock £15 million off profits within a year.

Because many of the independents rely on the margin gained from over-the-counter drugs, it was estimated around 15 per cent would go out of business because of the decision.

Source: LexisNexis

Question 6.3

What appears to be the overall impact of competitive pricing in the 21st century?

Product positioning and product life cycle as a determinant

Pricing will affect demand in many situations, and therefore issues in relation to product perception, product position and the stage in the PLC will be of the essence when designing appropriate pricing strategies. If you refer back to Unit 5 on 'Product operations', issues relating to price and profitability in the PLC are addressed.

Debtors and creditors as a determinant

Issues relating to liquidity, credibility, payment terms and cash flow will all influence the basis of pricing strategies. Pricing strategies will reflect largely the financial management of the company and will need to link closely to their key performance indicators.

The break-even analysis

The point at which an organization will become profitable will be one of the most important components of the decision-making process. Feasibility, viability, return on capital employed will all be linked to ascertaining the break-even point. Break-even charts can be extremely useful in evaluating proposals for new products or projects designed to improve profitability. They are based on the marginal approach and, being visual, produce an impact which figures alone rarely achieve.

This can be illustrated in a simple graph – Figure 6.4.

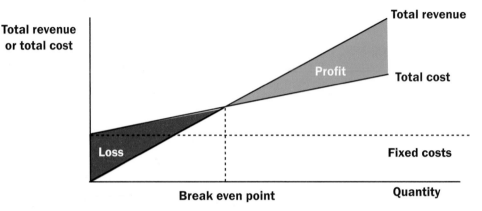

Figure 6.4: Break-even analysis

Break-even analysis involves looking at the break-even point of different price levels.

The break-even costs can be calculated simply as follows:

Break-even point = Fixed costs/(Price per unit – variable costs per unit)

Fixed costs are those costs that are constant; for example property rental, permanent fixed salaries, car fleets and so on.

Variable costs are those costs that change based upon the amount of products manufactured, the cost of raw materials and temporary labour.

Add the two together and you get the total cost of production.

This is the starting point for actually setting the price for many organizations. They would then go on to consider how their price should sit within the marketplace, taking into consideration the factors we have already discussed, that is the key influences on price both internally and externally.

To obtain an accurate price, it is essential that the organization establish an accurate cost.

As part of your studies within Management Information for Marketing Decisions, you will undertake the actual working out of break-even analysis.

While break-even analysis is an essential component of determining price and future approaches to pricing strategies, you should be aware that in essence, break-even will be a strategic decision. You as the marketer will be responsible for implementing the break-even objectives. However, it is essential that you understand the basic principles of using such models, in order that you clearly understand the basis of how the organization establishes pricing objectives.

Marginal costing and pricing

It is a given in pricing that sales revenue must at least cover the overhead costs before profit can be achieved. Therefore revenue should cover production, distribution and marketing costs and most likely make a contribution to the overall fixed costs of the organization.

Should a price be determined to recover the variable costs only, then the recovery is at the margin.

As a marketer you will need to establish what the marginal cost is of producing one or more additional units, in order that you ascertain the most cost-effective number of units to manufacture, to achieve profit.

Pricing objectives and strategies

Primarily, pricing objectives are set by companies in order to maximize sales revenue over and above costs in order to achieve profit.

Pricing objectives therefore reflect the basis of achieving profitability:

◆   **To achieve return on investment** – To ensure sufficient sales revenue to cover all associated cost bases and to pay back initial investment costs.

◆   **To maximize profits** – Companies who struggle to compete and have low market share may need to charge high prices to maximize profits.

◆   **To maximize sales revenue** – This will relate to setting prices at a level that will maximize sales turnover – more formally known as penetration pricing.

◆   **To achieve product quality leadership** – The basis of this objective will relate to providing the best quality product in the market in order to differentiate itself against its competitors, but will charge more than the competitors.

◆   **Market skimming** is where a company sets a high price to capture those customers who are willing to pay more for a product. Essentially this is more crudely defined as skimming the cream off, or targeting the top tier of the market. These people are likely to be the innovators, first in line in the adoption and diffusion process.

◆   **Survival** is, as it sounds, generally setting objectives that ensure survival in a highly competitive market. Therefore the aim is to generate enough income to cover all costs, potentially working on a break-even basis in order to stay in business.

One of the greatest challenges of pricing and the marketing mix is to define pricing objectives that allow for the achievement of gaining market share, achieving profitability, providing technical leadership, innovation and quality leadership. Balancing this can be very tricky.

As with all other components of the marketing mix, pricing objectives must be clearly defined in line with meeting the overall marketing objectives and corporate goals. The role of pricing will be to integrate fully and support all the other elements of the marketing mix.

Question 6.4

Explain why it is vitally important that pricing objectives reflect the marketing objectives and marketing strategy.

Strategic pricing

Two of the pricing objectives are highly strategic and will closely reflect the basis of the marketing objectives. It is therefore essential to understand the key characteristics of price skimming and market penetration.

When a new product enters into the market, it is likely that either one of these strategies will be adopted in order to aid market entry but, at the same time, to gain early ROI.

Price skimming has the following features:

◆ There is a relatively high price per unit.

◆ It is a good strategy to apply to new products and services with little price sensitivity (the development stage of the PLC).

◆ The price can be dropped when a market comes into existence.

◆ The market can be segmented easily.

◆ Profit is made on a per unit basis.

Price penetration has the following features:

◆ It offers a low price per unit.

◆ Price penetration is used when a large volume of the market share is involved.

◆ Profit is made through volume sales.

◆ Price penetration applies to 'me too' type products (copies of other market leading brands).

◆ Low price is aided by high promotions.

The two strategies above are key to ensuring supply and demand at a strategic level. But there is a tactical level of pricing that also needs to be considered.

Tactical pricing

Whatever pricing objectives the organization adopts, it will be important to define the appropriate strategy in order that they are achieved.

The development of appropriate pricing strategies will not only focus on the methods of costing, but also on the integration of pricing within the marketing mix. It will take into consideration external and internal influences which have been described earlier in the unit.

Tactical pricing provides the basis for the implementation of the marketing plan and its price-based objectives.

There are options to consider here:

◆ Quantity discounts

◆ Differential pricing

◆ Cost-plus pricing

◆ Demand-based pricing.

Quantity discounting

This involves the following:

◆ The principle that manufacturer prices are at their cheapest when large quantities are produced (economies of scale).

◆ Money is received quickly.

◆ Removing chances for the competition (in encouraging bulk purchase).

◆ Adding benefits for the customer.

A good example of this would be the purchase of print cartridges from the stationers. If a high usage or minimum purchase for a set period can be guaranteed then the customer may consider bulk purchase to obtain additional discounts. As the stationer does not have to store the materials for as long, it makes storage easier to manage and potentially reduces costs.

Differential pricing

This often involves the following:

◆ High fixed costs

◆ The relevant application of seasons and timings

◆ Benefit to both the producer and the consumer.

Differential pricing strategies set different prices for different markets, a point picked up earlier in this unit, and also within 'Product operations'. There is, for example, the differential pricing of Coca-Cola. Coca-Cola costs the customer different amounts depending on where they buy it – for example, it is likely to be more expensive in bars and cinemas than in petrol stations or supermarkets. Part of this pricing variance relates to including the cost of service and space as part of the overall strategy.

Other factors involved are as follows:

◆ Geo-demographics (i.e. geography and demographics) – where perhaps because of remoteness of a town, the cost of distribution is higher.

◆ The same products or services being sold in the same position at different prices geographically.

Cost-plus pricing

This involves the following:

◆ Covering the overhead costs, plus a percentage on top, to meet marketing/profit objectives.

Cost-plus pricing is usually used for projects that are more difficult to cost out, or actually take a long time for completion. It is also a useful pricing tool while markets are volatile, because you can always change the percentage on top of costs, and adjust it to meet market demands.

Cost-plus pricing is a simplistic approach which determines the cost of manufacture, plus a specified percentage above the price in line with the organization's requirements, which will ultimately achieve the selling price.

Eight stages to establishing a price

To summarize the key principles of pricing and to put your learning into a more practical context, Dibb *et al.* (2005) suggest that there are eight key stages to determining or establishing a chargeable price (Figure 6.5).

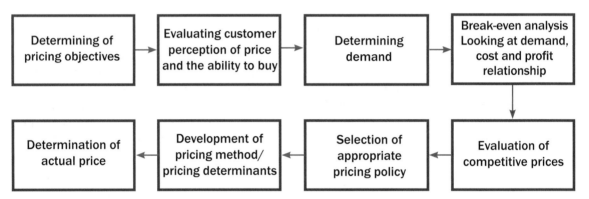

Figure 6.5: Stages for establishing price. Adapted from Dibb *et al.* (2001)

The route to setting higher prices

As a marketer you will always be challenged to identify a potential route for charging higher prices, as it is unlikely that profit goals will allow for the sustainable continuance of low prices. Some of the points to consider in doing this are as follows:

◆　　The strength of the customer relationship built by the salesforce – how does this impact upon the ability of the organization to negotiate higher prices?

◆　　Is the perceived value, that is the value proposition, enough to give the organization competitive advantage?

◆　　Does the marketing segmentation strategy highlight where some target groups are more or less price-sensitive than others?

◆　　How might the branding strategy allow for several price positions to be upheld in the market?

◆　　Are there any opportunities for skimming the market – price skimming?

Summary

The price element of the marketing mix leaves marketers aiming to achieve the ultimate blend of price, quality and perceived value. A balanced marketing mix will ensure the customer is getting the right product in the right place, at the right time, for the right price.

Customers are very fickle today and clearly understand that they have significant choice, and indeed power, in the marketplace and significant influence upon supply and demand.

Prices will vary according to what people are prepared to pay in different situations. Different prices might also reflect what customers can pay or are prepared to pay. However, from a management perspective, you are challenged to consider whether price is simply what the customer will pay, or a more flexible marketing tool than just that.

To understand the influence of price on the customers and competitors, a marketer must understand the need for significant ongoing research into the state of the external environment and the activities of competitors, and gain a key understanding of buyer behaviour and expectations.

The critical success factors in relation to price are to maintain the organizational objectives, yet endeavour to remain sensitive to the needs of the customers, ensuring that you can address their long-term needs, including the further development of new and innovative additions to the product range and lines. The key to price is to link the product quality with clear indication of value for money from the organization to the customer.

Pitching the price at the right level may be the difference between profit and loss or survival and failure, as pricing will reflect the long-term profitability and market share. To achieve a marketing-oriented approach to pricing, the organization should take into account a broad range of factors:

- Marketing strategy
- Value proposition
- Price–quality relationships
- Competitive pricing
- Costs
- Ability to negotiate higher prices
- External market forces
- The effects of globalization
- Product line pricing.

Further study

Recommended reading for this unit again comes from Dibb et al. (2005), Chapters 18 and 19. This will provide you with a very broad perspective of pricing. You will find these chapters very useful again when you study for Marketing Research and Information, as they explain some of the basis of the calculations.

Study tip

The basis of pricing in the context of Marketing Planning relates to understanding the concepts of pricing, the implications of pricing and possible approaches to implementation of pricing strategies in line with the corporate goals and marketing objective. The technicalities of pricing are covered in the *Management Information for Marketing Decisions* coursebook, which is where you will learn the actual basis of calculation. Therefore from an exam perspective it is likely that you will discuss potential pricing strategies, discuss influences on price and some of the strategic determinants.

In the exam, pricing is invariably included as an integral part of the marketing mix, with some individual pricing questions appearing on some, but not all, papers. For example in December 2007, there is consideration of price alongside product and distribution, with consideration of how it may be applied in virtual markets. This can be found in Question 5(a).

Question spotting and question prediction is a dangerous game, therefore always be well prepared, ensuring that you have a full knowledge and understanding of the subject in preparation for providing good robust answers.

Refer to the June 2006 exam paper, again Question 4, on establishing a price for a non-tangible product. Please note the integrative nature of these questions again. This should demonstrate to you the importance of application in terms of applying your knowledge and theory to a range of different situations, making recommendations and decisions.

Bibliography

Dibb, S., Simkin, L., Pride, W. and Ferrell, O. (2005) *Marketing: Concepts and Strategies*, Houghton Mifflin, 5th European edition

Unit 7
Place operations

Learning objectives

Place operations highlights the importance of distribution as a key factor in achieving the ultimate marketing mix. It is the final component and relates to ensuring that customers are able to gain access to and purchase their chosen product.

This unit reflects the same principal learning outcomes as the other marketing mix units, in terms of understanding the need to integrate the marketing mix tools and achieve effective implementation of plans.

From a place perspective, the indicative content reflects the following:

◆   Determine the channels of distribution and logistics to be used by an organization and develop a plan for channel support.

Syllabus reference: 3.9

Introduction

It is a known fact that without distribution 'place' the best product or service will not be delivered and the marketing mix will break down and fail. It was once said that the 'place' was one of the most powerful elements of the marketing mix, as it is the one way that we can both reach and actually service the customer.

Distribution is seen as a component part of the product. Therefore, in order to achieve total satisfaction, customer service will play an essential part in the overall achievement of customer satisfaction, retention and a sustainable competitive advantage.

Distribution works on two key principles:

1   It organizes the exchange process through distribution

2   It organizes communication.

Place plays a pivotal role within the marketing mix, and the key to success will be its successful integration within it, ensuring that customers get their products at the right place and at the right time. This will involve a range of alternative marketing activities based around promotion, price and the actual product design and packaging.

Distribution plays an important role, primarily because it ultimately affects the sales turnover and profit margins of the organization. If the product cannot reach its chosen destination at the appropriate time, then it can erode competitive advantage and customer retention.

An additional factor now facing distribution is the power of the buyers. As buyers we are becoming increasingly impatient, not wishing to wait for our products for any period of time. Therefore if distribution is a significant player in the decision-making process, the consequences of an inadequate distribution strategy may be catastrophic. There is an expectation in relation to delivery, in the same way there is with product and price. The combined package provides an expectation in the mind of customers and it also influences their overall perception of the value proposition.

Distribution provides many extensive new business opportunities and is currently at the centre of a range of strategic alliances, mergers, acquisitions, joint ventures and licensing agreements. In addition to this, the emergence and explosion of the Internet and other information communication technologies has put distribution on track to be one of the most lucrative business propositions of recent years.

Distribution requires a high degree of management skill, synchronization and integration with the overall organization, as it will be one of the major components in achieving a sustainable competitive advantage. Controlling the flow of products from the manufacturer or producer is no easy task, and as pointed out above, failure to control the flow effectively could decide the level of success you might enjoy in the marketplace.

Influences on distribution

Distribution is subject to a key set of influences in the same way as the other elements of the marketing mix. It is subject to external driving forces, internal forces and of course the forever-increasing power of the customer. Influences on place operations will therefore include the following:

◆ Fuel prices

◆ Environmental legislation

◆ Taxation

◆ Transportation choices

◆ National/global transportation infrastructure

◆ Nature of product and product characteristics – perishability and so on.

◆ Packaging

◆ Product life cycle

◆ Changing lifestyles

◆ The emergence of ICT

◆ Customer expectations

◆ Level of complexity in customer buying behaviour

◆ Competitive strategies

◆ Production targets

◆ Demand

◆ Market size

◆ Contribution towards costs

◆ Marketing mix components

◆ Customer services

◆ Technical support.

The list is tremendous and some of the factors have significant influence on the cost of distribution. Already in many organizations, distribution claims up to 50 per cent of the product costs, which is a considerable amount to absorb when designing appropriate competitive pricing strategies.

Logistics management plays a significant role in dealing with some of these influences and managing through them, in taking decisions such as appropriate order quantities, delivery methods, channel lengths, frequency of delivery, stock and inventory considerations, customer care and customer satisfaction. Each of these elements of logistics management will have a huge influence in achieving a balance between price and profitability.

Question 7.1

In what way do you think changing lifestyles have impacted on and influenced distribution strategies?

Marketing issues for distribution

Marketers need to be aware of the implications of distribution in respect of marketing. Distribution is ultimately about providing a service, a service of delivery to the customer, essentially getting the product from A to B. Therefore, there are some principal marketing issues that should be addressed.

The main marketing issue relates to channels. It is essential that you understand that the successful management of the supply chain will be achieved through selecting, motivating and controlling distributors and distribution outlets. However, if you reflect back on Porter's Five Forces, you will see that the marketer faces difficulty in achieving this, as the power of the supplier can be quite significant.

The other key component of successful distribution is meeting customer expectations in respect of delivery and service promises the organization might make. Think back to the importance of the value proposition. How does it position your business in respect of meeting delivery promises throughout the length and breadth of the distribution channel? The implications of achieving this will be a logistical challenge.

In order to achieve this wish list, a closely designed integrated marketing mix will need to exist. It will be essential that the underpinning support required by the distribution channel be in place in order to adopt both push and pull strategies in the marketplace.

Distribution channels

The distribution channel consists of a group of individuals or organizations that assist in getting the product to the right place at the right time. They enable the manufactured products to flow from the manufacturer to the end-user in many different ways.

Because of the nature of the marketing environment and the growth in international trade in what is termed the 'global marketplace', distribution can often be very involved, with a number of varying groups playing a key role in moving the products around.

Those groups are known as marketing intermediaries; they are really the middlemen. Intermediaries play a key role in ensuring that the manufacturer's target market is a group of very satisfied customers. Their role is to make sure that the product is available just when the customer wants it and from the place in which they want to purchase it.

Within each distribution channel there are a number of different levels and links, which will of course vary from channel to channel. However, as everything changes over time, the channels are predictably becoming shorter and shorter, with more and more people choosing to cut out the middleman in order to reduce costs and become more competitive.

The choice of channel is a strategic decision in the main and will have implications across the corporate organization in the way in which it does business. It most definitely impacts upon quality programmes, corporate development processes and, very importantly, resources.

Channel members

Intermediaries play a very important role within the distribution channel and the supply chain. In the main there are organizations such as transportation companies, merchants, agents, wholesalers, warehouses, retail outlets, to name but a few. Let us look at a brief overview of the function of each of them.

Wholesalers

Wholesalers are the middlemen at the early end of the distribution channel. It is very rare that they will sell directly to the end-user. They will buy products from the manufacturer, store them within their warehouses and sell the products on to the trade. This means that the wholesaler takes financial responsibility for the products; in fact they take legal title and physical possession of them. Producers will likely support the marketing activity through various push and pull strategies in order to ensure market demand increases.

Retailers

As a result of the technology revolution, the retailer is now not just on the high street but on the superhighway, the Internet. This is having a significant impact upon distribution, as you will see later in this unit.

The role of retailers is essentially the final stopping point for the product prior to its sale. Their role is to manage the transaction in which the buyer resolves to make their purchase decision and then the actual purchase. They will often act as the broker of information, the link between the customer and the producer, and the source of the customer relationship management.

Retailers have a highly prominent position in the channel and therefore potentially have the most challenging role in actually securing the transaction.

They may require considerable technical support, customer services backup, stock ordering facilities, technological systems underpinning the sales process, information and merchandise.

Distributors/dealers

Distributors and dealers are groups of intermediaries who are associated with stocking products for manufacturers and selling them on, including after-sales service and credit facilities. For example, when you purchase a Hotpoint washing machine, you may buy it from one of the big retailer outlets such as Comet or Currys; you may also buy an extended service warranty. The warranty does not come directly from Hotpoint nor from Comet, but from a third-party distributor.

Dealers are slightly different in that quite often they will specialize in selling one particular brand; for example, car dealerships are often associated with the manufacturer and therefore they sometimes sell on to the end-user, and the channel is somewhat shorter.

Agents/brokers/facilitators

Agents, brokers ad facilitators, as a general rule, do not take physical possession of the goods, but act on behalf of the manufacturer to sell their goods. Their main purpose is to bring buyers and sellers together. This is particularly common within international trade, where organizations do not necessarily have a physical presence.

Franchisee

Franchising is quite a common form of making a product available in the marketplace. The Body Shop was well known at one stage for franchising activities, as are Kentucky Fried Chicken and McDonald's. Franchising means that the franchisee holds a contract to market and supply a product or service that has been very strictly designed and developed by the franchiser. The franchiser will most likely have strict terms and conditions on store design, store layout and contents sold within the retail outlet.

Licensee

This is very similar to franchisee. The licensee pays royalties on sales or supplies to the licensor. The licensor is more often than not the manufacturer of the product.

Merchandiser

Merchandizing relates very closely to retailing. Merchandisers are responsible for store displays relating to different products. For example, most supermarkets now sell CDs in store. Many of the suppliers of the CDs employ merchandisers to go into the store to check supplies and set up promotional displays.

Why use intermediaries?

Due to the intensity of competition currently being experienced, many organizations are faced with cost reductions, resource reductions and often as a result, restructuring. So why, in the circumstances, should we continue to use intermediaries. What is the rationale that lies behind it?

Whilst distribution is highly expensive, naturally, there are a lot of add-on costs, such as those associated with marketing, administration, packaging, order processing and receiving and making payments. For an organization to undertake all of these activities will be quite costly.

Take the example of a producer with a network of links, a combination of retailers, wholesalers, agents and merchandisers. The network consists of 10 key buyers, who then distribute out to another 10 buyers; there are then 100 links in the network. The physical and logistical management involved might be horrendous. The costs will also be inextricably linked to the size of the network and the management exercise.

Therefore, the rationale behind the use of intermediaries in circumstances such as this is to invest in them and their activities in order that they take on the responsibility for marketing and administration within their network, further pushing the products out into the market. This may be a good value proposition to the suppliers, if the intermediaries are provided with some form of incentive such as heavy discounts or even profit-related returns.

Of course, while the financial benefits are significant, there are other benefits also, and other ways of adding value in the range of the customer–supplier relationship. The basis of these benefits can be segmented into three different groups (Figure 7.1).

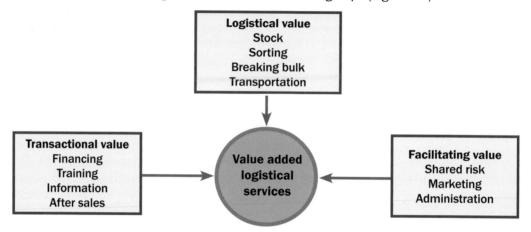

Figure 7.1: Valued-added services. Adapted from: Brassington and Pettitt (2000)

It is likely that in a large distribution network, channel members may have to perform a number of these value-added business functions to support their own organizational objectives. Should a manufacturer agree to supply an intermediary with their products, it may include securing a commitment from them to market their products appropriately to the target markets. Table 7.1 provides a more detailed basis of how the above value-added services might be undertaken.

Table 7.1: The role of the intermediary

Category of marketing activities	Possible activities required
Marketing information	Analyse information such as sales data. Carry out research studies
Marketing management	Establish objectives, plan activities and manage. Co-ordinate financing, risk taking. Evaluate channel activities
Facilitating exchange	Choose and stock products that match buyers' needs
Promotion	Set promotional objectives, co-ordinate advertising, personal selling, etc.
Price	Establish pricing policies, terms and sales
Physical distribution	Manage transport, warehousing, materials handling, stock control and communication
Customer service	Provide channels for advice, technical support, after-sales service, warranties
Relationships	Facilitate communication, products, parts, credit control, etc. Maintain relationships between manufacturer and retail outlets, and customer/consumer

Adapted from: Dibb *et al.* (2001)

Question 7.2

Explain with examples how the use of intermediaries can prove cost-effective in an organization.

The distribution channel and the customer

There are many variations in respect of the distribution channel structure (Figure 7.2); however, should intermediaries be deemed as appropriate in the business environment, the following channel structures would be available to you:

1   Passing of goods and services direct from the manufacturer to the consumer

2   Passing of goods and services via a retailer and then on to a consumer

3   Passing of goods and services from the manufacturer via a wholesaler and then directly on to the consumer

4   Passing of goods and services from manufacturer via a wholesaler, then on to a retailer and subsequently on to the consumer

5   Additionally, the manufacturer can distribute the products and services via an agent to a wholesaler and then follow the routes shown in points 3 and 4.

Quite often the types of channels of distribution used by organizations will depend upon the structure of the market, the size of the market, the complexity of the market and the geographical dispersion of the market, among other factors.

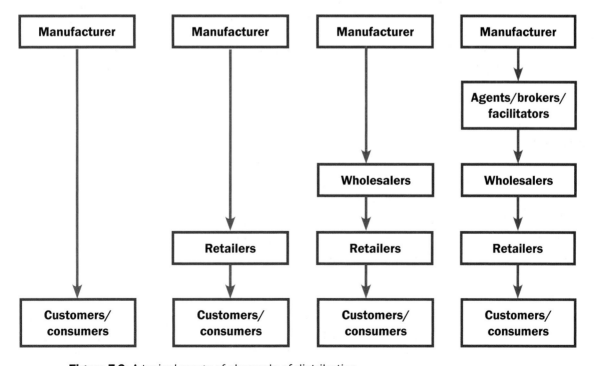

Figure 7.2: A typical range of channels of distribution

Selecting the channels of distribution

For a manufacturer to select a channel, they must consider the most appropriate one to meet their customer needs. They must consider the following:

◆ What are the product characteristics and how do they affect methods of distribution?

◆ Who are their customers?

◆ Where are their customers?

◆ What are their customer requirements?

◆ How, when and where do they want to buy their products?

◆ What are their competitors doing by way of distribution?

◆ What is the cost of distribution?

◆ What are the legal and regulatory constraints of distribution?

These are important issues and require significant levels of analysis in order to gain an understanding of the situation. Clearly some of these questions will form the basis of the marketing audit. Ideally the marketing mix has a clear focus on achieving customer satisfaction and achieving the profit objectives of the organization.

As competition is so aggressive in the marketplace, organizations will always look for new and improved ways of distributing their products. At the same time, retail outlets seem to be concerning themselves with providing as much as possible for the customer to save them going elsewhere, and obviously with the ultimate aim of securing a significant market share and increased profitability.

Supermarkets have moved away from just supplying food-based products to include fashions, music, electrical goods, cosmetics and so on. All of this is focused on meeting all of the above distribution factors. With the recent takeover of ASDA by the American-owned Wal-Mart, this kind of service provision is likely to grow and include an even broader range of products.

Intermediary selection criteria

There are two perspectives of intermediary selection, the strategic perspective and the operational perspective: strategic in relation to looking at the 'bigger picture' and 'operational' looking at the ability to implement the strategic marketing plan and distribution strategy.

Operational criteria

◆ Knowledge of local markets

◆ Appropriate premises and equipment

◆ Technological systems and processes

◆ Customer convenience

◆ Product knowledge and expertise

◆ Payment facilities

◆ Sales force structure, size and effectiveness

◆ Efficient customer service infrastructure.

Strategic criteria

◆ Plans for growth and expansion

◆ Resource capacity and future development

◆ Quality assurance processes

◆ Management ability

◆ Innovative

◆ Willing partnership

◆ Levels of loyalty and co-operation.

Applying these criteria to international supply chains

Later on in this text in Unit 9, there is some brief consideration of the implications of developing international marketing channels and supply relationships. However, it is important to note at this time that the application of the above criteria can be considerably more complex in international markets due to issues relating to cultural differences, that is the way in which organizations do business, structure themselves and commit themselves to relationships. Additionally, there are issues relating to resource requirements and fulfilment, that is does the international intermediary have the necessary resources and infrastructure to sustain a long-term supplier relationship.

It is a known fact that sometimes international intermediaries can be more fickle and establishing long-term supplier relationships based upon partnership loyalty and co-operation can be somewhat difficult to achieve, particularly when competitors offer preferential trade promotions to attract them away. Actually being able to tie an intermediary into a single supplier relationship can therefore be quite difficult.

One of the critical features of a channel network is to ensure that the country market analysed possesses channels which will provide the necessary services. Inherent within this will be the necessity to check financial stability, storage capacity for sufficient quantities of products, supply chain and distribution networks and whether the firm might invest in a dedicated network in order to supply the market.

Channel members tend only to be interested in closely defined or preferential supplier partnerships when high sales and high margins are available, which will contribute towards the competitive success of the company.

With a good distribution network established, co-ordination and control will need to be established. This task, even in a small firm, can be complex and must include ensuring that consignments and shipments arrive on time, that distributors are notified, that appropriate promotional mix activities are being undertaken and that the required financial reporting is in place. This will obviously include comparisons between budgeted and actual sales made and so on. Obviously with the increased use of telecommunications and computer networks the control and co-ordination and distribution across different countries are not very difficult tasks.

The balance of power within the distribution channel

The balance of power within the distribution channel is an interesting concept. As each party has its own set of objectives to pursue and its own agenda, fitting in with a partner organization can potentially cause conflict. Who then holds the balance of power? Is it the manufacturer because they have the products available for market? Or the intermediary, who may decide they do not want to sell on the product to retail outlets? Or is it the retailers themselves, who will decide on the most appropriate brand to sell to their customers?

Channel co-operation is critical and channel members need to be united. They should share information, agree to be directed to the same target markets and together maximize efficiency.

Often a channel leader will be identified to enable a co-ordinated effort of all parties in the marketing channel. Without co-operation, the member's objectives or the channel's objectives will not be achieved.

To become a leader within the channel, the channel member must want to direct and influence the channel's overall performance. To do this the channel leader must have significant power and driving force in order to succeed. To gain power in the relationship, the organization will likely of be a significant size, with major resources. It must be an expert in its field, and have the respect of the other channel members. It must be able to punish or reward other channel members effectively to get what it wants.

The channels will perform most effectively when they co-operate, co-ordinate and integrate their activities. Should they divert their gaze from the ultimate goal at any stage the channel will go into conflict and their effectiveness could be challenged and competitors could seize their opportunity to deflect customers to their products and markets.

Channel strategy

There are three types of market coverage:

◆ Intensive

◆ Selective

◆ Exclusive.

Intensive distribution means that as many available outlets as possible hold this product, for example chocolate, newspapers, bread and so on. Intensive distribution will mean convenience to the customer and increased customer satisfaction. The sale of groceries in petrol and service stations is an example of how intensive distribution has grown.

Key characteristics include the following:

◆ Maximum number of outlets covered to maximize availability

◆ Target outlets in as many geographical regions as possible

◆ Consumer convenience products

◆ High number of purchasers

◆ High purchase frequency

◆ Impulsive purchase

◆ Low price.

Selective distribution is different in that some products are only available from some outlets, for example electrical appliances, certain brands of clothes and fashion products.

Key characteristics include the following:

◆ Medium level of customers – but likely to be significant

◆ Less intensive distribution of outlets

◆ Retailers may require specialist knowledge

◆ Shopping-based products

◆ Medium number of shoppers

◆ Purchase is occasional

◆ Purchase is more likely to be planned

◆ Medium price.

Exclusive distribution is where possibly only one outlet in a certain geographic area supplies a product. This method of distribution usually relates to speciality products, for example special cars, specialist clothing and so on. Often exclusive distribution is relevant to niche products.

Key characteristics include the following:

◆ Relatively few customers

◆ Limited retail outlets

◆ Close retailer–customer relationship

◆ Speciality products

◆ Infrequent purchase

◆ High involvement and planned purchase

◆ High price.

Question 7.3

You have been asked by your manager to recommend and justify the most appropriate distribution strategy for a new palm-top product, which is a portable keyboard that can be plugged into the palm-top enabling it to be used as a mini-PC.

Vertical channel integration

An easy definition of vertical channel management, quoted by Hill and O'Sullivan (1999), is:

A distribution system where two or more channel members are connected by ownership or legal obligation.

A further definition is as follows:

A marketing channel in which a single channel member will co-ordinate or manage channel activities to achieve efficient, low-cost distribution, aimed at satisfying target market customers.

When you look at the varying distribution channels illustrated earlier in the unit, and you see the varying organizations involved, you will appreciate that in today's environment ,organizations, for reasons of economies and profit objectives, are becoming very interrelated.

A prime example of this would be a supermarket such as Wal-Mart, which is likely to service its own supermarket stores from its own network of central warehouses. This means that they own their own warehouses and their own logistics company.

This method of distribution ensures profit maximization is achieved across all areas of the business, with utilization of resources across the board. In doing this, the organization benefits from income vertically up and down the supplier/manufacturer chain. This particular strategy would invoke the demise of the middleman as the manufacturers endeavour to buy them out to service their own functions in-house wherever possible.

However, the vertical marketing system then undertakes the complex task of managing all associated management functions and all of the marketing mix activities in-house, which means that the marketing activities are much more closely related and integrated, and often therefore much more effective. These areas include the following:

◆ Product design and development

◆ Branding

◆ Pricing

◆ Promoting

◆ Stock control and storage

◆ Merchandising

◆ Transportation

◆ Retailing

◆ Customer services

◆ Finance/credit

◆ Warranties and guarantees.

Horizontal channel integration

Horizontal channel integration is easily defined:

> The combination of institutions at the same level of channel operation under one management.

This means that organizations that exist at the same level in the channel, for example the retailer level of the channel, may integrate with another organization by actually purchasing it. For example, there have been a number of significant mergers and takeovers within the mobile communications network, supermarkets (e.g. ASDA and Wal-Mart, Kwik Save and Somerfield) and the financial services sectors.

In this situation one business will purchase another business, either in the same field or in a similar o,ne, they will re-brand it, but pool resources such as marketing activities, marketing research, advertising, databases, personnel, distribution and warehousing. The net effect is that organizations can extend their market share both nationally and globally, while reducing their overhead costs significantly, but increasing their effectiveness, making them more competitive overall.

Physical distribution management

Distribution is an integral part of the marketing mix. 'Physical distribution management' (PDM) is the term used to describe the management of every part of the distribution process. It is extremely important, ensuring that products are moved from manufacturer to the point of sale efficiently, getting the correct product to the correct customer within a given timescale, as cost-effectively as possible. PDM can be contracted out to a specialist or developed as a function within the organization.

Part of PDM would include being aware of what your competitors are offering, as suggested earlier. Elements for consideration would include the following:

◆ Costs involved

◆ Methods of transport – road, rail, plane, shipping and so on.

◆ Routes used

◆ Stock, storage and stock control

◆ Protection and delivery of stock

◆ Timing – a key element

◆ Evaluating the effectiveness of distribution methods and being aware of alternatives.

Distribution is an integral part of the marketing mix. With the right distribution strategy in place, that is with the right mode of delivery, the right speed of delivery to the appropriate place of purchase, customer satisfaction can be significantly increased. Failure to deliver these practical points will result in the loss of orders and income to the company and long-term customer loyalty will decline.

The key objective of PDM is to find the most cost-effective way of meeting customer needs in relation to purchasing their product, whoever they are and wherever they are.

PDM includes the following functions:

◆ Customer services

◆ Order processing

◆ Materials handling

◆ Warehousing

◆ Stock/inventory management

◆ Transportation.

The key success factors of PDM include all elements of the marketing mix:

◆ **Product characteristics** – how do they affect delivery requirements?

◆ **Packaging** – can the product be transported?

◆ **Pricing** – how much does distribution add to the cost of the product?

◆ **Promotional campaigns** – creating an awareness of the product and where and how it can be purchased.

Timing is a critical element of PDM, as many companies work on the delivery of materials and components on a Just in Time basis (JIT). JIT is just as it sounds; it means that the manufacturer of products, or the supplier of raw materials, must deliver the necessary materials or components as and when required. For example, a window manufacturer, who makes windows for office buildings, will be making windows to order and will be required to deliver them at certain periodic times in the construction of the building. Because storing glass and the metal or plastic structures is difficult, the organization will deliver as and when the office block construction company needs it.

The concept of JIT was developed to encourage maximized efficiency of manufacturing. The process will reduce the storage space requirements, which is a direct cost saving to the organization, but it also means that the organization will only pay for the materials when they have taken delivery of them, rather than in a bulk order at the beginning of the contract. Both save significant amounts of money, which means that the cost savings can be passed on to the customer, making products cheaper to purchase.

JIT is very much linked to quality applications and improvements. Should the organization take a mass delivery of a component, and leave stock standing around, it could be damaged or problems with the delivery may not be discovered until it is too late. Therefore, quality assurance controls and measures can be implemented as the components are dispatched, which then aids the quality improvement process. This then enables organizations to work towards zero defects, which means zero wastage of time and materials, which means cost-effectiveness and quality improvement and ultimately a higher level of customer satisfaction.

Within the retail sector, JIT plays the same sort of role. You will note that retail outlets very rarely run out of standard stock products, because they have good stock control processes and systems that enable JIT delivery of those items.

Most retailers now work with electronic point of sale systems (EPOS). EPOS registers your purchase at the point of sale, that is the payment checkout. The product is scanned into the computer as sold and the computer automatically registers this as a stock reduction. When the stock reduction reaches a certain minimum level, the computer automatically generates a message to place a stock order for that particular product to be in store by a certain delivery date.

The EPOS system allows retailers to monitor frequency of purchase of certain products, which then enables them to forecast demand of their stock products. This in turn helps them plan for their stock requirement and come to appropriate agreements with their suppliers on delivery and storage requirements.

Push and pull strategies

The way in which products make their way to customers is a critical consideration to marketers. The push element relates to distribution and how personal selling links the supplier to the customer, pushing the product out to the market.

On the other hand, the pull strategy is very heavily reliant on advertising, packaging and sales promotions directly aimed at the consumer, effectively pulling them or attracting them to the product, encouraging them to purchase and forge a lasting relationship.

The huge growth in Internet marketing and direct marketing has really speeded this process up, with promotional incentives. For example, Marks and Spencer (M&S) are now giving discount vouchers to M&S storecard holders to encourage them to make additional purchases. Next Directory has introduced a variety of offers including free delivery or 20 per cent off on orders over £100. These are pull strategies. There has been a significant rise in pull strategies as a result of the surge in Internet-based shopping. It shortens the distribution channel and makes the response times quicker.

Key factors influencing push strategies might include the following:

◆ Levels of economic and financial stability

◆ Need for economies of scale

◆ Mature or saturated markets

◆ Consumer credit restrictions

◆ Political instability

◆ Intense competition

◆ High operating costs

◆ Indications of low market growth.

Key factors influencing pull strategies might include the following:

◆ Levels of economic and financial stability

◆ Innovative culture

◆ Underdeveloped retail infrastructure for the products

◆ High investment potential

◆ High levels of market growth

◆ Social stability

◆ Political stability.

As a marketing manager you will need to understand the importance of supporting onward suppliers in order to maximize economies of scale, associated profitability and benefits of a robust channel strategy.

The impact of the Internet on channel decisions

Distribution is currently subject to a fast pace of change as a result of the huge growth in ICT, and the majority of manufacturers and distributors have clearly been considering the above points in association with the new channel alternative of the Internet. Manufacturers and suppliers are being forced to reconsider the traditional routes to market that exist in favour of the Internet.

Question 7.4

What do you understand by the term 'disintermediation' and what are the overall benefits?

Evaluating channel effectiveness

It is essential that having selected an appropriate distribution channel and intermediaries, their efficiency, effectiveness and performance are continually managed.

Key performance and evaluation measures include the following:

◆ Regular reviews

◆ A forum for problem review and solution

◆ Monthly, quarterly and annual sales data analysis

◆ Average stock levels

◆ Lead and delivery times

◆ Zero defects

◆ Customer service complaints

◆ Marketing support – achieving marketing objectives, level of marketing activity, sales promotions, distributor incentives

◆ Spot-check of distributions further down the supply chain

◆ Annual performance audit.

For Internet marketing, typical methods of evaluating effectiveness might include:

◆ Number of leads

◆ Increased sales

◆ Customer retention

◆ Increased market share

◆ Brand enhancement and loyalty

◆ Customer service.

These are just some of the performance evaluations that you might implement. However, the tone and commitment to the distribution partnership will determine how much of this information should be provided in management reports, and the timings. Should the relationship be of a different nature, and perhaps the producer has less leverage, then some of the information required for performance evaluation could be significantly harder to come by.

Summary

The process of distribution is costly, complex and logistically challenging and will often involve many different groups of people or organizations. Right through the 1990s and continuing on into the new century, there has been a significant shift in distribution patterns, including the ongoing demise of many traditional middlemen. More and more organizations are merging, developing alliances and utilizing and pooling resources where possible, always looking at ways in which they can be more cost-effective, and expanding into broader geographical, in fact global markets. As the external marketing environment is so competitive, organizations have to find ways of increasing their market share and, obviously, increasing profits for shareholders.

Selection of the appropriate channel can give organizations the competitive edge over others by reaching customers in new and more innovative ways, particularly with the increasing use of the Internet.

Developing relationships between suppliers and customers is the essence of long-term customer loyalty. Should the marketing mix break down as a result of poor distribution strategy and management, then customers will go elsewhere.

Physical distribution management is a phenomenal task; it is complex, costly and critical. It has many facets, but its key role is getting the products to the customers, when and where they demand them.

One thing all organizations should bear in mind is that it is highly unlikely that customers will 'beat a path to their door'. The marketplace is vast and so is the amount of choice. Ensuring your product is visible when it should be will be one of the keys to marketing success.

Study tip

Distribution is raising its profile as a serious business function aided by the rapid evolution of e-commerce. You should be prepared to answer questions about any aspect of place operations. You should already be familiar with the basics of distribution in areas such as types of transportation and the roles of the various intermediaries through studying for Marketing Fundamentals, undergraduate studies or experience.

The concentration will be on the operation level of the subject, rather than a strategic level. Therefore it is likely that distribution-related questions will be about tactical implementation of distribution strategies that underpin overall marketing objectives and corporate goals.

Bibliography

Brassington, F. and Pettitt, S. (2000) *Principles of Marketing*, Thomson Higher Education

Dibb, S., Simkin, L., Pride, W. and Ferrell, O. (2005) *Marketing: Concepts and Strategies*, Houghton Mifflin, 5th European edition

Hill, E. and O'Sullivan, T. (1999) *Marketing*, Harlow: Longman, FT Prentice Hall

Useful websites include:

www.euromonitor.com

www.forrester.com

www.which.net

Unit 8
Managing marketing relationships

Learning objectives

The basis of this unit is to briefly focus upon the importance of managing marketing relationships effectively in order to maximize customer retention opportunities. This is also very much the focus of the Marketing Communications module and, therefore, the aim is to underpin the learning undertaken in that module.

Explain the importance of customer relationships to the organization and how they can be developed and supported by the marketing mix.

Syllabus reference: 3.11

The key to success within any marketing environment will be the realization that managing marketing relationships is crucial to long-term customer loyalty and customer retention, as is the necessity to manage each market differently in order to optimize customer relationships and the associated benefits.

Introduction

In the majority of situations, the basis of any type of relationship that is established is the way in which the supplier creates expectations. In creating expectations, you determine the nature and tone of the relationship and essentially you form and define customer behaviour in response to your organization and its product or service offerings.

The balance of optimizing customer relationships is a difficult one to manage, as quite often concentrating efforts on one customer or group of customers means that another customer might be neglected, ultimately to the detriment of the organization.

Pleasing the customer and creating customer satisfaction seem to become a greater challenge almost daily, as organizations strive to achieve some form of competitive advantage. Customers become more demanding, assert their buyer power, and their expectations are continually rising, all the time making the value proposition more difficult to achieve.

With the growing influence of a number of key driving forces through SLEPT factors in the market, managing the marketing relationship is becoming a more turbulent affair. Every concept of every relationship now appears to demand more of the organization. The role of stakeholders, the growing influence of social responsibility and ethics, and internal marketing factors are now squeezing organizations from every angle, in order that they please all of the people all of the time.

The emphasis is now on knowing your markets, knowing your individual customers, and being able to address them directly. Thus having 'an electronic footprint' of them is essential if you are to establish a robust long-term relationship with them.

Ignoring the issues of managing relationships will ultimately leave organizations and marketers in a very vulnerable position.

One of the main reasons that organizations will, however, start to make positive moves towards managing marketing relationships is in order to maximize their effectiveness by retaining existing customers rather than focusing consistently on new customers. Long-term relationships provide the basis of consistency, synergy and achieving satisfaction. The long-term profitable benefits to the organizations will be considerable. For example, a 5 per cent reduction in customer defections can improve profitability by an excess of 25 per cent.

Relationship marketing

> ## Definition
>
> **Relationship marketing** – is to establish, maintain and enhance relationships with customers and other parties at a profit so that the objectives of the parties involved are met. This is done by mutual exchange and fulfilment of promises (Gronroos, 1994).
>
> **Relationship marketing** – refers to all marketing activities directed towards establishing and maintaining successful and relational exchanges (Morgan and Hunt, 1994).

The fundamental principle upon which relationship marketing is founded is that the greater the level of customer satisfaction with a relationship – not just the product and service – the greater the likelihood that the customer will stay with and be retained by the organization.

For relationship marketing to succeed in any organization, there will need to be a cultural shift, as discussed in Unit 3 on 'Marketing planning, implementation and control', away from the old transactional style of marketing to the more dynamic and rewarding basis of relationship marketing.

From transactional to relationship marketing

A more conventional approach to marketing has been the old transactional marketing, whereby the functions of marketing, customer services and quality have been separate entities within the organization. However, the disintegrated approach to marketing meant that the potential to optimize marketing relationships was being lost, as the lack of co-ordination between the three functions gave way to a fragmented approach to achieving customer satisfaction. Ultimately, and in many instances, this started to prove problematic with many organizations as they found they were suffering lack of market share compared with the more relationship-focused business.

There are therefore a number of significant differences between the concepts and the contexts of transactional and relationship marketing, as illustrated in Table 8.1.

Table 8.1 The shift in relationship marketing	
Transactional focus	**Relationship focus**
Orientation to single sales	Orientation to customer
Discontinuous customer contact	Continuous customer contact
Focus on product features	Focus on customer value
Short timescale	Long timescale
Limited emphasis on customer service	High customer service emphasis
Limited commitment to meeting customer expectations	High commitment to meeting customer expectations
Quality is the concern of production staff	Quality is the concern of all staff

Source: Peck *et al.* (1998)

Principally, the key difference in the management of the relationship is that the basis of it will be a long-term relationship, a long-term view achieving long-term customer loyalty.

In order to establish and construct a relationship programme, or indeed a relationship chain, there are four factors that the organization will need to concentrate on, each of which we have covered in other units:

1   Defining the value proposition (Unit 5).

2   Identifying appropriate customer value segments (Unit 3).

3   Designing value delivery systems (Unit 7).

4   Managing and maintaining delivered satisfaction (all units).

For an organization to succeed it is, of course, essential that the value proposition meets the expectations of the customers, that the expectations in their minds meet those in the mind of the supplier and that there is little scope for customer uncertainties, a concept that you will come across in selling. Therefore, the value proposition needs to fill any gaps in expectations.

Market segmentation has been a continuous thread throughout – the more closely defined the target markets, the more the likelihood of success. The more you know and establish in the relationship with your customers, the closer you get to delivering what they really want, again closing the expectations gap.

In Unit 4 some time was spent on the definition of value: establishing values – core values and peripheral values. For relationship management to work, defining the method of actually delivering that value will be essential. This will include a range of delivery systems and channels, and these should be appropriately tailored to the customer needs. Of course, with the growing influence of digital marketing and service technologies, it will make it far easier for you to perhaps support a diverse range of customers. However, a word of warning – you should be aware of the fact that while it gives you strength to manage customers, so too does it give a competitor strength. The switching process from one company to another can often be fast and painless.

Because the quality and strength of customer relationships is vital to the survival and profitability of all organizations, it is essential for competitive advantage to be sustained, customer loyalty to be achieved, and the process of delivering customer satisfaction to be clearly defined to avoid any potential gaps in customer perception of the value proposition and their expectations.

While this seems quite broad, with every group of customers or each individual customer, these are core issues in sustaining the relationship. This applies to the context of each customer group that will be the focus of this unit. It is, therefore, essential that at this stage you actually have an understanding of how broad that scope can be.

The scope of marketing relationships

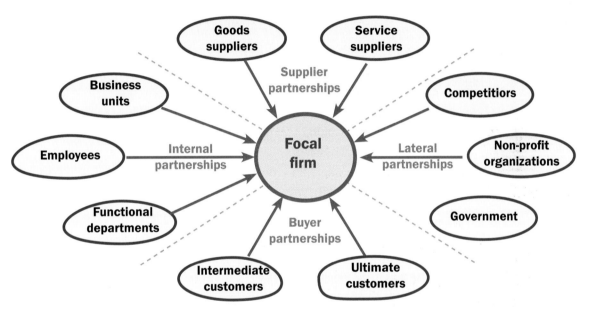

Figure 8.1: The scope of relationships. Adapted from Morgan and Hunt (1994)

The scope of managing marketing relationships is significant (see Figure 8.1), stretching as it does across four key groups: customers, suppliers, internal markets and stakeholder markets, each defined in terms of relationship marketing partnerships.

In addition to this, the scope broadens once more, as you look at managing marketing relationships in the broader context of business sectors:

◆ Organizational markets

◆ Service markets

◆ Not-for-profit markets.

Each of these particular elements is the focus of other units in this text, where some issues pertaining to relationship management are discussed.

However, in brief, the critical issues relating to each market sector are as follows:

Organizational markets – Require high levels of relationship management due to the intensity and time dimensions of the process of purchase. The market is essentially less fickle and more rational, which provides the basis of establishing closer links. Closer links mean working towards gaining preferred supplier status. The basis of achieving this will ultimately mean long-term supplier–buyer relationships, effectively putting a relationship on a strong footing.

Essentially relationship marketing is about collaborative relationships, working together in optimizing opportunities and maximizing potential.

Service markets – Relationship marketing in the context of services is the major imperative, as at the core of any successful service delivery will be the relationship between the service provider and the service consumer. Never before has the power and strength of that relationship become so relevant. The whole basis of its success rests upon the key factors of relationship marketing, as defined in Table 8.1:

◆ Continuous customer contact

◆ Focus on customer value

◆ Long timescale

◆ High customer service emphasis

◆ High commitment to meeting customer expectations

◆ Quality as a concern to all staff.

Not-for-profit markets – Relationship management is the critical success factor and should be the core of these markets. In order for charities, for example, to succeed they need to establish long-term relationships so that they can sustain three key factors:

1 Donors – The givers of money and equipment to support their work.

2 Volunteers – The people who give time and effort and avoid company overheads.

3 Client – The users of the charitable service; the charity needs to gain trust, understanding and often long-term relationships in order to undertake the work at the heart of their organizations.

Question 8.1

Think about the scope of your own organization or one you know well, and make a list of groups of individual customers with whom you have relationships – you might be surprised at the balance of the group.

Planning for relationship management

A marketing relationship does not just happen, evolve or emerge, it has to be planned. As with all other aspects of marketing, it requires a structured approach to ensure that relationship marketing does maximize business potential, provide the basis of profitability, and create sustainable competitive advantage, through robust and long-term customer, supplier and stakeholder relationships.

In order to plan for relationship marketing, there needs to be an understanding of some key factors: customer loyalty, the dimensions of quality, building trust and the basis of continuous improvement.

Customer loyalty

To achieve customer loyalty is highly challenging, as it looks at the loyalty of all customer groups that are involved in the relationship marketing process. For relationship marketing to be truly implemented and be part of the business culture, it has to focus on all customer groups.

We have already established that relationship building is a long-term process and, in order for customer loyalty to be achieved, there are a number of key identifiable stages that the relationship moves through. This is more formally known as the 'Relationship marketing ladder' of customer loyalty (see Figure 8.2).

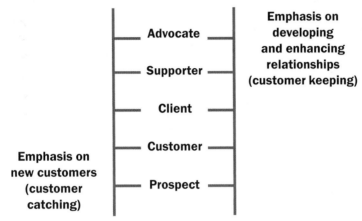

Figure 8.2: The relationship ladder. Adapted from: Peck *et al.* (1998)

The ladder highlights the process from targeting the customer, to adoption, to developing the relationship from customer to long-term client. From here, it is then essential to encourage them to become both a supporter and advocate of the company, in order that they can become marketing tools, on your behalf. Thus, you not only retain them, but also use them to grow your market.

The recent addition to the ladder is that of partnership. In the organizational marketing context, partnership is a very positive stage to move towards, in order to secure optimization of opportunities to be exploited for the benefit of both the supplier and the buyer organizations.

Customer loyalty, however, has two dimensions: long-term loyalty, which is the basis of a true relationship marketing scenario, and false loyalty. This will essentially be driven by a number of key factors:

◆　Limited completion of the task

◆　High switching costs

◆　Proprietary technology

◆　The attraction of some loyalty scheme.

The key objective in this context, therefore, will be to actually switch the power base of loyalty to a more long-term relationship and, indeed, partnership.

Customer loyalty, of course, is very interlinked with brand loyalty, which was discussed in Unit 5.

The key dimensions of relationship marketing

In Unit 10 you will look at the basis of services marketing, that is to ensure that quality is at the core of the business and the relationship with customers.

Therefore, there are some key dimensions upon which an organization must deliver in order to provide a basis for a relationship.

◆ **Reliability** – Ability to perform the promised service dependably and accurately

◆ **Responsiveness** – Willingness to help customers and provide prompt service

◆ **Assurance** – Knowledge and courtesy of employees and their ability to inspire trust and confidence

◆ **Empathy** – Caring, individualism and attention to customers

◆ **Tangibles** – Physical facilities, equipment and appearance of personnel.

In order for the relationship to be established, the quality gap must be filled, that is the difference between the customer expectations and the organizational perception of what is being delivered.

A relationship based upon trust

Morgan and Hunt suggested three dynamics to trust within a relationship (Figure 8.3).

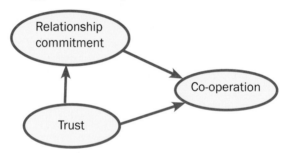

Figure 8.3: What builds trust? Adapted from: Morgan and Hunt (1994)

These are three quite simplistic components that would form the basis of any relationship, personal or business. The basis of trust provides the opportunity to develop a relationship that includes co-operation, leading to relationship commitment. While principally they should be the basis of relationship marketing aims and objectives, typically these three components can often be overlooked, perhaps assumed or even ignored. However, in Figure 8.4 you can see the benefits of building a relationship on trust, as you can save on relationship termination costs, gain many benefits and look towards a relationship based on shared values. Opportunistic behaviour will be a great benefit of partnerships in a relationship management context.

Communication is an absolute, as the more inward- and outward-bound communication that exists, the more you will find out about the customer, their needs, wants and perhaps their competitive experiences, all of which will only serve to strengthen the basis on which you might operate.

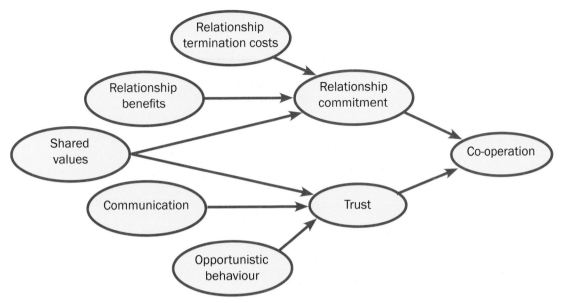

Figure 8.4: Relationship model. Adapted from: Morgan and Hunt (1994)

Customer retention management

The most simplistic view that any organization could take of customer retention manage-ment is that the way to keep customers is to keep them satisfied. Some organizations think that this means zero defects, others are realizing the increasing importance of this and are really looking at ways in which retention is not just a concept but a reality. According to *Loyalty Today*, 51 per cent of all British shoppers possess a loyalty card and those who shop at supermarkets which offer them, 70 per cent have a card. However, the reality is that few buyers are 100 per cent loyal within any one year.

Peck *et al.* (1998) have developed a number of techniques for measuring customer satis-faction and essentially linking them directly to profitability. Principally, what they are doing is measuring customer retention, where customer satisfaction is measured at the rate at which customers are kept.

Peck *et al.* suggest that a retention rate of 80 per cent means that, on average, customers remain loyal for five years, whereas a rate of 90 per cent pushes the average loyalty up to 10 years. And as the average life of a customer increases, so does the profitability to the firm. They go on to suggest that long-term established customers are more profitable for six reasons:

1   Regular customers place frequent, consistent orders and, therefore, usually cost less to serve.

2   Long-established customers tend to buy more.

3   Satisfied customers may sometimes pay premium price.

4   Retaining customers makes it difficult for competitors to enter a market or increase their share.

5   Satisfied customers often refer new customers to the supplier at no extra cost.

6   The cost of acquiring and serving new customers can be substantial. A higher retention rate implies fewer new customers need to be acquired, and they can be
acquired more cheaply.

Here, you see some of the benefits alluded to within Figure 8.4, so therefore a relationship
based on trust can gain commitment and co-operation, with all of the other add-ons as
previously discussed.

Customer retention in consumer markets

In consumer markets, customer retention schemes are in the main focused around loyalty
cards. Most people, on average, will have at least five loyalty cards on the go at any one time.

Loyalty cards became highly popular in the mid- to late 1980s as the intensity of competition began to rise in the supermarket wars, closely followed by banks and credit card
companies. For example, the American Express Blue Card gives you a penny back for every
pound you spend on their card, at the end of the year. Boots followed suit with their loyalty
card, which proved to be very beneficial to the customer. With double points and special
offers, the Boots card has been branded a success by its customers.

The latest example of this type of loyalty bonus is the 'Nectar' card sponsored by Deben-
hams, Sainsbury's, BP and Barclaycard. After getting off to a rather rocky start due to issues relating to website registrations, and the crashing of the Nectar website, the Nectar
card has been relatively successful in consumer retention markets, however, so have organizations such as Tesco's, who also host their own Tesco's Club Card. See the overview
of the Nectar card launch and the basis upon which it operates, with sponsoring organizations working together to achieve customer loyalty.

Case study: Nectar cards

In March 2002, Sainsbury's, in conjunction with a number of key sponsors, launched one
of the most successful loyalty arrangement packages ever, the Nectar card. This is a new
type of reward card – one which lets you collect points at more than one place, rather
than using lots of cards in different shops. So now it's easier for you to earn more points
than ever before. And the more points you have, the more rewards you'll be able to enjoy.

All you have to do is hand over your Nectar card whenever you shop at Sainsbury's, or
eat at the Beefeater or Brewers Fayre and wherever you see the Nectar sign at BP. You
can also earn points when you shop by phone or on the Internet. And from time to time
you'll be able to earn bonus points to boost your total ... which means you could enjoy
even more great rewards.

When you pay at the till at Sainsbury's or BP, your Nectar card will be swiped and any
points added to your account. When you pay by Barclaycard anywhere in the world, your
points will be added to your Nectar account each month (once you have registered your
Nectar number with Barclaycard). Shop with your Barclaycard at Sainsbury's or BP and
you'll earn two lots of points.

Once you've collected enough points for the rewards you want – whether it's free meals,
great days out, flights abroad, cinema tickets – the choice is yours. You can even use
your points to save money at Sainsbury's or Argos.

Since launch, Nectar provision of loyalty arrangements has been extended to many more companies, including:

Ford	Vodaphone	Threshers
Magnet	Brewers Fayre	Beefeater
Talk Talk	Thompson	Adams
Dolland and Atchinson.		

To see all others log on to: www.nectar.com

Customer retention in organizational markets

We have already touched upon some of the issues relating to this within this unit, and will develop the issues relating to customer retention management in other contexts later in the book. However, there are five basic principles that an organizational market should consider:

1   **Technical support** – Providing added value to clients in industrial markets.

2   **Technical expertise** – Providing expertise in design and engineering can be a USP of the organization and add to the value proposition.

3   **Resource support** – Ensure that a range of versatile resources are available to support the relationship, that are cost-effective and efficient, and that could ultimately see the development of an alliance when business opportunities are presented (the basis of partnerships).

4   **Service levels** – These appear to be of growing importance and will relate in particular to time, delivery and product quality.

5   **Reduction of risk** – Giving as much insight into the product proposition as possible through exhibitions, trial use and product delivery guarantees.

Customer retention in not-for-profit markets

The basis of customer retention in not-for-profit organizations is covered in some depth in Unit 11.

Essentially, one of the key considerations is that marketing activities in not-for-profit markets need to be very focused at each of their customer groups, as we ascertained earlier, those being donors, volunteers, client/users.

It will be essential that the charity understands their target markets and segments them exactly, as each of them will manifest different customer retention characteristics, particularly as their personal reasons for charitable involvements will be very diverse.

Key relationship marketing issues will include the following:

◆   Analysing acquisition and retention costs

◆   Managing customer retention and customer acquisition activities concurrently

◆   Recognizing how emphasis needs to be placed on all markets in order to achieve the success the objectives demand

◆ The need to have adequate information sources about each of the customer groups.

Of course, within the not-for-profit sector there are some far broader strategic issues that typical organizations will grapple with, such as the challenges of the functions of management and marketing, developing and understanding the basis of market segmentation strategies and finally the scope of their mission, which in many instances can be huge.

All in all, the challenges of both relationship and retention management in the context of marketing are quite daunting.

The marketing mix for customer retention management

As you will be beginning to conclude, the foundation of success in managing marketing relationships and customer retention marketing is the value proposition. Therefore, it is essential that the use of the marketing mix as a key set of tools be optimized in order to have maximum impact upon the customer base, meeting their expectations and retaining them and your competitive advantage.

Therefore, the following marketing mix suggestions should be considered. They relate back to, and build on, your studies in other units.

Product extras

◆ Product and service augmentation and innovation – guarantees of standards and service levels, preventive maintenance

◆ Customizing the offer – relationship building

◆ Cross-selling other products in the product line or portfolio.

Relationship pricing

◆ Price incentive for increased customer spend and perhaps customer share

◆ Price sensitivity – what are the issues with price sensitivity – is it a relationship issue?

◆ Perceived value – the value proposition versus the price.

Specialized distribution

◆ Priority customer-handling – For example, British Airways offers Executive and Standard check-ins

◆ Preview evenings – M&S, House of Fraser, Laura Ashley – typical tactics in relationship marketing

◆ Exclusive or selective distributors

◆ Multiple accessing options, that is the Internet, retail outlets, direct marketing.

Reinforcing promotions

◆ Sales-force responsiveness

◆ Loyalty schemes – reward cards, membership benefits, sales promotions, magazines

◆ Tailored direct marketing.

Managing internal marketing relationships

Definition

> **Internal marketing –** Can be defined as 'marketing by a service firm to train and effectively motivate its customer contact employees and all the supporting services to work as a team of people to provide customer satisfaction' (Kotler *et al.*, 1998).

The fundamental component of achieving successful relationship marketing is the infrastructure of the organization – the culture, leaderships, skills, resources, synergy, co-ordination and co-operation of the employees within the organization. Without these key factors being addressed by the organization, success in the external market is likely to be limited.

The overall aim of internal marketing, therefore, is to ensure that everybody within the organization contributes towards developing a marketing-oriented, customer-focused culture in order to improve levels of services to customers.

It is necessary that an integrated approach towards achieving customer satisfaction is taken by the whole of the organization to optimize the skills, talents and abilities that employees have on offer to meet the needs of the external market.

In Unit 3, we looked at the importance of internal marketing as part of the implementation process, and saw that, indeed, internal components and infrastructure needed to be in place in order for the corporate goals and marketing objectives to be achieved.

Therefore, the key to managing internal relationships is having a rational understanding of the key factors listed below, in order to establish a basis for the relationship between employees to be built in the context of trust, co-operation and commitment.

The same benefits also operate in the internal context of marketing, with perhaps the difference being that employee relationship termination may well result in the employee switching to competing organizations. Should an employee move to a competitor, they take with them a lot of inside knowledge of their previous employer, which ultimately will influence them within their new role. This should obviously be avoided.

Internal stakeholders

Internal stakeholders are people who are likely to be involved in internal marketing and those who operate within the boundary of the organization and who have an effect on the organization's overall performance. The stakeholders are likely to include shareholders, directors, management and the workforce. As stakeholders, they expect to receive some reward for their efforts, through either payment or share options.

The way in which staff are paid can often have a significant bearing upon their overall performance and often the provision of a stake in the organization is a good incentive and motivational factor.

Internal relationship marketing techniques

In the main, most organizations now recognize the pivotal importance of internal marketing in respect of achieving robust customer relationships with their external customers.

However, organizations do need to address a number of key issues in relation to successful implementation, all of which have been covered within Unit 3. As a reminder, these are the key components of internal marketing success:

◆ Create an internal awareness of the corporate aims, objectives and overall mission.

◆ Determine the expectations of the internal customer.

◆ Communicate to internal customers.

◆ Provide appropriate human and financial resources to underpin the implementation of the marketing strategy.

◆ Provide training in order that employees have the appropriate skills and competences to undertake the task at hand.

◆ Implement a change in tasks and activities appropriate to the objectives of the organization.

◆ Provide a structure whereby cross-functional integrated teams across business units can work together, in order to aid communication of business activity relating to the achievement of corporate goals.

◆ Provide the systems and processes that enable successful delivery of services and products, enabling employees to successfully implement them and achieve organizational success.

◆ Maximize the opportunity for customer interaction through effective management of service levels, for example response times, reply processes.

◆ Institute internal monitoring and control.

For internal marketing to be successfully implemented, a planned approach is essential to allow evaluation and measurement of the successful execution of the plan.

The plan could be designed with the following headings:

◆ Internal vision

◆ Aims and objectives

◆ Internal marketing strategy

◆ Segmentation, targeting and positioning

◆ Marketing programme (to include all elements of the marketing mix)

◆ Implementation

◆ Monitoring and control of the success or failure of execution.

Question 8.2

Why is it important to have highly motivated personnel in order to successfully implement a relationship marketing programme within the organization?

Importantly, in terms of managing customer relationships, internal marketing forms the basis of the 'relationship management chain' (Figure 8.5).

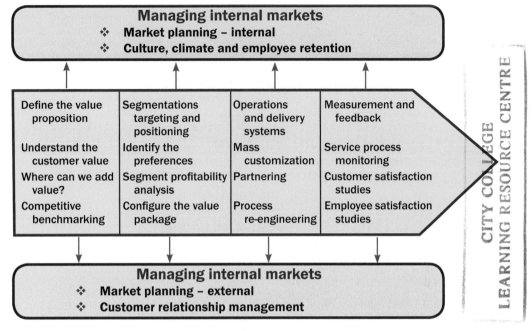

Figure 8.5: The relationship management chain. Adapted from: Peck *et al.* (1998)

Essentially, to establish a really effective relationship chain within the organization will require a focus upon a number of critical issues – to which we made reference earlier:

◆ Defining the value proposition

◆ Identifying appropriate customer value segments

◆ Designing value systems

◆ Managing and maintaining delivered satisfaction.

The relationship marketing plan

It is essential that an organization manage the scope and range of relationships within the marketing environment, in order to achieve all-round success.

As the management of relationships in each of the markets we have defined is critical to the achievement of the overall customer retention objectives, there must be crystal-clear linkages that bridge the objects and the markets (see Figure 8.6).

In order to achieve a meaningful relationship marketing plan, you have to consider the needs of each of the individual markets in order for it to be successfully implemented. The linkages between each audience should be clear, and they should all be directed towards the same overall purpose. The successful implementation of such a plan will most likely impact upon the achievement of retention goals.

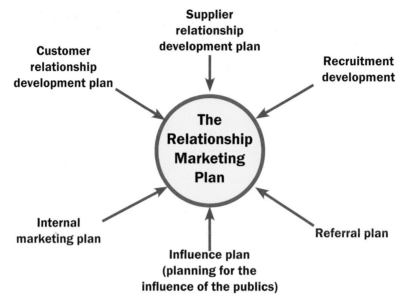

Figure 8.6: The relationship marketing plan. Adapted from: Peck *et al.* (1998)

Summary

The move from transaction marketing to relationship marketing has meant that the marketing planning process has now taken on a new set of dynamics. It is no longer purely based around developing a marketing mix to meet organizational goals, it is much broader in perspective, and the task much bigger.

Essentially, organizations which are truly committed to developing a relationship marketing approach will need to be supported by a structure, culture and overall organizational climate that will enable each of the functional business units within the organization to align and co-ordinate themselves to develop an integrated approach to the achievement of the overall marketing objectives of every market.

Principally, the role of the relationship marketing plan is to ensure that there is a synergy, consistency, coherence and cohesiveness, and a 'pan-company' approach to the implementation of the marketing plan.

Study tip

Question 4 in the June 2007 examination paper question 3(a) asked for students to 'explain the importance of customer relationships to an organisation and how they can be developed and supported by the marketing mix'. This is an integrated question and required learning from Units 4-7 on the marketing mix, also requires learning from this unit, with students demonstrating a clear understanding of the principles of relationships marketing.

These types of questions require an in-depth understanding of relationship marketing, which can be applied in any given context.

Further study

There are some useful articles that appear from time to time in Marketing Business in respect of relationship marketing and customer retention.

Bibliography

Gronroos, C. (1994) From marketing mix to relationship marketing: Towards a paradigm shift in marketing, *Management Decision*, 32(2), 4–20

Kotler, P., Armstrong, G., Saunders, J. and Wong, V. (1998) *Principles of Marketing*, FT Prentice Hall

Morgan, R.M. and Hunt, J.D. (1994) The commitment-trust theory of relationship marketing, *Journal of Marketing*, 58, 43–8 (July)

Peck, H., Clark, M., Payne, A. and Christopher, M. (1998) *Relationship Marketing: Winning and Keeping Customers*, Oxford: Butterworth Heinemann

Unit 9 International marketing

Learning objectives

With the ongoing evolution of global markets, it is of primary importance that the function and practice of marketing in an international context is considered.

The underpinning indicative content, that is the syllabus areas to be covered, include:

◆ Explain how marketing plans and activities vary in organizations that operate in an international context and develop an appropriate marketing mix.

Syllabus element: 4.1

Introduction

In order to survive in the marketing environment in the twenty-first century, alternative methods of growth, expansion, diversification and differentiation are playing an increasing role in everyday business. Expansion into international markets is one of the more common ways of fulfilling growth and market development objectives.

Around the world, managers are realizing the increasing necessity for their organizations to develop skills, awareness and knowledge to enable them to manage the international market development process. That knowledge and understanding includes an insight into the expectation of international customers, their cultures and their existing levels of awareness of products and services that you might offer.

As an international marketing manager the demands on you will present an interesting challenge as you strive to understand the cultural diversity of doing business in other countries.

One of the many misunderstandings in the business environment is that international marketing is exclusively for large organizations. This is a great misconception, as the whole world is a marketplace, presenting many profitable marketing opportunities for all. Every country and every region offers new and exciting challenges, and a different range of marketing opportunities, which in essence will arise from its own particular needs. Understanding these needs as a marketer is of pivotal importance. Marketing after all is the process of identifying, anticipating and satisfying customer requirements profitably.

Why go international?

For many organizations going 'international' will ultimately be to fill a gap that will affect the organization's ability to expand in the long term. These gaps in organizational performance will be due to a number of reasons:

◆ **Intensity of the competition** – An organization may expand, first, because there may be less intensity of competition overseas, or second, because some organizations are finding the intensity of competition so virulent in their own country, that they are unable to survive without an alternative strategy.

◆ **Saturated domestic market** – As competition continues to intensify, it is likely that businesses can no longer sustain the level of competitive advantage and market share, therefore the alternative is to look for market growth and market development opportunities elsewhere.

◆ **Product life cycle differences** – As a product moves through its life cycle it is subject to many levels of change, in functionality, style and quality. However, in order to avoid deletion from the product range, international markets provide new opportunities for the same product, perhaps for a different use, or alternatively there is a cultural and time lag in the country. For example, long after the Hillman Minx had been obsolete in the United Kingdom it was a common sight on the roads of Tehran, Iran. So while the product has expired in most of the Western world, there has been life thereafter.

◆ **Excess capacity** – Where an organization is operating successfully in the domestic market, but operating below optimal capacity, then there is excess capacity available to produce more products for different markets. Particularly important here would be issues relating to marginal costing. If economies of scale were appropriate, marginal costing could reduce the price significantly in order to overcome the barriers of entry into new markets.

◆ **Comparative advantage** – Organizations may establish, as a result of their research, that they actually have comparable advantage over their international rivals, perhaps in their own domestic market. The advantage might be skills based, technology based, access to raw materials and so on.

◆ **Financial reasons** – There are a number of financial reasons why an organization may decide to take the international route. These might include investment incentives, availability of venture capital and grants from local authorities.

◆ **Organizational issues** – On many occasions, early entries into international markets can almost happen by default. Organizations involved in mergers or acquisitions may find that their partners in the product have international operations, of which they then become a part.

◆ **Geographical diversification** – This will likely happen as a result of some of the other factors covered. To avoid competitive intensity, saturated markets and so on, the organization will expand geographically into new areas.

Levels of international marketing

The decision to exploit international marketing opportunities will be a strategic one; it will be linked to corporate and financial goals and will involve considerable financial risk. Therefore the decision must be an informed one. Strategic evaluations will be considered and the exploitation of any opportunities will have to be justified, with the provision of a high level of substantiating information.

The key to making the right decision will be gaining understanding of the different levels of international development available, backed by market research into the chosen countries to ascertain the strategic fit between the hosting nation and your own organization.

The various levels for international marketing are as follows:

◆ **Domestic/regional marketing** – which involves the company manipulating a series of controllable variables such as price, advertising, distribution and the product in a largely uncontrollable external environment that is made up of different economic structures, competitors, cultural values and legal infrastructure within specific political or geographic boundaries. For the United Kingdom, this is a challenging issue, particularly with the very close links relating to our relationship with continental Europe through the European Union. While in normal domestic or regional settings there is only one common language to deal with, for example within the United States; Europe has the situation where in some respects there is no one dominant language and while English is widely spoken, it most certainly is not a prerequisite for joining the EU. This immediately erects communication barriers.

◆ **International marketing** – which involves operating across a number of foreign country markets in which not only do the uncontrollable variables differ significantly between one market and another, but the controllable factors in the form of cost and price structures, opportunities for advertising and distributive infrastructure are also likely to differ.

◆ **Global marketing management** – which is a larger and more complex international operation. Here a company co-ordinates, integrates and controls a whole series of marketing programmes into a substantial global effort. Here the main objective of the company is to achieve a degree of synergy in the overall operation so that by taking advantage of different exchange rates, tax rates, labour rates, skill levels and market opportunities, the organization as a whole will be greater than the sum of its parts.

◆ **Export marketing** – is where the organization trades its goods and services across national and political boundaries. There are two types, direct and indirect.

    ◆ **Direct exporting** – is where an organization sells their goods and services directly to a host country. This will mean that they will need to invest much resource, time and effort in establishing business links within international markets. This may mean establishing a physical presence in the market-place.

    ◆ **Indirect exporting** – is where an organization with limited resources trades internationally through the most simple and low-cost method available. Quite often their profile will be raised through a number of market entry methods, for example the use of an agent, or an export house.

To clarify this a little more, let us look at the differences in domestic and international marketing, as shown in Table 9.1.

Table 9.1: Domestic versus international marketing

Domestic marketing	International marketing
Main language	Many languages
Dominant culture	Multi-culture
Research straightforward	Research complex
Relatively stable environment	Often unstable environment
Single currency	Exchange rate problems
Business conventions understood	Conventions diverse and unclear

The international marketing environment

International marketing carries with it a high element of financial risk, as there are many uncertainties, some of which are significant and often many times greater than those facing a company operating in just one marketplace. Therefore, it is of primary importance that before entering any overseas marketplace, the organization has a thorough understanding of its nature and characteristics. This is effectively undertaking a marketing audit, but in an international context.

Earlier in this book within Unit 2, 'The marketing audit', there was some discussion about the nature and extent of the external marketing environment. The environmental influences that should be considered in the context of international marketing are still the same, namely SLEPT, but let us look at how it balances out for international considerations.

Figure 9.1 illustrates some of the considerations of international marketing.

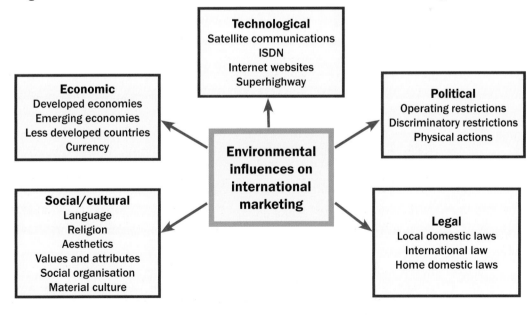

Figure 9.1: Cultural framework

Social/cultural factors

Cultural differences are apparent from one end of the United Kingdom to the other, or one end of China to the other, but between different countries it would appear that in some instances they are enormous. You will find a range of different social interests and a variety of different customer behaviour patterns. Failure to understand them on the part of the organization could end in disaster, as it did several years ago when McDonald's moved into Iran. Some Iranians were less than delighted at Western intervention and it resulted in significant damage to the buildings.

Cultural differences are very significant, with considerations of religion, languages, education, symbols – these differences are often termed 'cultural gaps'. Clearly these will cause operational problems with the marketing mix and the ability to develop global brands. For example, Pepsi-cola had to change its 'Come Alive with Pepsi' campaign theme as in Germany it was translated as 'Pepsi Out of the Grave'!

These factors present many challenges for marketers in terms of their ability to meet such a broad range of customer needs under the social and cultural banners. While product specifications – the tangible element of the mix – might be almost identical, the services mix – the level of customer services and technical support required – may be very diverse, dependent upon the infrastructure and expectations of the host country.

The challenges will be across the whole range of the marketing mix, not just the traditional elements of pricing, distribution and advertising but also the 3Ps of the services mix, which will present significant challenges for the marketer.

Religious cultures present a very interesting challenge, particularly in Middle Eastern countries, where the role of women is different to that in the Western world. Marketers must be very sensitive to the varying levels of cultural diversity if they wish to be successful in international marketing terms.

Question 9.1

Identify two countries that you are familiar with and draw up a list of potential social/cultural differences. You should do this by identifying four cultural characteristics and then compare and contrast them across both countries.

Legal environment

Legal systems will invariably be different, in terms of context, content and meaning. You may have to think of law as being the 'rules of the game' for international trading.

There are four key considerations for international law:

1   **Domestic laws in the home country** – At the same time as working within international law requirements, you also have to consider your own country's legal requirements.

2   **Local domestic laws** – These are all different. The only way to survive through the legal systems abroad is to employ external agents, experts in the country, to manage the legal side of the business for you.

3   **International laws** – There are many international laws that affect the marketing of products and services overseas. For example, international conventions and agreements, trade embargoes, International Monetary Fund (IMF) and WTO regulations, treaties, patents, trademarks and so on.

4   **Laws and international marketing activity** – These laws will affect each element of the marketing mix in different ways; it could be product patents or advertising restrictions, many of which exist in the Middle East.

There have been many interesting legal cases relating to international marketing and also cases of major organizations giving up on trying to achieve new market entry strategies because the red tape has been too difficult to get through.

Economic environment

There are fairly wide extremes in relation to the economics of varying countries. For example, from Ethiopia, where average earnings are considerably less than $100 per annum, through to North America, where the average monthly earnings are in excess of $2000. The differences between Southern American economies and those of the Asia Pacific Rim are considerable. A further example of differences in economies is that in Tokyo you have to work for less than 25 minutes to buy a Big Mac from McDonald's, whereas in Mexico City you have to work for 80 minutes to buy exactly the same product.

Three categories of the economic environment

◆   **Developed countries** – This includes most of the Western world. The NAFTA (North America Free Trade Agreement) countries, the EU and Japan account for over 80 per cent of trade in the Triad economies, the Triad being a global triangle within which trade exists – three different groups of cultures and economies coming together.

◆   **Emerging economies** – Countries and regions such as India, China, South America (in particular Brazil) are defined as emerging because of the change in direction of their internal economic policy and growing demand for every type of Western product, for example mobile phones, cars, computers. All of these present significant marketing opportunities, but also significant marketing mix challenges, as the marketer deals with the wide range of international trade issues.

◆   **Less developed countries** – Typically in these the per capita income is extremely low, which inhibits the amount of funds for regeneration in the economy. Common characteristics of such countries are poor communications networks, poor transportation system, high levels of poverty, low levels of education and health care.

Currency/interest rate risks

World economic instability and currency variations are potentially very damaging to organizations. A rapid drop in one particular currency can wipe away almost immediately the benefit of doing business abroad, in fact it can be the difference between organizations managing to sink or swim. This is something that has been very much in the forefront of everyone's mind since 11 September 2001 and also the conflict on Iraq that began in Spring of 2003 and still continues.

Rises or falls in interest rates can also have significant effects, as we have seen in the UK in the past, where high interest rates make international trading difficult, as UK products and services are expensive.

With the 2008 credit crunch biting the USA hard, the situation globally is very testing at this moment in time, with governments shoring up banks, borrowing to try and get them through a difficult situation.

The value of the dollar is low and the exchange rates between the UK and Europe are not at all favourable, with the euro being at its highest level to the pound in March 2008.

Political

In Unit 2 of this text, we explored the volatile nature of politics in respect of the external environment. As we watch world events unfold, it is only too clear to see that international markets can be significantly erratic and volatile politically. For example, in the wake of the sad and prominent events of September 11, we saw the United States forging very close ties with countries from within the European Union. However, in March 2002, there was a political eruption over the exporting of steel into the United States, as they sought to enforce tariffs on the importation of European steel. This has created a significant backlash. In addition to this there is complete disruption at one of the critical political domains, the United Nations, where in essence, critical countries such as France, Germany and Russia have taken a stand against many other European countries in relation to the War on Iraq in 2003, creating significant tensions in the European political environment.

Technological environment

The biggest single influence of recent times on international trade has to be the Internet and the technological revolution. Principally, the effect of the Internet has manifested itself by reducing the world to a global village, with trade, communication and information being easily and readily available.

With the evolution of satellite, digital and mobile/video phone technologies, the marketplace has become much more accessible, without there necessarily being a physical presence. The continuing levels of innovation may go some way in the future to easing some of the burdens on international trade, as there may be a sharp decrease in trade barriers as a result of the Internet.

Question 9.2

List five ways in which the Internet will aid international trade.

Know your markets

Marketing research is critical in all markets, but when trading overseas, and effectively operating in a vacuum, the need for comprehensive information is essential. There are two components to marketing research:

1   The need to understand customers and their buying behaviour

2   The need to understand the marketing and operating environment.

International research is complex and difficult to manage. It is costly and time-consuming and the outcome is not always very meaningful. The consequences of collecting incorrect or inappropriate information could be immeasurable.

Organizations failing to carry out effective marketing research could find themselves missing significant market opportunities, or alternatively finding that the supposed opportunities identified do not exist. Either way, without the right information on the proposed market, the organization could lose out.

The role of the international researcher for the organization will be to produce a clear overview of the current state of the marketplace. This should include examining issues such as the SLEPT factors, demand for products, ability to pay, levels of competitor activity, ability to meet the political and legal requirements of the host country and, of course, the technological ability of the country concerned.

There are three key functions an international market researcher should undertake:

1   **Scanning international markets to identify and analyse the opportunities** – This will include looking at accessibility, profitability and market size of existing markets, latent markets and potential markets.

2   **Building marketing information systems to monitor international environment trends and patterns of trade** – This includes the collection of primary and secondary data and ongoing external audits to monitor the pace of change or the stability of the host economy.

3   **Carrying out primary research for specific reasons** – This would include potentially carrying out test marketing and measuring the feasibility and viability of trading in the host country as well as the impact that this trade would have on the marketing mix and the implications of changing the mix to meet a range of different customer needs.

The key to successful market entry is to ensure that markets are scanned and analysed, and comprehensive market profiles are built up and detailed country studies undertaken.

Understanding the external marketplace

We have already looked at the intricacies of analysing the external environment, through the use of PESTEL or SLEPT. However, there are some specific market performance indicators in relation to key economic indicators that you might need to ascertain the position of. They include the following:

◆   Population size and growth

◆   Population density and concentration

◆   Population age and distribution

◆   Disposable income and income distribution

◆   Economic activity – where is the concentration of economic/financial generation?

These indicators will highlight to you the economic position of the country and its status in relation to its level of development, for example emerging economies like India, or less developed economies, such as Ethiopia.

Other indicators include areas such as

◆   Natural resources

◆ Topography

◆ Climate

◆ Energy and communication

◆ Urbanization

◆ Differential inflation levels.

Clearly, understanding these indicators will give you a broad brush picture of the state of the host nation you are considering, which provides a sound basis on which to judge the level of perceived risk in market entry.

Market entry strategies

Market entry strategies are based around a strategic decision taken to trade internationally. Ultimately it will form part of the overall corporate and marketing strategy. However, it is useful to understand the basis of the different entry strategies.

Having established the following facts, the organization should be able to choose the most appropriate method of international expansion:

◆ The company objectives in relation to the size and value of the market

◆ The financial resources required to commence trading

◆ The existing marketplace

◆ The level of competition that exists

◆ The nature and characteristics of the market

◆ Pricing issues

◆ The nature of the product/service

◆ Timings.

Dealing these issues should enable the organization to decide on the most appropriate method of trading internationally.

◆ **Licensing** – The positive side to licensing is that it requires relatively low levels of investment. Licensing is usually based around a contract that enables a second party, the licensee, to produce products or services, have technological know-how, research and development information and trademarks that belong to another organization, namely the licenser. Both parties sign an agreement that then outlines terms and conditions for the use of the above.

The advantages include a low level of commitment, reduced market entry costs and the ability to enter smaller markets in a more cost-effective way.

Disadvantages could include being tied into a long-term relationship, particularly if conflict evolves, and competition from the licensee.

◆ **Agents** – Agents are effectively overseas sales personnel, who operate in a range of markets on behalf of different organizations. Agents will usually work on a retainer basis with commission or on a commission basis. Their role is to create an awareness of your organization and the products and services it has to offer, ultimately with the view to securing a sale.

Agents are often very successful as they are operating in their local marketplace which then reduces some of the barriers to entry that organizations often face when trying to gain entry into new markets. They should be selected for their financial strength, their contacts within the host country, the nature and extent of their relationships with organizations and their skills, abilities and resources.

◆ **Franchising** – is a very common way of operating overseas. Think about how many outlets McDonald's, KFC and Pizza Hut and so on have around the world. You can probably see from those examples the success of franchising on a global scale.

◆ **Company acquisition** – This actually refers to gaining market entry by buying an existing company in the country where you wish to trade. The advantage of this is that you are buying an existing going concern and therefore the infrastructure is in place, but the financial risk involved is considerable.

◆ **Wholly-owned subsidiary** – Probably one of the most expensive methods of international business is setting up a wholly-owned subsidiary, which means that the organization will effectively set up a fully fledged business overseas. This will include very significant overheads and is therefore a very costly option.

◆ **Joint venture** – Is really a variation of the above, but instead of a total investment into another country, your organization may choose to buy into another country, through a joint venture, potentially buying up to half of a compatible business. This is a very common practice. There are many advantages of this process, as organizations share market research, product development, marketing planning and implementation, capital and resources both human and financial. You will often find that organizations join forces for competitive reasons, or for technological know-how.

There are also many disadvantages, such as trust with the other partner, differences in aims and objectives and strategies. One partner may hold a greater stake than the other; that in itself can cause much conflict.

Question 9.3

Explain the differences between international and export marketing.

Case study: Capital PR – promoting diversity in marketing

A mandarin-speaking organization employed a company called Capital PR to navigate its way through cultural differences and language barriers when the public relations firm organized a major trade exhibition for Australian companies seeking tender opportunities for the Beijing 2008 Olympic Games.

The company coordinated a three-day trade mission to Beijing called China Stadia 2004. Capital PR co-ordinated the displays of 27 exhibiting companies. The aim of the programme was to give Australian companies an opportunity to win contracts relating to the Olympics. They employed a range of strategies which included utilizing diversity, including the linguistic skills of bilingual members of staff. They recognized that by embracing productive diversity practices they can extend substantial economic growth.

The company, by using linguistics and cultural skills awareness and knowledge, were able to expand export markets, overcome prejudices and develop harmonious customer relationships. They developed approaches to cross-cultural relationships, something increasingly important to all western economies in order to aid growth.

This case study is a good demonstration of utilizing the marketing mix. By utilizing strong 'people' skills, they were able to combine the extended marketing mix, with the 4Ps of the marketing mix to open up new market opportunities. They were able to identify that fast, accurate and effective communications with clients is essential to success. They were culturally aware, diverse in business practice, and innovative and creative with these assets.

Source: Australian Government – Department of Immigration and Multicultural and Indigenous Affairs

Potential barriers to entry

In any new international marketplace, there are a number of barriers to entry that organizations must consider how they will overcome.

Barker and Kaynak (1992) list the following important areas:

◆ Too much red tape
◆ Trade barriers
◆ Transportation difficulties
◆ Lack of trained personnel
◆ Lack of export incentives
◆ Lack of co-ordinated assistance
◆ Unfavourable conditions overseas
◆ Slow payment by buyers
◆ Lack of competitive products
◆ Payment defaults
◆ Language barriers.

By selecting the right market entry channel, many of these barriers may possibly be overcome; therefore careful consideration of the most appropriate entry method for the most successful outcome is crucial. The more informed the organization, the clearer the country profile, the easier it will be to identify the best method for the organization.

The implications for marketing plans

Again, from your earlier studies you should be very familiar with marketing plans and the marketing mix. What you need to consider now, looking at them in an international context, is how in some instances, organizations may need to amend their plans and mix to meet the needs of the particular market.

One thing you must be clear on is that it does not matter where in the world you operate, or have a physical presence, the concepts of marketing and customer orientation are exactly the same.

When trading internationally, organizations will clearly need to break their markets down into a number of different segments, which in turn become target markets.

While the organization may have one set of corporate objectives, which include international marketing, it is highly likely that they will have a number of varying plans and strategies to reflect the local demands of each country. In turn this means that the marketing mix could also be different.

The organization produces products or services for the benefits their customers want to gain. Therefore, it is critical to ensure that the organization's product offering fits the requirements of the host country. For example, almost every country in the world uses irons or hairdryers. While the main functions, characteristics and mechanisms are the same, the power supplies and sockets are different. Therefore, an organization must reflect on this element and amend their products accordingly. Should they do this, it would flag up a change to the product element of the marketing mix.

The key question the organization must then ask is should their product offering be standardized or differentiated?

Product life cycles and product positioning will also vary according to the country of operation. This will be due to issues such as market demand, market growth, the pace of change and competitive activity.

Under 'product' the issue of branding will also have to be considered. Organizations will need to consider the benefits of branding and whether or not their brand is meaningful in the country in which they operate.

Product

New products for international markets will effectively need to go through the same new product development process as within the domestic country setting. Product opportunities should be referenced against aspects relating to its development such as:

- Manufacturing requirements – home and abroad
- Marketing research
- Ability to purchase the product
- Customer needs, wants and expectations in relation to the product
- Fit with existing product portfolio
- Trademark and patenting agreements for overseas
- Local and international safety standards
- Technology demands
- Technical support
- After-sales support
- Whether or not it should be standardized or adapted for local use.

Pricing

Clearly, pricing will be an issue where there could be significant variances. This could be because of currency exchange rates, international or local legislation, distribution and storage costs, as well as the cost of manufacturing the products.

In many instances, organizations could be subject to varying taxes and tariffs, which will affect their pricing policy. Obviously the method of payment and speed of payment will also be a critical issue.

The influences on price will be very similar to the ones highlighted in Unit 6, 'Price operations', but careful consideration must be given to the economic situation and economic indicators within the host country.

Being able to control the pricing strategy in international markets will depend upon the degree of regulation employed on a local basis. However, controlling prices will be an essential activity in order to sustain market share, competitive positioning and a degree of continuity within the chain. Issues of price sensitivity will vary from country to country, but cultural diversity will have an influence on the perceived value proposition.

Place

The big factor in this area will be accessibility and its cost. There are many logistical challenges with distribution, including warehousing, storage, transportation network and so on. The selection of the appropriate market entry strategy will influence the way in which distribution can effectively be managed.

Clearly, with the growing importance of the Internet, the dynamics of distribution are sure to change in the coming years, and while there is some instability, currently organizations such as Amazon have proved it can work. Management of channel members will require serious consideration and could prove to be a logistical nightmare. However, the following points should be taken into account:

- Set-up costs of the channel and members
- Level of investment required
- Level of incentive required
- Synergy with the local/domestic channels
- Management and control of the overall process.

Promotional mix

This area is possibly the most interesting and the most complex to deal with, because of the nature of social/cultural differences from country to country. There are many challenges to be faced under this banner. These include the following:

- Language
- Image
- Relationships
- Corporate identity
- Product image
- Company image

- Methods of advertising
- Tolerance of advertising
- Marketing ethics
- Available media
- Adult literacy levels
- Accessibility of information
- Agencies.

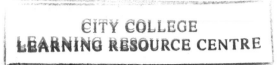

As a result of so many different facets of culture within so many different countries it is highly likely that the organization will need to develop a range of different marketing and promotional mixes to match the host country's market.

Again the importance of defining a good country profile is highlighted. This should be based around a wide range of issues critical to the successful development of a marketing strategy. This then ensures that the organization achieves a true marketing and customer-oriented focus, producing products they want, where they want, when they want, at a price they want to pay and responding to promotions that are meaningful.

Question 9.4

Choosing a country of your choice, discuss how you perceive the effects of economic and environmental trends on international produc t development.

Globalization

In the final part of this unit, we consider the advantages and disadvantages of global marketing and discuss whether plans and mixes should be global and whether we should be 'thinking global and acting local'.

For a long period of time we have heard terms such as the global village, the border-less world. This was an idealism of the 1990s but the surge towards standardization has been considerable as organizations see the potential for cost saving through economies of scale. Organizations constantly struggle to find the balance of just how far they should go, how much they should standardize, how much should they adapt to meet the needs of the global market.

So far there has only been limited success in developing a standardized global marketing strategy. It has been suggested that the only likely place for this type of strategy to really succeed is on the Internet, where the world is a global village. The same product, price, distribution channel and promotional campaign are used across the globe.

Often people associate organizations such as McDonald's or Coca-Cola with being truly global. While their brand is global, they do have variations on a theme to meet the customer expectations of the market they operate within. While they are global in market coverage, they localize in both tastes and language; they are global, but local.

Globalization is often characterized by the standardization of the marketing mix, and while this in essence would seem the most cost-effective and efficient way to move forward, it may not be the most competitive.

Standardization versus adaptation

Standardization

An organization seeking to globalize would have to consider standardizing almost all of the following elements:

◆   Market access

◆   Industry standards

◆   Technology

◆   Products

◆   Services

◆   Promotion

◆   Distribution

◆   Customer requirements

◆   Competition

◆   Communication.

The implications of standardizing the organization's approach present the marketer with a significant challenge, as moving towards a standardized marketing mix has no guarantee of success in all markets.

Adaptation

In many respects, standardization may seem the easiest approach, that is one product and one approach for all; however, in the real world this is not always possible and therefore adaptation has to be considered.

Adaptation can mean that the whole or part of the marketing mix has to be changed to meet the changing needs of different nations.

Adaptation of the product involves many companies in changing their products to meet local needs and conditions. For example, Nokia is known to have customized some of its phones to meet the needs of every major market.

As for promotions, some organizations will again either adapt the promotional strategies for each of their companies or change. There are known and obvious difficulties with not adapting promotions, as culturally there are many areas that are taboo. One of the greatest causes of conflict in promotional activities can be something as simple as the use of colour. For example black is thought to be unlucky in China, whilst white is a mourning colour for Japan and green is associated with jungle sickness in Malaysia.

Furthermore the names of products can also cause conflict and misunderstanding. One of the biggest product name changes was that of the Snickers bar from Marathon, to actually 'standardize' the name of the chocolate bar product.

Pricing creates many a tension in international markets as many companies find it difficult to set international prices. One of the main problems for those companies trading internationally is that of the cost of distribution. If the company is to be profitable in its dealings then the cost of distribution should be passed on to the customer. However, if the company wishes to be extremely competitive, then this becomes a slightly more challenging issue.

In recent times it is evident that economic and technological forces have had a significant impact upon global pricing. Closer to home, we have seen the introduction of the euro over the last couple of years reduce the differentiation in prices across Europe and the price and indeed value is now more transparent and measurable. Added to all of this, the opportunity and ability to shop online means that prices are now more evident and that as such 'price transparency' is now required.

We have already alluded to the fact that there are issues with distribution. For many companies the challenges of distribution and the cost of distribution can often make international trade more prohibitive and difficult to achieve successfully and competitively. Channels of communications vary so much from country to country, however, that there is often no choice but to tailor and adapt distribution requirements to meet channel needs for both the consumer and the B2B customer.

Clearly, the ultimate decision whether or not to standardize or adapt products can only be based upon knowledge and a wide range of information about each foreign market, its channels, features, cultures and characteristics.

Benefits of globalization

There are number of advantages and disadvantages associated with globalization. The advantages are that globalization is more straightforward, in that it seeks to use one set of tools to meet one global set of customers. This provides economies of scale, supposed fairness and equity and potentially greater accessibility, and could potentially lead to the organization being very competitive on a cost basis. But you may ask yourself: do we want one product for all?

Clearly, there are a number of disadvantages associated with standardizing the mix, as it could prove to be a very inhibitive practice that could cause immense difficulty when trying to meet the needs of so many different facets and such extreme target markets.

The key success factor in achieving any marketing strategy, including globalization, is to ensure that the organization keeps a constant watch on the global marketing environment.

Organizations should monitor change, identify strengths and weaknesses, opportunities and threats and then aim to build a strategy based around customer satisfaction, increasing profitability, head marketing share and achieving global competitiveness.

As the world becomes a smaller place through the power of ICT, true globalization and complete standardization may one day be achieved. In the meantime, thinking global and acting local is the most a customer- and marketing-oriented organization can achieve.

Summary

The issues relating to international marketing and globalization are considerable. But the key to its success is to remember the purpose of marketing. It is critical to the organization not to see international markets as a special project or view them in isolation.

Critical to any decision in relation to international marketing is sufficient information on which to base a decision. Organizations should never underestimate the power of market research in giving them a snapshot of the bigger picture. That picture will show the many different facets of the target country, which is when the organization identifies whether to globalize or localize.

Because marketing is dynamic and ever-changing and because of the growing partici-pation of the Internet in the marketing environment today, globalization will continue to be an objective for which many organizations should strive.

To remain competitive the organization will need to make a number of major decisions based on who their market is, where their market is, the status of the economy of their markets and the opportunities they present.

Staying ahead of the competition will be critical and therefore for many years to come organizations will increasingly need to develop and use a range of marketing informa-tion, market entry strategies and overall marketing strategies to keep the balance be-tween globalization and localization, and customer satisfaction.

Further study

In addition to reading this text, and your recommended text, you may find it helpful to read some of *International Marketing Strategy* by Isobel Doole and Robin Lowe (2004), in particular Chapters 3, 4, 9, 10 and 11. This book is the recommended text for Inter-national Marketing Strategy and the Postgraduate Diploma level.

You will see in the exam question below that you are asked to provide an example of excellence in respect of continuous assessment. It is therefore advisable that you fol-low the press – *Marketing* and *The Economist*, among others – to observe the nature of international marketing and also the successful implementation of international mar-keting strategy across the world.

Study tip

As a result of the growth in international marketing, clearly it is playing a more promi-nent role in our everyday lives. The examination of Marketing Planning is no exception. One of the key tips to consider is that whenever the situation permits you to, include reference to internationalization and globalization as being key market driving forces in the economy. Virtually every exam paper has an international marketing question on it, and this should be a good indicator to you to highlight its importance.

Bibliography

Barker, T. and Kaynak, E. (1992) An empirical investigation of the differences between initiating and continuing exporters, *European Journal of Marketing*, 26(3) 27–35

Dibb, S., Simkin, L., Pride, W. and Ferrell, O. (2005) *Marketing: Concepts and Strategies*, Houghton Mifflin, 5th European edition

Doole, I. and Lowe, R. (2004) *International Marketing Strategy*, Thomson Learning

Kotler, P., Armstrong, G., Saunders, J. and Wong, V. (1998) *Principles of Marketing*, FT Prentice Hall

Unit 10
Industrial/ business-to-business, FMCGs and services marketing

Learning objectives

This is one of three units looking at the application of marketing in a number of given contexts, to help you understand the broad diversity of marketing, given different situations, different markets and different customers.

The indicative content of the syllabus is as follows:

4.2 Develop a marketing plan and select an appropriate marketing mix for an organization operating in any such context as B2B and services.

3.12 Describe how a plan is developed for the human element of the service encounter, including staff at different levels of the organization.

3.13 Explain how the physical evidence element of the integrated marketing mix is developed.

3.14 Explain how a plan covering the process or the systems of delivery for a service is developed.

4.14 Determine an effective extended marketing mix in relation to the design and delivery of service encounters (SERVQAL).

Syllabus elements: 4.2, 4.4, 3.12, 3.13, 3.14.

Business-to-business marketing

Introduction

There are varying terms to describe the B2B markets; however, one of the more commonly used ones is 'organizational markets'. Principally, this is where the buyers within the organizations buy on behalf of them. This could include a range of different products from computer equipment, forgings, welding, stationery and various plant and equipment that might be needed in order to get the job done.

Organizational markets include organizations such as manufacturers, hotels, hospitals, conference centres, wholesalers and sometimes retailers, local authorities, government bodies to name but a few.

There are many implications of organizational markets, but in short they include:

◆ Geographical diversity – they can be spread very far and wide

◆ Size of the decision-making unit

◆ The issue of 'preferred supplier status'

◆ Size of purchase

◆ Frequency of purchase

◆ Negotiation of contracts

◆ Lead time between order and delivery.

One of the most important factors that you must identify with, particularly from a forecasting position, is that industrial demand in B2B markets is derived from consumer demand. If you think of any consumer product, you should be able to work out that the need for the production factory, the raw material supply and the transportation services all depend on the demand for the product. They would disappear if the consumer demand for the product actually declines.

The same applies to every industrial product, although it is often difficult to visualize the extent of supply chains, with the different manufacturers and their network of suppliers and distributors.

Organizational buying

Organizational buying behaviour, like that of a consumer, will be very much influenced by a range of different factors:

◆ The amount of money available

◆ The size/volume of purchase

◆ The level of risk involved

◆ The timeframe for decisions

◆ The buying situation

◆ The purpose of the purchase

◆ Competitive offers

◆ Credit terms and conditions of purchase

◆ Delivery lead times

◆ Packaging

◆ Environmental factors

◆ Supply and demand

◆ Inelastic demand

◆ Fluctuation in demand

◆ SLEPT influences

◆ Organizational objectives

◆ Individual and interpersonal.

As a marketing manager, it is essential that you understand the different degrees to which you could find yourself involved, within organizational markets. You will find that in many organizational markets many products are bought on a repeat purchase basis, possibly the same order sizes, qualities and quantities. There is little difference between these transactions and the consumer buying, and the selling situation will be based upon 'order taking' perhaps rather than order making.

However, for some rebuys, in particular modified rebuys, the process will often be more involved and perhaps require more technical advice, sales support and negotiations. Past experience will have a big effect on the decision and the DMU will be strongly affected by technical matters.

It is in the 'new buy' or 'new task', which involves perhaps the buying organization embarking upon a new project or a new job, that marketing must be used to its full effect, so we shall look closely at the information required, the time and resource involvement the contract might require, and the level of technical support. Essentially, as a marketer you will need to identify the level of involvement the contract will entail.

While it is vitally important to understand all of these influences, it is also essential that you are aware that one of the key influences in the buying process is the actual buyers themselves.

Understanding the nature of business-to-business buyers

Quite clearly, the role of an industrial buyer in an organizational market is going to be at the opposite pole from that of a typical consumer. Their objectives and motivations are going to be entirely different, as they are based around the organization, its function and its customers. Generally they are better informed, more demanding, more technically minded, and they also manifest more rational behaviour than consumer buyers.

However, while their focus might be the organization, as a marketing manager you should be aware that sometimes their own personal goals and hidden agendas might actually influence the purchasing decision. While the motivation is supposed to be organizationally focused, some buyers do gain psychological satisfaction from the purchase process. Essentially, they are human and their human and personal feelings will on occasions influence the decision.

The organizational/industrial buyer will be very interested in the overall value proposition; they have a duty and responsibility to the organization and stakeholder alike, to execute the best deals for their business. For a typical buyer, the key considerations in relation to the value proposition will include quality, delivery, service and price. The range of products available and the level of innovation an organization demonstrates will also play a role in influencing their thinking.

For large and more specialized products, you should expect a buyer to require significant amounts of data, market information, performance specifications, technical specifications, and it is also likely they will require a great deal of consultancy-style support in order that they have the complete picture and can make a fully informed decision.

Because of the nature of their role, they will also involve themselves with competitor organizations and therefore will be fully aware of different options and alternatives available. As a marketing manager, you will therefore need to understand clearly the nature, scope and threat the competition will provide.

When all is said and done, organizational buyers are probably far more rational than individual buyers, they are less likely to be compulsive buyers, but what they will be is informed, demanding and focused upon achieving the best deal for the organization.

To give you a somewhat clearer picture of the high level of involvement in the organizational marketing context the Howard Sheth model of industrial buying might be helpful (Figure 10.1).

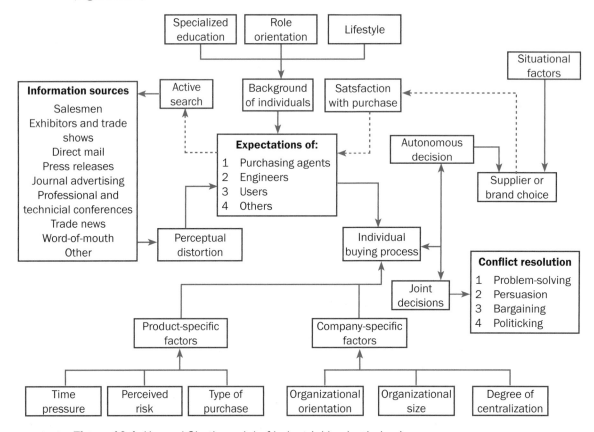

Figure 10.1: Howard Sheth model of industrial buying behaviour

Question 10.1

With your knowledge of the selling process gained in Unit 4, outline the nature of the sales relationship that would be developed in the purchase of a motorway maintenance contract, to be managed and co-ordinated by a large civil engineering consultancy.

Market segmentation for organizational marketing

As many companies supply to a wide range of industries it is wise to segment the market so as to serve a specific market segment more thoroughly. It is equally essential to specifically target your products at special groups in organizational markets as it is in consumer-based markets.

Segmentation criteria may include:

◆   **Type of industry** – It may be possible to specialize, but even if this is not possible there may be common characteristics in some industries. For instance, aircraft manufacturers need specific certificates, which can only be supplied by approved companies; other industries have their own special needs.

◆   **Size of company** – The 'size' of a company may be measured by turnover, number of employees, output or capital employed. Many large companies have professional buyers, so they tend to evaluate their suppliers differently.

◆   **Type of product or service required**.

◆   **Type of buyer** – Some big companies allow their branch factories to buy, others do not. Some companies put limits on the value to which the branch factory buyer can go without asking for higher authority.

◆   **Geographical location** – There may be some parts of the country which have specialist needs, in which case you can segment them on that basis.

For gaining a clearer insight into both geographic factors and demographic factors, a look at the following additional criteria might be of assistance:

◆   SICs

◆   Census of the population (most recently in April 2001).

To understand the nature of the organizational requirements you will need to know:

◆   The nature of the benefits sought

◆   The degree of formality of the buying organization

◆   The people involved in the buying process.

Segmentation, however, is not perhaps as commonly used in organizational markets, and while it is an ideal, often the markets are limited in size, which makes it perhaps a little less appropriate.

The buying and decision-making process in organizational markets

It is here that the most important difference between industrial and consumer buying becomes almost self-evident. Traditional consumer-based markets aim directly at the customer or consumer, i.e. the end-user, and therefore understanding customer satisfaction levels is essential. However, in organizational markets the motivations are different. The key to customer satisfaction is ontime delivery and the quality of the products arriving undamaged in order to meet production deadlines. It involves heavy-duty distribution requirements, stock handling, serious packaging and, of course, tightly negotiated deals.

The sales lead is likely to originate from a requirement within the company that emerges as a result of either the buying organization tendering for work (and therefore needing technical specifications and prices) or orders that have been placed by customers, and the buyer may have to buy raw materials, components, services, machines and even, perhaps, some design work.

There are a number of problems relating to organizational decision-making that perhaps put some of the above into focus:

◆ **Precipitation** – Why is the decision being made, what is it supposed to achieve, what are the benefits, what are the cost cuttings available?

◆ **Product specification** – Quality, quantity, characteristics, attributes, service levels, pricing.

◆ **Preferred supplier** – It is likely that supplier selection will be based upon a short list of known suppliers, creating a major barrier to entry for new suppliers. They will almost definitely have some key criteria that they will work on based upon past experience of their supplier base.

◆ **Commitment** – Will the chosen supplier be committed to the process, deliver on time, understand the nature of the problem?

Within the buying process there are a number of roles that might emerge based upon the level of technical specification being presented. Therefore, in a highly technical specification sale, the following roles might be very significant:

◆ Supplier relationship management

◆ Supplier sourcing

◆ Evaluating tenders

◆ Negotiation

◆ Financing

◆ Order placing

◆ Performance evaluation

◆ Purchasing.

From the internal perspective of a supplying organization, that is a supplier to the organization market, you will additionally be involved in liaison with production and engineering divisions:

◆ Research and development processes and findings

◆ Assessing return on financial investment, managing methods of financing, costing and any borrowing in relation to the purchase

◆ Marketing of the products.

The process of the supplier–buyer relationship is quite a complex web and does in the main require a level of mutual understanding and co-operation and support on both sides.

The decision-making process

You will be familiar with the consumer decision-making process, as explained in Unit 5, so Figure 10.2 will need little explanation. However, what it does do is explain which elements are relevant to new tasks, modified rebuys and straight rebuys (repeat purchases).

	Buy classes		
	New task	**Modified rebuy**	**Straight rebuy**
1 Problem recognition	Yes	Maybe	No
2 General need description	Yes	Maybe	No
3 Product specification	Yes	Yes	Yes
4 Suppliers' search	Yes	Maybe	No
5 Proposal solicitation	Yes	Maybe	No
6 Supplier selection	Yes	Maybe	No
7 Order-routine specification	Yes	Maybe	No
8 Performance review	Yes	Yes	Yes

Figure 10.2: Buy grid. Adapted from Worsam (2000)

The buying centre – the decision-making unit

Like consumer markets, organizational markets have a decision-making unit or a buying centre. However, the dynamics and scope of the task are considerably higher.

The roles of a typical decision-making unit for an organizational market are as follows:

- **User** – The machine operator – the person who actually uses the product.

- **Influencer** – Typical influencers will be users, suppliers, research and development staff, accountants, buyers, sales representatives, external consultancy representatives and so on.

- **Decider** – On this occasion it is more likely to be 'deciders'. These might include a management team, a tendering committee, an individual buyer, shareholders – this will vary depending upon the extent and financial involvement of the decision.

- **Buyer** – The person who will handle the internal supplier sourcing, information seeking, and who will handle negotiations with the suppliers.

- **Gatekeeper** – This is likely to be a member of the secretarial or administrative staff, handling the flow of information inbound and outbound through the organization.

Question 10.2

What are the distinctive differences between a consumer decision-making unit and an industrial decision-making unit? (Refer to your studies in unit 4 for information about the consumer DMU.)

Relationship marketing in organizational markets

A poor purchasing decision from an organizational buying perspective could be fairly catastrophic, and therefore every opportunity has to be taken to ensure that the risk inherent in the decision, and therefore in the relationship, is reduced.

The history and previous experience of the organization will be an imperative to the final choice of supplier that an industrial buyer will make, amid other key factors. However, gaining preferred supplier status gives a positive stance, so that when the tendering process has a close outcome, the strength of the preferred supplier relationship secures the deal.

There are three key components linked to the relationship marketing stance:

1   **The durability of the relationship** – The length of time over which a supplier–buyer relationship will continue (in some industries a purchase can take 12 months and above to secure).

2   **Economics** – The investment of time and money in the relationship actually enhances relationships and preferred supplier status opportunities.

3   **Social dimensions** – Because of the duration of the relationship it is likely that it might take on some form of social dimensions. While this is inevitable, mixing business with pleasure can sometimes cause conflict. Having said this, some supplier–buyer relationships, according to research, extend beyond 20 years.

Essentially there are likely to be two approaches to managing the supplier: adversarial and collaborative.

Adversarial – the characteristics pertinent to this approach include the following:

◆   Regular price quotes
◆   Little co-operation
◆   Quality and delivery thresholds meet lowest denominator
◆   Emphasis on lowest unit price
◆   Multiple suppliers.

Collaborative – the characteristics of this approach will include:

◆   Few suppliers
◆   Long-term and long-standing relationships
◆   Partnerships
◆   Frequent planned communications
◆   Integrated approach to operations
◆   Quality and timescales designed in and met
◆   Emphasis on the value proposition but the key being value for money – that is the lowest cost for the highest quality.

Question 10.3

Why is it important for a supplier to establish a strong relationship with the buyer, and what are the benefits overall?

The marketing mix for organizational marketing

As with any consumer products, there is a need to tell the organizational buyer that your product exists, just as in any other type of marketing, and the specific nature of most organizations makes it fairly easy to segment the total market. However, telling the customer that your products exist is a different matter when dealing with these buyers; they are usually professional people, probably having or aiming to have a qualification as good as yours, and they are just as ambitious as you are.

Some advertisements will be useful 'to put the company on the map', but the organizational buyers will be more interested in brochures/catalogues or complete information packages explaining the company's portfolio of products and services, and price lists for standard products.

Product

The product may range from tiny components through to massive projects such as a ship or aircraft. Obviously, there is quite a difference between marketing small screws, in packs of several hundred each, and the marketing activities that go into a large construction of a car park or motorway.

For a product that has been designed for a specific customer, all the features required are already there, and the marketing manager can concentrate on other things. There are also products that are built to agreed international standards so that they can be interchangeable, at least in theory, because the standards usually specify the dimensions and minimum performance ratings.

Place

The demand for a distributor can be very challenging, particularly with very large products, or indeed very heavy products. There is likely to be a wide distribution network, which will be similar in many ways to the wholesaler/retailer system used in consumer marketing. Therefore, some of the key areas of managing a distribution channel covered in Unit 7 will be comparable in this situation.

In addition, some manufacturers will make their products so that they exceed the minimum performances shown in the standards. This added value does distinguish the product from the rest, and can be a valuable selling point if your distributors are trained to use it.

Price

Pricing will take on a different dimension, and will be based around a variety of different methods, from negotiation through to tendering. It is often quite complex and highly competitive. You will find that there is less likelihood, however, of organizational markets switching due to price, as reliability is equally important.

In respect of available budget, this will of course vary from one business to another, but it is likely that the scope of the budget will be limited and not as significant as in some consumer-based markets.

Promotion

The major uses of the promotional mix are shown in Figure 10.3 and the mix itself is shown in Figure 10.4.

Types	Use
Public relations	As in all forms of marketing, to secure favourable mention and restrict and/or counter unfavourable. With trade press and industry-specific features in the major newspapers there is ample opportunity to create PR opportunities.
Press advertising	National press is broadband and not often cost-effective, with the obvious exceptions of those organizations who operate in the customer markets and thus allow the industrial marketer to ride along if brand extension has been achieved.
Trade press	Highly targeted. Most effective for awareness and to stimulate a first response perhaps via a reader's enquiry service. Major opportunity for linked advertising and PR. Quality of trade journals varies widely.
Direct marketing	Mainly direct mail because many lists exist. Need to be careful to select with care and shorten where possible. Can be very important to develop one's own list and protect it rigorously.
Directories	Very valuable for services in particular. Yellow Pages and Talking Pages are extremely effective for certain businesses. Beware not to subscribe to an unknown directory and never pay for space without having ordered it first.
Exhibitions	Most valuable in many areas. An opportunity to display product, to meet with existing customers, to develop and qualify leads and to sell (many forget that they can sell from a stand!). Also a valuable opportunity for competitive contact and research. Should be used positively, never simply to 'show the flag'.
Brochures, sales literature	Educational and informative, they should supplement, not to be expected to carry the whole message. A range of mix and match, targeted literature will be needed in most areas.
Audio-visual	Can be simply educational and ephemeral but can also be used to positive effect if designed to achieve something that is otherwise difficult, such as a visit to a remote location. Can be mounted in the buyer's office using easily portable equipment as part of a sales pitch.
Computer	Few salespeople are today properly equipped without the ability to interrogate a database whilst with the buyer. Quotations can be printed on the spot, as can contracts. Via a modem, a link to a senior manager can be established and a deal struck. Computers will support audio-visual presentations that can easily be tailored to need ahead of each visit.
Sales promotion	It is possible in some markets to add a 'temporary inducement at point-of-sale'. Not to be confused with discounts, however, unless SP gifts are of low value they may be perceived as bribes. It is better to target them on benefits to the organization or the department, not on the buyer.
Give-aways	Can be useful as reminders of phone numbers and so on. They also provide an opportunity to make contact. Probably the best are the long-lasting ones such as desk pads and diaries - but these benefit from tailoring to need rather than simply being bought off the shelf with the buyer's initials added (i.e it is better to invest quite heavily and do a proper job because the give-away says a lot about you and your organization).

Figure 10.3: Major uses of the promotional mix

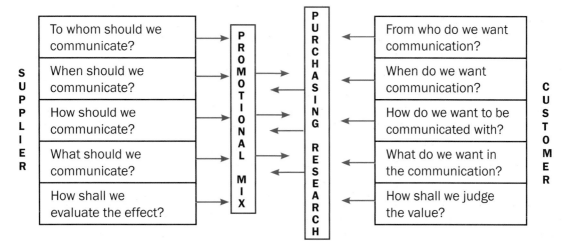

Figure 10.4: Role of the promotional mix. Adapted from Hill and Hillier (1977)

There are many sources of support and things that can be done to help the sales repre-sentatives and these usually involve the provision of quality catalogues, where they are appropriate, or such items as films to show your products in use. Such films and brochures can give clients a better idea of how to use the products and some of them will be flattered if you can feature their products along with your own.

The role of the salesforce could be quite intensive and involved, from actually establishing the lead through until the order placement. This might involve qualifying leads, sorting and evaluating them against an established criterion.

Quite often the promotion consists simply of the knowledge of the salesperson, and he or she must be able to help designers or get someone in who can.

For the large construction projects, which take months or years to complete, the marketing team must match the DMU in terms of rank and status, in the early stages at least.

In the organizational marketing sector, marketing takes on a totally different meaning. Many organizations still do not embrace marketing in the same way and do not necessarily have organized or structured marketing activity. This often means that marketing can be random and ad hoc in nature.

Industrial organizations will need to develop a competitive advantage, indeed a competi-tive edge. Therefore, in many sectors a serious cultural change may need to be initiated in order for those sectors to impact seriously upon the competitors and maintain their stake within the marketplace.

Developing a marketing strategy for FMCGs

Clearly, when any FMCG company is developing a brand in today's market it is likely to be sold far afield. In the United Kingdom, this will include across Europe and many other parts of the world. Therefore, when considering the development of new products and brand strategies, we should not be insular in our approach, but more global in our vision.

To do this, significant investment is required. A key writer, Lynch (as noted by Brassington and Pettitt in *Principles of Marketing*, 2000) declared the following criteria to be essential for building that brand, both at home and on a European basis:

1   **Resources** – It is estimated that a marketing communications budget of not less than $60 million is needed for three years to establish a brand.

2   **Quality** – The need for consistent quality in both the product and the brand name is critical. Logistical and administrative procedures supporting the product should not be underestimated and are vitally important.

3   **Timing** – According to Lynch, it will take at least five years to establish a Euro-brand, as opposed to a shorter term on a national basis.

When you consider these three criteria very closely, this puts Euro-branding out of reach of many organizations. Additionally, many organizations may find it difficult to deal with cultural and language differences across Europe and the rest of the world. Just consider this statistic for a moment: only 40 per cent of all adults in Europe understand the English language, yet it is the most widespread language.

The net impact of this, which is also critical, is that packaged goods must take on a multilingual stance, or a non-verbal approach, or substantial amounts of expenditure will become necessary on packaging for the same products in a number of different languages.

The FMCG market is particularly competitive. Take, for example, the number of Coca-Cola-like drinks that are available, or the number of different brands and types of toothpaste, or washing liquids and powders, or even petrol. This, in itself, is an indication of how serious it is for any organization to develop an appropriate product and brand strategy.

Further considerations for FMCPG (fast-moving consumer packaged goods) organizations are the use of brand names and product names, and whether they should be used independently or combined: for example, Cadbury's Creme Eggs or Cadbury's Flake; or Heinz Baked Beans, Walkers Crisps. Each of these organizations uses the brand and product name simultaneously. The brand name and the product are then closely associated. This means that the brand and the product develop an integrated approach and a message that associates the two. Often the message will be related to quality of the product, assists the organization in developing a competitive position, or even takes away the price-sensitive nature of the market. For example, many people will buy Kellogg's cereals over and above supermarket brands, yet Kellogg's are more expensive.

When Cadbury brings out new products, consumers associate the product and the brand. For example, there is Cadbury's Caramel Bar, now there is also Cadbury's Nuts about Caramel. It is therefore potentially easier to introduce new products or extend product lines, based upon the success of existing products and brand associations.

On the other hand, there are also many benefits attached to existing as two separate entities, as practised by Lever Bros, Smith and Nephew, Johnson and Johnson to name but a few.

◆   The benefits of independent branding and product association include preventing the downfall of a company from damage to a particular product. The damage is limited to the product rather than the brand.

◆   It can also allow greater activity with packaging and promotions generally, when organizations are not restricted to using the same company corporate image on every element of their activities.

◆ It allows for the product name to become a generic term. A good example here is that in the United Kingdom, we call paper hankies 'tissues'. In Iran, all tissues are known as Kleenex. It doesn't matter what the brand is; the brand has become the product. This is an interesting concept when considering marketing brands and products internationally.

◆ When an organization is test marketing a new product, through the NPD process, it will not be damaged in the same way should the product fail the test-market process.

The list of advantages and disadvantages is endless.

Earlier on in your studies, we considered a broad range of factors associated with the marketing mix, such as the PLC and the new product development process. Interestingly, many FMCG products have an extremely long life cycle. For example, look at Kellogg's Cornflakes, Heinz Beans, Heinz Ketchup, Mars, Persil and so on. All of these brands have products that have gone on for years and years, both in Europe and indeed broader international markets. By the same token, there are products under these brands that have had face-lifts, modifications, new and more innovative versions introduced, but all based around the original concept.

Therefore, new product development plays a critical role in ensuring that new and interesting products are always being developed, but the financial support and infrastructure to do that come from the significant success of existing products. Many of the products within the FMCG market would fall into the 'cash cow' category, generating significant income, with the initial investment long gone.

Of course, the success of any product is not singularly based around just the product and branding element of the marketing mix; it is based around the success of a well-developed and integrated marketing mix. Therefore, we should also consider the other elements of the marketing mix and how they impact upon FMCPGs.

Place

When developing a new brand, it is imperative to consider the nature of the product and then its distribution requirements. Many of these factors will be based upon the characteristics of the product.

First, an organization must consider whether its strategy will be intensive, selective or exclusive. In the case of most FMCPGs, the distribution strategy will be intensive. This means that the majority of FMCPGs appear in many outlets. For example, chocolate bars appear in just about every food shop, petrol station, leisure outlet, newsagent, supermarket, corner shop, chemist, and even in places such as Petsmart. Chocolate is therefore subject to intensive distribution.

The advantage of this distribution method to all customers is that the product is accessible anywhere, in an instant. A new slant on this, of course, is that you can do your shopping for FMCPGs from your home, through the Internet. This puts a completely new dimension on the consideration of distribution strategies for any significant FMCPG organization.

When using this type of distribution strategy, the organization will, of course, be clear that market coverage is far more important than the type of store selling the product, hence the number of non-vehicle-related products within petrol stations.

While an intensive strategy is the way forward and has been for decades, one critical element that must be considered is quality. This is not particularly a problem for tinned packaged goods, but with more perishable items or frozen goods, manufacturer quality standards must be considered. Poor handling of such products can be costly to the organization, not only in terms of mistakes made, but also in respect of damaged reputation.

A further element of intensive distribution relates to the channel choice. Often with FMCPGs it is extensive and involves a lot of intermediaries. The most typical channel is shown in Figure 10.5.

Manufacturer ⟶ **Wholesaler** ⟶ **Retailer** ⟶ **Consumer**

Figure 10.5: Traditional distribution channel.

Having said this, where large supermarkets are involved, the situation may be slightly different and could cut out the middlemen, making the channel more cost-effective.

Intensive distribution is probably the most efficient way of making the product as widely available as possible, but total distribution costs may be high, especially where small retailers are concerned and unit orders are low.

The marketing mix for FMCGs

Price

For a marketer in an FMCG sector, pricing will be an extremely difficult component to manage. You will be aware that the FMCG sector is intensely competitive, with many like organizations striving for market share. Concepts such as price skimming are less likely to be relevant in this particular market, and it is more likely to see loss leader, penetration marketing or even promotional pricing activities being undertaken in relation to FMCGs. Competitive pricing is also an issue. You see this regularly, with one coffee producer offering extra reward points in association with the supermarket, whilst another producer will give you 20 per cent extra free, or indeed reduce the recommended retail price accordingly.

Pricing is a volatile area. FMCG organizations will need to be highly responsive to consumer needs and market demands. In many respects, FMCGs can be subject to supply and demand elements, particularly based on raw material values, which makes the competitive demand harder to manage.

Promotion

One of the most common forms of communication in the FMCPGs area is advertising and sales promotion. As you have already seen, a considerable amount of money is invested in this sector every year.

Consumer-oriented appeals are probably the most challenging that an agency may face, as the level of competition is so massive in the marketplace, with every organization wanting to differentiate from the direct competitors. The main purpose of this approach is to get consumer attention by association. For example the use of Jamie Oliver as a UK celebrity chef, in association with Sainsbury's, or David Beckham in association with Nike, and Kate Moss and Top Shop. However, this can work against organizations for example H&M fashion chain dropped Kate Moss at the time of allegations of drugs abuse. An organization must be sure about its linkages before embarking upon what may be a potential PR disaster.

Case study: Kate Moss and brand association

Philip Green, who owns Top Shop's parent group Arcadia, has in recent times secured an association with Kate Moss in order to build Top Shop in to a global brand. Kate Moss is a fashion icon in terms of the United Kingdom...and this is what Top Shop is all about in terms of fashion. Top Shops customers identify with her.

It's the kind of partnership other brands would kill for. The model's style and selling power are legendary. She can carry anything from a charity bag from Superdrug that costs just £2.99 to a Balenciaga Lariat bag and sales will go through the roof.

She is more influential than many designers working today – whatever Moss is seen wearing will almost always become a huge trend for girls in their teens or twenties to thirties and beyond. She has made skinny jeans de rigeur – until of course she made an appearance at London Fashion Week wearing vintage Chloé flares which will no doubt spark a huge mania for 70s-inspired denim.

Kate Moss is currently at the height of her profession – despite her troubled past over the last couple of years – and is starring in at least 14 campaigns in 2007 including Burberry, Dior, Longchamp, Louis Vuitton, Calvin Klein jeans and Versace.

The introduction of awards schemes has been one of the key factors in the development of sales promotions. For example, Sainsbury's and Boots both encourage you to go to booths within the stores to swipe your card, to get the best incentive bargains of the day.

Common sights are 'Buy one, get one free', 'Gain 500 extra reward points', 'Get 2p per litre off petrol' – and so the promotional battle goes on.

In the FMCG market, the main elements of sales promotions are as follows:
◆ Display materials
◆ Packaging
◆ Merchandizing
◆ Direct mail (coupons, competitions, premiums).

Marketing of services

Delivering services is people's business: only great customers and great employees can guarantee great service quality (Hans Kasper).

There are a number of problems and challenges associated with the management and implementation of service organizations, relating to a wide range of factors such as the gap between expectations and what is delivered, evidence on the service proposal being limited and different perspectives on what constitutes quality service.

In order that an organization can deliver any form of service, they will need to recognize what that actually means in practice.

The purpose of this part of the unit is to address the particular issues associated with service delivery and how the process of continuous improvement is essential to the successful implementation of service offerings.

Services defined

Dibb *et al.* (2005) define a service as

> An intangible product involving a deed, a performance or an effort that cannot be physically possessed.

You may recall that when examining the 'product' element of the marketing mix, we briefly looked at the intangible element of the product and noted that the product itself was normally tangible, that is, had a physical dimension to it.

Services are usually divided into two main sectors:

1   **Consumer services** – Include marketing in non-profit-making organizations such as education, health, charities and government. Profit-making sectors include financial services, personal and professional services, leisure, entertainment and tourism.

2   **Business services** – Include repairs and maintenance, consultancy, leasing/contract hire, transportation, recruitment, advertising, marketing research, financial services, to name but a few.

The structure of the services sector

A good benchmark of the significance of services marketing both home and abroad is the number of people employed in various service jobs.

The service sector is growing and evolving rapidly. For example, in the United Kingdom, over 64 per cent of the workforce are employed in a services related industry and in Europe as a whole, over 61 per cent of the workforce are in the services industry.

One of the main reasons for the significant growth in the services sector is related to lifestyle. It would appear that while a potential economic slowdown might be looming, the services sector will possibly suffer a little less than areas such as manufacturing, as services are now a core part of everyday existence.

In the main, people are spending more of their income on insurance packages, financial services packages, convenience services, travel and leisure and many organizations provide employees with private health packages. People now buy time. It is a known fact that in today's time-starved societies, families 'purchase time'. To enable time-starved families to spend quality time together many more people were buying services such as laundry, cleaning, gardening, takeaways and so on.

Service characteristics

The difference between product and services

There is a distinct difference between the marketing of goods and services. The one common factor is that customers purchase goods and services for one reason only – they want the benefits a product can provide. Having said that, it is critical that you understand the difference between the two.

Services have four main characteristics:

1   Intangibility

2   Inseparability of production and consumption

3   Perishability

4   Heterogeneity.

Let us look briefly at each characteristic in turn.

Intangibility

Services are intangible, because there is no physical product, nothing to be seen, touched, tasted, smellt or heard before being purchased. The difficulty being, therefore, that the customer will be unable to perceive, imagine or fully understand the nature of what they are to receive.

The challenge for the service provider, therefore, is to ensure that they determine the extent of intangibility and how, if necessary, tangible elements could be included to aid the understanding and expectation on the part of the customer.

A key characteristic of intangibility is that once that service performance has taken place, it cannot be used again. The performance was for that occasion only. For example, the training that you have undertaken cannot ever be delivered in exactly the same way again; it will never be repeated word for word in the same way, because effectively you have consumed the service. If the quality was poor or the standard of the course director was poor, nothing could be done about that particular performance. It could be improved for the next time, but the service would then be a different service.

Inseparability

There is a definite distinction between products that are bought and used over and over again by the same customer, and that of services which are essentially consumed as they are purchased. A simplistic example of this might be having your hair cut or staying in a hotel. Should you decide to have your hair cut by one particular stylist, then it is not possible for another client to have the same hair cut at the same time, because you have purchased it and consumed it. Another example of this would be the use of a hotel room. If you use the hotel room on the night of 1st June then nobody else can use it that night; you have consumed the service the hotel provided on the occasion.

The implication for this particular component is that the involvement of the customer in the production and delivery of the service means that the service provider must take care in what is actually being produced.

Perishability

Because services are produced and consumed at the same time, they are perishable, that is they cannot be stored for later sales or later usage. If the service is not used then, it cannot be used again. Again a hotel is a good example of that. If you did not use that room on the night of the 1st June and nobody else booked in the room, it could not be used again on that night, because that night has now gone. If the hair appointment isn't filled, and the time passes by, then effectively that appointment has perished, gone forever.

The implications of this relate to fluctuations in demand. Those which are unexpected pose a serious threat to the organization, in that they actually lose potential income, as a result of the time of use of the service passing by.

This is quite a serious problem for the service sector. Should the appointment not be booked, the bed not slept in, the car not hired or the flight seat remain empty, each of the providers of that service have seen the service perish and therefore they cannot gain any income from time not used. This is why you can purchase last-minute flights or holiday deals, as organizations would rather take less income for the provision of the service than no income at all.

Heterogeneity

Heterogeneity, or variability effectively means difference. Going back to the example of a training course, there could be two training courses running on the same day, the same materials are being used and the rooms being used are exactly the same. The difference comes in the delivery. Each of the course directors will be different. They will have different appearances, different personal characteristics and different styles. It is unlikely that you would ever receive exactly the same service twice.

From a business perspective, the implication is that marketing services then become a difficult task, as each time you sell a service, there is no real guarantee that the service will be as good as you may say it is, as it is often down to human behaviour, or unfortunately and all too often true, human error. It is difficult to determine the quality and level of service provided, as the service is not a product that can be quality assured before dispatch; it is produced as it is consumed. This also makes pricing the service very difficult.

The main difference between products and services is the tangible versus the intangible. Tangibility does to a degree give you guarantees of performance, quality and value for money. Therefore, marketing a tangible product enables you to balance the marketing mix more successfully, and you are then able to deliver a key set of standards to the customer.

The uncertainties of service

As we have established, delivering service quality presents a tremendous challenge to the marketer on a day-to-day basis. From a customer's perspective, it can be very difficult to qualify what you expect from a quality service because your personal expectations will quite often differ from others. However, from a marketing point of view, it is you and your perspective as a customer that will define how the service quality expectations are defined and delivered.

It is therefore necessary to stop for a moment and consider the interface between the service and the customer.

The main characteristics of this process can be identified thus:

◆　　The customer is physically or virtually present, at the place where the service is delivered

◆　　The service and delivery process are interdependent (simultaneous production and consumption).

Within this interface it becomes clear that a potential 'uncertainty' arises between what the customer actually wants and what the customer is actually going to be provided with.

According to Mudie and Cottam (1999), this uncertainty arises for a number of reasons, but mostly because service deliverers fail to understand, for example, the following key customer inputs:

◆　　Physical state of body (e.g. for a fitness clinic)

◆　　Mental state of mind (e.g. for an education service)

◆ State and complexity (e.g. of a car for detecting faults during a service)

◆ Capacity (e.g. of clothing and carpet fabrics to withstand chemical treatment)

◆ Amount and nature of customer information (e.g. for medical diagnosis).

Essentially what happens is that in the above situations it becomes clear that the service provider is unsure about the customer's state of mind, which in turn, can affect their pre-paredness for creating and delivering an effective service.

During the service delivery, the customer can actually be portrayed as posing problems for an organization by being disruptive, rude, ignorant or even arrogant and essentially fail to comply with the service demands. Principally, this is due to the lack of understanding in the interface situation and potentially the wrong fit being delivered – that is the wrong service to the right customers.

Question 10.4

Explain your understanding of 'customer uncertainty'.

It is very rare that organizations ever supply either a pure product or a pure service, it is more often a combination of the two. For example, if you buy a new car or TV, you rarely just buy the product. It is normal for products to have warranties and customer services sup-port as part of the value-added element of the product. This essentially means that there are two components to consider, the core service and the peripheral service.

The core service relates to the core technical feature of the service; for example, if you are travelling by train, the service will be to get you to your destination in a safe and reli-able manner. By the same token you are taking the CIM Advanced Certificate in Marketing Course, and the service is to provide you with a learning package that provides career enhancement, self-achievement and actualization. Essentially, therefore, the core service is what is at the heart of the package, and every effort should be made to communicate this to your customers.

The peripheral service, however, is almost like the distribution channel, it is the way in which the service is supported or implemented, that is the check-in desk at the airport, the ticket office at the railway station. Therefore, the peripheral service relates to the facilita-tion of and support of the core service.

Meeting customer expectations

Understanding customer expectations is the same as understanding customer buying behaviour. However, on this occasion understanding the behaviour and perceptions be-fore and after the event is essential, in order to understand whether the service exceeds, equals or indeed fails to meet expectations.

According to Mudie and Cottam (1999), service organizations need to understand and recognize the importance of the first law of services, which states:

Satisfaction=perception−expectation

However, as you can imagine, this is likely to be quite a subjective measure, as everybody's interpretation is probably different.

Measuring consumer perceptions in the service industry is essential in order that continuous improvement can be adopted, and that the appropriate market mix is designed. Essentially, the role of the organization will be to determine the views of the customers, against the perception of the organization.

The service mix – physical evidence, people and process

The marketer has a full tool bag when it comes to marketing services; there are the traditional 4Ps: product, price, place and promotion. In addition there are the physical environment, the people and processes – the other 3Ps that ultimately give the opportunity to establish a high-quality service provision on behalf of the organization.

The physical environment – physical evidence

The physical element of the marketing mix relates to the physical environment, the place from where the services are prepared and delivered. For example, the restaurant where you go to have a meal out is the physical environment. The restaurant is where the service is delivered and consumed.

From a marketing perspective, it does help support the marketing of services as the physical element of the service brings some consistency and guarantee of quality and does enable the basis for a brand to be established and built upon. There are many examples of this, for example with chain restaurants such as Pizza Hut, BeefEaters, Brewers Fayre and so on. They are all well-known brands where the physical environment has played a significant role in relation to service delivery. Increasingly, in the hospitality industry there is a growing emphasis on the image created by the physical environment and it plays a significant role in the USP of the organization.

The physical environment can be represented in quite simple ways, through staff wearing uniforms, similar interior design and often the same menus, special offers and promotions. This is reassuring for the customer, to know that the brand is meaningful and familiar.

Therefore, when establishing a marketing mix for services, the physical environment plays a significant role in stabilizing the quality perception of the organization, similar to the way in which a product can.

You should be aware that services can be administered both mechanically, for example on the Internet, or through automated voice handling mechanisms, but also through a physical human contribution.

The importance of people to the marketing mix

The people element of the mix is quite complex in that the one big inconsistency in planning for the marketing mix is human nature. The role of customer-facing personnel is very difficult and demanding and at times extremely frustrating. Therefore, it is difficult not to let that frustration show and affect the level of customer service then being delivered.

The people element of the marketing mix in today's marketing environment is critical, as customer service is seen to be one other major value-added component of the customer's overall purchasing experience.

Managing the people aspect of the marketing mix requires a high degree of interpersonal skills and a strong internal marketing programme, whereby the internal members of staff, 'people', have their roles and responsibilities and overall contribution to the purchasing process communicated to them. For them to be effective and for the organization to go some way towards guaranteeing quality, the people aspect of the mix must include the following:

◆ **Investing in staff and training** – Product and organizational training

◆ **Empowerment of staff** – Encouraging staff to be involved to make a contribution

◆ **Internal marketing** – Communicating to them and motivating them to achieve

◆ **Decision-making capacity** – To enable staff, within their empowerment factor, to make decisions relating to the delivery of the service.

Sadly, one of the most significant impacts upon the service industry, the Internet, is reducing the number of people involved in customer service delivery and is effectively very process-oriented.

Process

The process element of the marketing mix will always need to be managed with the customer in mind. What are their expectations, their needs and wants in relation to the service experience?

Process is about developing processes for the delivery of service that will add value to the customer experience. For example, when staying in a hotel, you would expect the booking in and out process to be concise, fast and efficient. To add value to the customer experience when staying in hotels, many of them put your bill under the door for your information, overnight, which makes checking out faster and efficient.

The process of booking a holiday or flight should be the same. The customer requires the whole service to be a positive experience; therefore, processes are critical to that value-added aspect of the product or service.

It is important that organizations develop systems that allow the service provider to ensure a seamless transition throughout the customer service experience, and an approach that allows inputs and outputs from the customers to be handled effectively. Processes should in essence be 'invisible' not evident, but essential to the customer experience.

Well-designed processes are needed as the service is delivered to ensure that the customer gets through with minimum fuss and delay, and that all elements of the service are properly delivered.

This will, as mentioned in the hospitality context, take into account the use and collection of information, payment procedures, queuing systems and task allocation.

This is of major importance to the financial services industry where much effort has gone into ensuring that services are more accessible to customers, via telephone and Internet service provision. The way in which security systems and processes have been designed to enable customer security, and also providing 24/7 access for customers in their own home and whenever and wherever they want it, has been ingenious and is now one of the biggest online success stories of all time.

As a result of the success, banks are aiming to create further flexibility and offer incentives to encourage customers to use Internet banking, including such things as reduced interest charges.

The impact of the Internet upon process

One of the reasons that many organizations are being drawn to the Internet is for the advancement and continuous improvement in customer services, but also to ensure that customer service is more cost-effective to deliver.

Currently, on the process side of the marketing mix, the Internet is still causing many aggravations and frustrations. You have probably heard of or experienced the process of filling your shopping basket online, only for the server to go down and 30 minutes shopping input to be lost. While this is a technological problem it is also a service process problem, which means that organizations need to understand the technology requirements, time-out settings and so on, on personal computers and give more guidance and advice on purchasing a service through this mechanism.

Question 10.5

Explain, with examples, the importance of the 3Ps of the services mix.

The marketing mix in the context of services

The marketing mix does play a role, as has been suggested now on a number of occasions, but the lack of tangibility poses a serious problem to its design and implementation.

Product

You have to convert this to think in terms of benefits, but there are also often products associated with services and the products may have a big influence. The 'product' of dry cleaning is the cleaner clothing, or the benefit of clean curtains that would not fit in your electric washing machine. The benefit may also be psychological rather than physical.

Price

Price reflects quality levels, whether we like it or not. The basic idea of charging as much as customers will pay may be reasonable for products where customers have a choice of whether or not to buy the product, but would that be reasonable for essential services, such as business consultancy, secretarial services, medical and dental treatment? This is actually like asking the question 'How long is a piece of string?' The price charged for a service will be based around the service value proposition, the levels of tangibility that might offset concerns about levels of intangibility. Therefore, when the delivery of a service provides a tangible benefit, pricing becomes more objective. Of course, other factors such as demand and market forces will play a significant role.

Evaluating value in terms of price is always highly subjective; however, the price of a service can create demand and entice customers.

In a more traditional manner, travel companies do charge according to demand – if you travel by rail at peak periods you pay a lot more than you would if you went later in the day. The same applies to electricity – there are much lower 'off-peak' charges in the night because the demand is lower then, but the generators still have to run.

Place

One of the key characteristics of services is that the actual service provider may deliver them directly to you. However, there are a lot of services that do not involve the customer being present because they are of a virtual nature. You can transfer money via the Internet or telephone banking, you can order flowers, all of which are away from the place of service delivery. However, physical evidence can play an important part in this, for example within a bank, hotel or restaurant, when the role of the place becomes quite important.

Promotion

Promoting services is more difficult where the level of intangibility is higher, and there is a likelihood of customer uncertainty being aroused.

We are all subject, on a daily basis, to a surge of advertisements, promotions and direct mail in relation to financial services, pensions, holidays, flights, rail travel – the list is endless. There is probably a close correlation between the level of advertising for services and that for products. The justification of the core service has to be at the heart of the message for customers to listen, retain and respond.

Positioning will be a big issue in establishing the core values of the service, and therefore this will need careful consideration in the context of any promotional activity.

Principally, whatever the promotion, 'Don't promise what you can't deliver'.

The key components of designing a services mix

While we have looked at the importance of the 7Ps in relation to the marketing mix, we also need to consider the 11 design elements that run in parallel with the 7Ps. Mudie and Cottam (1999) suggest that the following design principles are considered:

1 **Customer contact** – What is the level of contact between the organization and the customer during the delivery of the service?

2 **Service mix** – How many service offerings will there be, how effective will they be, what will the services portfolio consist of?

3 **Location** – Should the service go to the customer, or the customer be drawn to the service?

4 **Design** – Practical design extends from basic logos and letterheads through to uniforms, physical structures and therefore is a component of the 7Ps.

5 **Technology** – What technology will be required for the delivery of the service – will it be reliable, what are the customer expectations and what will the impact be?

6 **Employees** – Success will hinge on the organizational culture, the level of support, the strength of internal marketing, the appropriate and adequate resource base to support them in their work.

7 **Structure** – The structure will go a long way towards determining the organizational culture and establishing lines of command.

8 **Information** – Good MIS systems will be useful in ensuring that appropriate levels of information are available to support the service delivery and understand customer expectations.

9   **Demand** – The level of demand for a service will affect the standards of delivery.

10   **Procedures** – As in process – it is essential to understand the nature of the processes required for successful execution of the service.

11   **Control** – The only way in which continuous improvement can be understood and
quality standards measured is through a range of monitoring and control processes.

The case relating to Argos below highlights the potential a successful services mix offers,
including for the customer the best value for money through convenience, good service
and accessibility to new technologies.

Insight: Argos – The unique shopping experience!

Argos' unique shopping experience is popular and successful because it is focused
around meeting customer needs. Argos has gained competitive advantage over rivals
by differentiating itself on the basis of providing the best value for money for customers through the most convenient shopping experience. The market has been carefully
segmented according to the way in which customers use the stores to make purchases.
Argos' strategy is to continue to grow through attracting new customers while rewarding existing customers for their loyalty. By embracing new technologies in a busy world,
Argos continues to provide the channels that are most appropriate to the modern retailing experience.

The importance of service quality

People, physical evidence, process – these three elements of the marketing mix are critical to the delivery of exceptional service quality. They are responsible for reducing waiting
times, avoiding long check-in lines at the airport, getting quick answers on financial services packages, to name but a few.

It will always be difficult for a service-related organization to deliver 100 per cent quality, but
with the complete marketing mix at its disposal, service should be improving all the time.

When it comes to marketing a service versus a product the considerations are the same
for delivering service quality (see Figure 10.6). Service-related organizations should always
consider:

◆   What the customers expect.

◆   Service specifications (in the same way as there are product specifications).

◆   Employee performance – quality of their delivery, training needs.

◆   Managing customer service expectations – making sure quality is achieved.

SERVQUAL aids the measurement of service delivery and seeks to measure quality within
the service sector. It looks closely at five factors as listed below and shown in Figure 10.6:

1   **Reliability** – Ability to perform the promised service dependably and accurately.

2   **Responsiveness** – Willingness to help customers and provide a prompt service.

3   **Assurance** – Knowledge and courtesy of employees and their ability to inspire trust
and confidence.

4   **Empathy** – Caring, individual attention the organization provides its customers

5   **Tangibles** – Physical facilities, equipment, appearance of personnel.

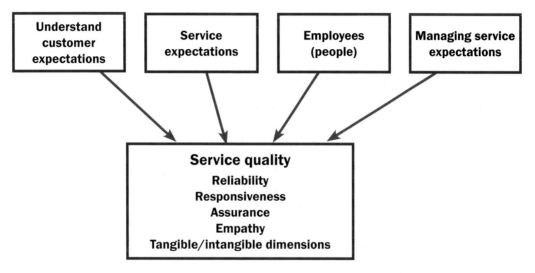

Figure 10.6: The dynamics of service quality – SERVQUAL

SERVQUAL measures the gap between customer and management perceptions of the quality issue.

The gaps, highlighted by B.G. Dale in *Managing Quality* (1994), are as follows:

Gap 1 – Consumers' expectations ←→ managers' perceptions of consumers' expectations

Gap 2 – Managers' perceptions of consumers' expectations ←→ service quality specifications actually set

Gap 3 – Service quality specifications ←→ actual service delivery

Gap 4 – Actual service delivery ←→ external communications about the service

Gap 5 – Resources.

Quality and reliability are often used synonymously. Part of the appeal and acceptability of a product or service will depend on its ability to function satisfactorily over a period of time, and also with a measure of reliability.

Principally, quality can be used as a tool for competitive advantage, and can be a powerful strategic weapon within the organization.

Managing the differing levels of quality in services is, as we have established, more difficult than for goods overall, as a result of issues relating to levels of tangibility and intangibility.

Quality management has to be based around the three key elements of the services marketing mix: the people, the physical evidence and the process. Analysis of performance in each of these areas would help the organization ascertain their position both from a customer perspective and a competitive perspective. High scores or ratings in each of these is likely to be a positive factor. If it is the reverse, there are some severe financial penalties to face.

Quality measurements and quality objectives are highly important and will be the basis in establishing customer perception and achieving customer satisfaction. Principally, promises that are made should be kept.

Performance relates to the delivery of the product by staff, and it is essential in that respect that there is strong internal marketing support in order that the ethos of the organization shines through, that staff are highly motivated and influence the basis of consumer perceptions of the service.

Implementing a quality culture

Quality can be used as a tool for competitive advantage, and can be a powerful strategic weapon within the organization. This would include addressing the following elements:

◆ Innovation

◆ Status

◆ Leadership

◆ Rewards

◆ Values

◆ Developments of a learning organization

◆ Empowerment to achieve challenging goals.

The successful measurement of a quality culture may manifest itself in the following ways:

◆ People see for themselves the need for quality management tools

◆ Motivators and champions start to emerge

◆ People talk of processes and not of functions

◆ People volunteer to take on tasks, which previously have involved considerable management intervention.

The quality guru Claus Moller suggested that there are 12 golden rules to aid quality implementation and improvement, all of which are particularly pertinent to the delivery of good quality service:

◆ Set personal and corporate quality goals

◆ Establish personal accountability

◆ Check how satisfied customers are with your efforts

◆ Regard the next link as a valued customer

◆ Avoid error

◆ Perform tasks more effectively

◆ Utilize resources well

◆ Be committed

◆ Learn to finish what you have started

◆ Control stress

◆ Be ethical

◆ Demand quality.

Moller emphasized the need for administrative procedures to improve rather than an improvement in the delivery process, as it is often the one that lets the other down. He further emphasized the need to use checklists, personal performance standards, ideal performance levels and actual performance levels (Moller, 1988).

Essentially, quality is the key to success and in the context of services people are the key to achievement.

Monitoring and evaluating service

There are a number of key issues that impact upon quality measurement:

◆ The difference in perception between employees and customers

◆ The inseparability of production and consumption

◆ The individuality of employees' performance and customers' perceptions.

There is a proposed formula for measuring these components:

Customer expectations – Service organizations' perceptions of customer expectations

Customer experience – Service organizations' perceptions of customer experience.

This is based on the different expectations of 20 customers receiving the same service, and is probably very subjective as each of them will feel differently and therefore the analysis could be rather inconclusive. However, while the feedback might be diverse, it is likely that some useful information might manifest itself in order that future improvements might be made.

To be able to continuously improve the level of service offered, to understand the gaps, the confusion, the customer uncertainties, the following monitoring and evaluation processes could be implemented:

◆ **Marketing research** – To gather information about services, and delivery of them

◆ **Data collection** – Frequent reviews

◆ **Observing respondents** – as they receive the service

◆ **Interviewing respondents** – To understand their perceptions and expectations versus their experience

◆ **Customer satisfaction surveys** – Questionnaires to monitor customer satisfaction

◆ **Mystery consumer experience** – Include a mystery person in the delivery of the service

◆ **Evaluating dissatisfaction** – Examine the main causes of customer dissatisfaction

◆ **Monitoring image** – How is the image of the service perceived

◆ **Performance appraisals** – Of staff involved in the delivery of the service

◆ **Employee group discussions** – Internal marketing practice.

Question 10.6

Why is it important to evaluate the delivery of services?

Summary

Marketing to organizations and industries is different in practice from consumer marketing, but uses the same principles. The demand is managed differently and the buying process has to be accepted as it is. Quite often, the delivery in the time promised is more important than price alone.

The range of marketing opportunities is very wide and the range of products can be bewildering. The buyers are professionals, and their motives for buying are quite different from those of consumers. Instead of looking at their own individual needs they will be accountable to the organization for making the right purchase decision in order for the supply chain to function satisfactorily.

The 4Ps can still apply to marketing to organizations but with a different emphasis. Distribution of some products is similar to that for consumer goods, but there are also some quite big differences.

There is a stronger need to maintain a competitive edge, because of the professionalism of the buyers and the competitors.

The importance of services in the modern economy is shown by the fact that Britain, and most other developed countries, are now service economies, with more than 50 per cent of gross spending being on services and 64 per cent of the UK workforce employed in services.

Services have to be marketed but there are more differences than similarities with the marketing of products. The problems arise from the features of services – their intangibility, inseparability from the provider, perishability and the impossibility of stocking up for future sale. There is also the potential variation of quality due to the fact that people, who vary in performance day by day, provide the services.

The marketing mix for services includes the 4Ps of product marketing, with the addition of people, physical evidence and the process or methods of providing the service. However, the importance of the 11 elements of design should not be underestimated.

Ultimately, as with all marketing strategies, plans and implementation of various marketing mixes, the quality of the product and service provision should be a matter of 'excellence'.

Study tip

Because of the growing importance and influence of services in the economy, it is natural that this should be reflected in the syllabus and the examination. Therefore a total grasp of the subject will be vital.

By the same token, business-to-business applications play a major role and are frequently the source of exam questions.

The test will be of your ability to apply marketing in a variety of different contexts, this means organizational marketing, services marketing, international marketing and not-for-profit-marketing. In doing this you will develop very versatile marketing skills that will make your transition from one industry to another a little smoother than perhaps it might be.

Further study

In addition to reading your recommended text, you will find it useful to gain a more in-depth understanding of some of the services issues by reading the following chapters from *The Management of Marketing Services* by Peter Mudie and Angela Cottam (1999) – Chapters 1, 3, 5, 10, 11 and 12.

Bibliography

Brassington, F. and Pettitt, S. (2000) *Principles of Marketing*, Thomson Higher Education

Dale. Barrie. G., (1994) *Managing Quality*, Wiley, second edition

Dibb, S., Simkin, L., Pride, W. and Ferrell, O. (2005) *Marketing: Concepts and Strategies*, Houghton Mifflin, 5th European edition

Hill, R.W. and Hillier, T.J. (1977) *Organizational Buying Behaviour*, Palgrave Macmillan

Moller, C. (1988) *Personal Quality*, Time Management International

Mudie, P. and Cottam, A. (1999) *The Management of Marketing Services*, Oxford: Butterworth-Heinemann

Worsam. M (2000), *Marketing Operations*, Butterworth Heinemann

Unit 11

Not-for-profit, SMEs and virtual marketing

Learning objectives

This unit looks at the role of marketing within not-for-profit organizations, SMEs and virtual markets. The profile of all three has gained in prominence in the past 10 years.

The indicative content in relation to this unit includes:

4.2 Develop a marketing plan and select an appropriate marketing mix for an organization operating in any context such as voluntary, not-for-profit and SMEs.

4.3 Explain how marketing plans and activities vary in organizations that operate in a virtual marketing place and develop an appropriate marketing mix.

Syllabus reference: 4.2, 4.3

Charities – not-for-profit marketing

One of the certainties in life is that we need money to survive, as few things in this world can be either acquired or achieved without money. The key role of any charity therefore has to be to generate income in order to achieve the aims and objectives defined by the board and management of the charity. Increasingly, charities are recognizing the value of marketing, and there has been a distinct change, as more and more charities emerge into the arena of different forms of retailing, sponsorship and event organizations. However, their approach to retailing takes on very different dynamics to that of a traditional retailer.

Charities as retailers work very much on a non-business-marketing basis. The shops are stocked with goods that mainly have been donated, and so the necessity to purchase stock does not exist at the same level. In addition to this, charity shops are manned by volunteer workers; therefore payroll costs are a minimum in comparison to mainstream retailers.

Many of the bigger charities involve themselves in 'high-profile charitable events', for example Children in Need, Red Nose Day and the London Marathon, or various 'party in the park' type events, or major rock/pop festivals, probably the most significant event of this type being 'Live Aid' run by Bob Geldof. In hosting and managing these events the benefits include considerable publicity, in terms of both TV and press coverage, and usually fairly significant donations.

One of the major differences between profit-making and non-profit-making businesses is that their perspective on life provides for an interesting range of dynamics. As profit-making business are very focused on making money, charities are focused and dedicated to changing people's lives and really making a difference in the most horrendous situations.

Case study: Ronald McDonald House Charities

Ronald McDonald Care Mobile Programme

In 2000, to help address the growing need for access to health care for millions of children worldwide, Ronald McDonald House Charities launched a fleet of Ronald McDonald Care Mobiles, paediatric healthcare units delivering free medical and dental care directly to underserved children in their own neighbourhoods. By 2008, 32 mobile healthcare unit were in operation, making this one of the most extensive mobile healthcare programmes ever undertaken.

Ronald McDonald House Charities launched the first Ronald McDonald Care Mobile outside the United States in Buenos Aires, Argentina. Through this programme, McDonald's see that they can be part of the solution to the serious healthcare access problem facing children today.

The Ronald McDonald Care Mobile helps reduce reliance on expensive and inappropriate health resources, such as hospital emergency departments. The programme also provides continuity of care by providing follow-up services and referrals to primary care physician, dentist or paediatric sub-specialists and helping eligible families to enrol in a government assisted health insurance programme such as 'Insure Kids Now'.

Background of Ronald McDonald Charities

Ronald McDonald House Charities has helped more than 10 million families in 30 countries around the world. This not-for-profit organization creates, funds and supports programmes that directly improve the health and well-being of children. The charity makes grants to not-for-profit organizations and provides support for all Ronald McDonald Houses and Mobiles.

Source: Lexis-Nexis

Typically the board for a charity will comprise of a number of professionals who will be ultimately responsible for the effectiveness of the organization in supporting appropriate causes. They will be responsible for allocation of funds, utilization of resources and a number of specialist activities that the charity might be planning to embark upon.

The source of funds for not-for-profit organizations will come from a range of government bodies, lottery funds, trust funds and in some instances, corporate funds from large organizations that support the specific work of the not-for-profit organizations, particularly if there is vested interest in their work.

That covers all the services we mentioned above, but it could also cover a lot of the most visible charities, such as the Red Wings Horse and Donkey Sanctuary, which runs a thriving mail order business. Profits from the mail order business are reinvested directly back into the business for future care and development work.

Marketing planning for charities

Setting objectives

You will have noticed by now that all marketing activities start with some measurable objectives, and so it is with charities and non-profit-making organizations, although the measurement of achievement is not always so straightforward.

The prime objective of charities will reflect their desire to enhance the quality of lives. For example, a typical objective might be 'To serve the needs and wants of the 'users' through the financial contributions, time and support of the public donor'.

The objectives in general terms tend to be used as an umbrella for several more specific objectives, which deal with problems that occur from time to time. This makes the measurement of achievement of the objectives, in the marketing sense, difficult. Marketers are used to dealing in money terms, or units sold, but that is not possible for the work of, say, helping to save sea birds from polluted seas, or of saving an old building so that future generations can enjoy the view from the balcony.

Essentially, the most likely aim of charitable organizations will be to achieve surplus funds through donations and sales of merchandized products, so that they can use the income generated to achieve their objectives. Therefore, the role of the charitable trust board and its members will be to ensure that the income is properly and appropriately managed.

The objectives set will very much be formed on the basis of the nature and purpose of the marketing audit undertaken. This auditing activity will be essential in determining the scale of the charitable needs in the 'users marketplace' to gain a full understanding of the level of donations required and how they might be appropriated in the future. This essentially allows organizations to clearly define their 'marketing opportunities'.

Typical auditing will obviously be upon a SLEPT basis, but with a particular focus on some of the following areas:

◆   Other similar charitable activities (competitive charities)

◆   Research into focused areas of needs

◆   Breadth and depth of the situation

◆   Economic situation of area of country involved

◆   Taxation benefits for charitable giving

◆   Facts and figures in relation to the number of potential users in one market

◆   Resources available

◆   Scale of user needs

◆   Levels of charitable giving in these areas previously

◆   Level of publicity in relation to user problems

◆   Political influence and involvement in particular area of need and available funding

◆   Social responsiveness to charitable giving

◆   Legal loopholes for charities

◆   Trends on the most popular forms of attracting donations.

These are just a few examples of information that might be needed to underpin the objective-setting and strategy development of the charitable organization.

Marketing segmentation and targeting for charities

The market segmentation process for charities consists of closely targeting individuals who are able to support the charity through donations of money, equipment and time in order to assist them in meeting the objectives of the charity and meeting the needs of their users.

The key targets for charities will include the following:

- **Donors** – Those who give funds and equipment
- **Volunteers** – Those who will give their time and effort to support the charitable cause
- **Clients** – Users of the charitable trusts, funds and services.

Obviously in mainstream marketing of profit-making organizations the segmentation process is very scientific, and focuses on the whole range of marketing mix activities, such as targeting customers for different variations of the marketing mix.

Charity marketing has to offer some benefit, and that is not always easy to visualize. The flag days have the answer – you put some money in the box, and in return get a flag to stick on your clothing to show that you have paid up. Because the feeling of well-being that comes from donating some of your hard-earned money soon wears off, it is essential for the charity to provide a tangible indicator of your generosity, usually in the form of a flag or sticker, which serves as a tangible reminder of your willingness to support the charity concerned.

That is one aspect of the marketing activities of charities, but there is a further vast 'target market' in companies. If some of the profits made by companies can be donated to charities, the improvement in funding might be quite dramatic. This is rather different from appealing to the individual – the company has no conscience and cannot get the benefit of 'feeling good' because of having donated some money.

Marketing planning and control

Planning is as vital to charitable organizations as it is to any commercial venture, as it is necessary to take a structured approach to implementation in order to achieve the objectives defined by the charitable board.

However, planning takes on two dimensions:

- To generate high levels of income from donations
- To allocate and apportion funds to particular products efficiently and effectively.

It is essential that considerable control be implemented over the planning process, in order that levels of accountability can always be achieved. Therefore, monitoring and control processes should be implemented in order that evidence of fund management can be provided. Objectives will be SMART in the same way as commercial objectives are.

While there has been a focus on voluntary workers earlier on, there are paid staff who deal with corporate fund-raising and therefore have played a different role, because they have to show the public and charitable stakeholders that they are above reproach in the way in which they manage charitable funds. However, there are also donors who like to gain high profile coverage of their donations, and who like to see that there is a measurable commercial benefit in giving money or lending facilities to a charity.

It is likely that many of the significant donors will want ultimate recognition for their contributions, as this is a way of reaping commercial benefits. Therefore, publicity of this nature has to be jointly managed by the charity and the organization for mutual benefit and gain. Charitable managers must therefore ensure that the credibility of the donor is satisfactory in order that there is no backlash of public support, due to the dubious nature of donors.

However, the approach taken to marketing planning is slightly different in nature, while the marketing mix does have similar characteristics. Therefore, it is essential at this time to look at the nature of not-for-profit organizations and compare and contrast them with profit-making organizations, before looking at the combined approach to the marketing mix. In respect of control, there will be a number of key areas that the charities should involve themselves in the measurement of

◆ The environment in which they operate

◆ Consistency and quality in the level of service offered

◆ Customer satisfaction

◆ Competence of staff and ability to manage and implement programmes effectively

◆ Effects of internal and external communications.

Question 11.1

Explain three key methods of acquiring donations for charities.

Question 11.2

Who are the three important audiences a charity needs to target and why are they so important?

What is a non-profit-making organization?

While there are a number of definitions for non-profit-making organizations, they are not universally agreed.

Definition

Non-profit-making organization – An organization whose prime goal is non-economic. However, in pursuit of that goal it may undertake profit-making activities.

Charity is not the only form of 'not-for-profit-making' organization. There are many other types of organizations. Bodies such as the armed forces, police, probation service, ambulance service and a number of support societies are also not-for-profit organizations.

The determination of non-profit-making realistically relates to the focus and objectives of the business. The whole ethos of not-for-profit organizations relates to the use of funds for particular reasons; they are accountable for the specific allocations of funds against objectives. Accountability in not-for-profit organizations is a serious business.

Not-for-profit marketing versus profit marketing

A not-for-profit marketing organization typically faces a very different range of challenges in terms of both managing and marketing their business. In the absence of a product or service to sell in the same way as profit-making organizations, its marketing focus is primarily to provide a range of products and essential support services for little or indeed no charge to the user. It will usually have multiple objectives and multiple publics, to whom it offers multiple services, but the funder of the service is different from the receiver.

Principally, profit-making organizations focus their attention on a number of profitable markets that have very tightly defined profitable targets. This purpose of the profit-making will be not only to cover their overhead costs from the income generated from the sales of products and services, but to provide a dividend for shareholders and to generate funds for investment in growth and diversification opportunities. Profit-making organizations, such as B2B, consumer, industrial or services-related industries, have in the main been the focus of marketing in the context of this book.

While the focus of profit-making organizations' customer base is customers and consumers, the focus of a charity will be on the receivers, the people who benefit from their services, who indeed then effectively become the 'user'.

For not-for-profit organizations, marketing is now playing a pivotal role in raising considerable funds that will not only serve the 'receivers' end of the service, but also fund the management and resourcing of the charity. There has, however, been a lot of controversy about mismanagement and misuse of funds within charities.

Therefore the focus of marketing for non-profit-making organizations will principally be on attracting substantial donations, equipment and voluntary support in order that they can achieve the defined objectives of the organizations.

Many non-profit-making organizations have very scarce resources and often struggle to achieve their corporate objectives, but the challenges they face are very demanding and very different, as the stakeholder audience is often extensive.

The motivational factors influencing not-for-profit marketing and profitable organizations

All organizations, both profit and not-for-profit, will benefit from having a clearly defined understanding of the customer base, that is consumers or users. Therefore, in that respect, there are many similarities in the motivation of both profit-making and non-profit-making organizations in that they both need income to survive.

The profit-making organization needs income to enable it to survive, to aid continuous improvement and to meet profit objectives and shareholder objectives. The non-profit-making organization also needs income to survive, and to continue to provide a considerable service to needy and worthy causes, but the income is channelled in different directions.

The main difference in respect of motivation is the use of the word 'profit'. Both organizations are committed to generating as much money as possible, but effectively the use of that money is very different.

The non-profit-making organization does not make a profit for its owners or shareholders. Whatever the source of income, if there is any surplus it will be directly invested back into the organization whereby all money will go into supporting the work of the business.

Therefore, while motivational factors may be similar to a degree, the word 'profit' creates different dynamics for the diverse nature of the organizations. So while profit motivates profit-making organizations, the focus of delivering a range of invaluable services is the main motivation of not-for-profit organizations.

Marketing planning for not-for-profit marketing

Setting objectives

The nature and dynamics of objectives for this particular sector differ again. For example, the objectives of a church might be to 'inform the public about the doctrine of the church and encourage a growth in church membership'. This is particularly relevant as recent statistics have shown a drastic reduction in church membership in the last 10 years.

The most likely source of funds in the case of not-for-profit organizations may be from government sources, lottery funds and local authorities or industrial support for the purpose of the project. In addition to this, income might be generated by membership subscriptions and charitable donations. In the Church of England, for example, the money will come from church offerings, donations, investments and tax benefits, among others.

Setting objectives and controlling them may prove difficult for the marketer working in not-for-profit organizations. A marketing manager employed by a charity may have the same type of ambitions as his or her opposite number in a profit-making organization, and he or she may not think that its objectives will provide the career advancement opportunities that he or she wants.

Marketing planning and control

It is essential that in order to control the achievement of objectives, through the implementation of the marketing plan, not-for-profit managers use the range of information that they should have collected through undertaking some form of marketing audit, to define objectives and implement a range of controls.

Controls will be based around the product/services mix, in order that quality is maintained and standards delivered. In addition to this, financial controls must be in place to ensure that funds are pulled in, in order to achieve the objectives defined by the organization.

While the principles are the same, sometimes, because of the nature of the organization and the number of volunteers involved, the waters become a little muddied and the overall objectives of the organization fail to be achieved.

Objectives, while SMART, can be difficult to measure. While they might be related to creating awareness, it will be difficult to determine the level of awareness as perhaps advertising is not measured in the same mechanical way as it is with commercial organizations.

However, in organizations such as universities, a business-like approach is now taken to planning and control, with an increasing emphasis on accountability, quality and service levels. They have had no choice but to change the way they operate to be much more business-oriented and focused.

Managing the marketing mix: charities and not-for-profit organizations

Charities and not-for-profit organizations are more similar to services than to manufacturers, and it may put their marketing into perspective if we try to see how the 7Ps of service marketing fit in with their activities. However, one thing that should be considered in developing and optimizing the effect of the marketing mix is the ability for each charity to retain some form of competitive advantage, in terms of gaining preference for charity giving to their own organization.

◆ **Product** – Is equivalent to the benefit that charities provide to donors; the feeling of well-being, either for an individual or for the staff and management of a commercial enterprise.

◆ **Place** – You may think that 'place' is not important to the collectors of money for charities, because all money is of equal value wherever it comes from. However, in some instances it is vitally important, for example with the need for charity shops to play a significant role in income generation. For Oxfam in particular this is a vital source of income, therefore distribution of stores on as intensive a basis as possible is desirable.

◆ **Promotion** – Is very relevant, as has been seen earlier in the text, with sponsorship, publicity and PR playing a major role in the marketing activities. There is a heavy involvement in direct marketing and specifically targeting home-owners to donate to charities on a regular basis.

Promotion of non-profit-making organizations is increasing and becoming much more high profile in order that they may gain support, membership and potentially donations to further enhance the work they undertake. This may be more focused in terms of specialist journals relevant to the organizations and direct mailing base.

◆ **Price** – As a concept, price will vary between charities and non-profit-making organizations. For charities, price will hold two interests, the amount of money generated and the cost of programme implementation.

However, the not-for-profit-making local authority assesses the amount of money they will need for the next year, then works out the amount to be charged to each household.

◆ **People** – People certainly matter in charities and in non-profit-making organizations: the charities depend on non-paid-for help from volunteers, and the work that they do, in marketing terms, is very much 'people-oriented'. The various non-profit-making organizations are people-oriented too. There are people involved in the interface with the public, naturally, and the characteristics of these people can make the marketing activities more, or less, effective depending on how well they relate to other people.

◆ **Physical evidence** – Is needed – if you know what a charity will achieve with your donation you may feel disposed to give more money, and when you have to pay for the services of the local authority, without much choice, you do expect to see some physical evidence of the use of the money.

◆ **Process** – In charity and non-profit-making organization terms, process is about making it easy to donate money. The charities collect money in the street, or on the doorstep, and they all show donors how to make their contribution more effective. The days of the street collection may be numbered, as people complain that there are too many of them, and the increasing use of direct debit has reduced the need for door-to-door collections' although some charities still use this methodology.

The non-profit-making organizations seldom have to ask the public to be donors, because their funds come directly or indirectly from some form of public source, but their dealings with the public must still be smooth and efficient. The public are often in the position of customers and owners, although the ownership is indirect.

Case study: Red Nose Day

Since Comic Relief began, we have raised, through the Red Nose Day, over £400 million and have given to over 7000 projects. This money has helped poor and disadvantaged people in the United Kingdom and Africa turn their lives around. Sixty per cent of this money is spent in Africa and 40 per cent within the United Kingdom.

Comic Relief support a range of activities. In Africa the six key areas of focus include the following:

1 People affected by conflict and wars

2 Women and girls

3 People living in towns and cities

4 Disabled people

5 Pastoralists – people who traditionally make a living from raising cattle, goats and sheep – and hunter-gatherers

6 People living with and affected by HIV and AIDS.

In the United Kingdom the key areas of focus include the following:

◆ Young people who are struggling with various crises in their lives such as being homeless, sexually exploited or coping with mental health problems

◆ Women and children experiencing domestic violence

◆ Refugees and asylum seekers who have fled their countries because of persecution. They arrive in the United Kingdom with nothing and need to rebuild their lives

◆ Older people who are treated without dignity and respect, whose rights are ignored and who are, in some circumstances, experiencing abuse

◆ People living in local communities who are working together to tackle poverty and disadvantage to make their area a better place to.

In 2007, Red Nose Day was expected to be supported on its big charitable day in March, by Sainsbury's, TK Maxx, Walkers Crisps, Andrex, Kleenex, British Telecom, Müller, Baby Bel and Ernst and Young, to name but a few. Their success is massive, as Red Nose Day has a major national cult following, in employing organizations, schools and hospitals, it is a national giving day!

This level of input and support requires significant marketing effort to not only get the donations but also the level of national participation for such a project. It is a true story of charity success which is now as much part of British Culture as the British Breakfast of bacon and eggs. The marketing mix and marketing effort has been innovative, creative and co-ordinated in order to bring such a national level of support in to play.

Go to www.rednoseday.com for more information.

It is appropriate to mention the changing nature of some non-profit-making organizations. We have mentioned the way in which some charities have taken up marketing activities, with good effect, and it is evident that since the 1990s there has been a growing move to make the non-profit-making organizations more accountable for the money they spend.

Different marketing adoption in not-for-profit organizations

In Table 11.1 you can see the variety of ways in which the adoption of marketing has been implemented in a range of different not-for-profit organizations.

Table 11.1 Marketing's adoption	
Colleges and universities	1. The product range is under constant review, the physical environment is of concern and more efficient methods of teaching are being devised.
	2. Promotion has sharpened and the importance of internal marketing is being recognized.
	3. Staff needs, both teaching and support, are identified using HRM techniques; recruitment ads are more professionally produced and placed; selection is more concerned with effectiveness than qualifications. Training is budgeted and encouraged.
	4. Funding sources are targeted and marketing plans developed to maximize the probability of achievement. Trans-EU funding requires a long-term commitment. Commercial sponsorship needs activities targeted to meet the sponsor's needs.
Hospitals	1. Excess demand and budgetary constraints are causing hospitals to allocate their resources very carefully.
	2. Sponsorship and the aid of voluntary groups such as 'Friends of the Hospital' has to be solicited and the benefits be seen to be valued.
Doctors	1. Excess demand and budgetary constraints are causing doctors to consider which patients they can afford to accept on to their lists.
	2. There is a growing resentment in the population because the tradition of open access is now restricted. This presents a serious need for doctors to use marketing to show that they are not responsible for Government actions.

Charities	1.	Funds must be solicited from a variety of sources.
	2.	Beneficiaries of the charity must be located and encouraged to apply and/or accept support.
	3.	Internal marketing must co-ordinate and motivate the individuals who work for the charity either in an employed or voluntary capacity.
Social organizations	1.	Many long-standing organizations such as the YMCA, and churches are losing members and suffering from lack of income. Marketers face the twin problems of redefining mission and corporate policies to provide what people require today, and securing the necessary funds to generate an upturn in membership.

Question 11.4

You are a marketing manager for a well-known charitable organization. You have been asked to justify to the Board the reasons why the charity should not employ an advertising agency to undertake promotional work on their behalf.

Study tip

Question 4 in the December 2003 Marketing Planning paper was set in the context of not-for-profit organizations and explored the concepts of relationship marketing as a mechanism for increasing donations. Therefore it is important from an examination perspective to understand the relative importance of other business contexts and be prepared to respond in an applied way to examination questions in relation to them.

Marketing for Small to Medium Enterprises

The next stage of this unit is looking at the marketing for SMEs. For many SMEs, marketing is a wide-ranging term which covers the process of identifying potential buyers and gaining their purchasing commitment in order to facilitate and generate sales; whilst ensuring such sales are profitable. In many respects this approach is no different from much larger corporations, and at times the approaches taken to developing marketing strategy and plans can also be similar but obviously, on a much smaller scale.

Offering products or services that have a real demand is central to the operation of an effective marketing strategy. It is important to identify the market for a product or service in order to be able to correctly satisfy their needs.

Developing unique selling points which differentiate a product or service or even a company from its competitors is essential – whilst creating a corporate image that is clearly recognizable. Success in marketing can be measured by increases in sales, turnover and profits.

Frequently small businesses in particular misjudge their markets and do not achieve expected sales targets. This often leads to insufficient cash flow and poor profits. An effective marketing strategy and a real understanding of the marketplace is imperative in order to grow and develop a successful business.

Marketing strategy and planning for SMEs

Small- and medium-sized enterprises, like large FMCG companies or not-for-profit companies, need to be specific about each objective and consider how they will reach each objective, how often they will review it, what it will cost and the results expected from these actions.

The benefits of a marketing plan are that they highlight the things that the company was not aware of, thus preventing the making of costly errors. It sets out clear marketing objectives and allows the company to look back and find out what had gone wrong and enables them to put things right.

It is imperative to know the strengths and weaknesses of the business. The best way to assess them is to use SWOT (Strengths, Weaknesses, Opportunities, Threats) analysis. Strengths include having a large customer base, viable range of products, skilled staff, low-cost base, a good information technology system, a strong balance sheet and so on. Weaknesses are generally the opposite of your strengths.

Opportunities may be weak competition, a growing market, availability of new grants and lower interest rates. These are external market forces. Threats are generally the opposite of what you see as opportunities. SWOT analysis will provide lots of answers which SMEs are often not aware of.

Identify the factors critical for success. This may mean reviewing how new products are developed, improving quality, reducing costs or providing better customer care. Set your objectives, look at the options, consider the practicalities and check that your plan is achievable.

The marketing plan is an integral component of all business plans and it is something that many SMEs, particularly very small companies, often overlook. The marketing plan is of importance in documenting and setting targets and objectives for the business whilst acknowledging potential competitive issues. It is advisable to refer to the marketing plan and indeed the business plan from time to time to establish whether the targets and objectives are being met. A marketing plan is a prerequisite when applying for a loan or a grant and is often the one time when small companies seem to get remotely near to any form of planning activities.

Outline marketing plan for SMEs

Many smaller organizations find it difficult to understand the importance of planning and even more so the types of information and activities involved in creating a marketing plan. Below is a list of activities SMEs should undertake when preparing a plan.

1 Collect data and review the plan as a whole.

2 Decide on the content.

3 Plan the design and layout.

4 Write it up clearly and simply.

5 Assemble all the finalized information for your marketing plan.

6 Include a competitor's comparison table.

7 Prepare a SWOT analysis.

8   Include objectives.

9   Include sales forecasts.

10   State the marketing strategy.

11   Provide a detailed plan of action.

12   Include a timetable for implementation.

13   Put in some key controls in order to monitor the plan.

14   Keep the plan to between 10 and 20 pages.

The marketing mix for SMEs

Product

All products have a pattern of demand. Initial demand may be limited, although effective marketing efforts should ensure growth in demand. However, this demand will eventually peak and decline. This usually results in the product being discontinued. This process is termed the 'product life cycle'. In every market, as new products are introduced, older ones become obsolete. New products usually replace older ones, although in some cases changes in purchasing patterns can result in markets disappearing altogether.

Effective advertising and sales promotion can help to increase demand for SMEs and extend the life of older products. This is a commonly used approach by much larger corporations and has been successful; there is therefore no reason why it cannot be equally so for small businesses. However, please note that this is not always affordable, so SMEs do have to be creative with their promotional budgets.

The best way to protect SMEs against all products declining at the same time is to have a portfolio of products at different phases of their life cycles. This helps to spread the marketing and development workload more evenly whilst ensuring a more constant flow of income. Again this is the strategy followed by a larger organization, but some SMEs do have a broad portfolio of products and it is therefore important to spread development costs where possible as it becomes a drain on very valuable resources.

Place

Many companies use wholesalers and retailers rather than sell direct to customers. The reason for this is that they do not have the resources to sell direct to large numbers of customers.

Most small- to medium-sized manufacturing businesses prefer to invest in the production side of their business instead of the distribution side and are unable to afford their own distribution networks and are reliant on outsourcing to others. In distribution there may be several layers of intermediaries. Once they have selected their distributors, they will need to work hard to motivate them so that they will promote and sell their products. This really relates to the issue of volume and profit for the intermediaries, in order to make it worth their while.

It may be necessary to evaluate these distributors in terms of sales quota attainments, promotion of their products and services offered to customers.

Price

When trying to establish prices, consideration should be given to whether high or low volume sales would be achievable. High volumes usually require lower pricing in order to sustain sales. It may be useful to draw a break-even chart to illustrate the relationship between the cost of production and profits. Markets are often sensitive to price changes.

Price wars are often deemed as something that only happen with larger organizations, but this is not so. Even the local hair salons, small family furniture stores and many other smaller businesses often involve themselves in small-scale price wars on a local level, some of them even trying to take on the larger organizations to gain local market share. These types of price wars can prove to be costly whilst forcing down the long-term willingness of customers to pay the true value of a product or service. For example, local furniture stores taking on bigger furniture chains will struggle to achieve the economies awarded to large organizations for buying bulk stock. It can therefore be financially stretching and could cause severe financial damage to the organization. When discounting products or perhaps offering discounts on a regular basis, setting a higher selling price can help to maintain margins. Also, selling certain products or services at a loss may encourage sales of other products whilst gaining market share and brand awareness. The following factors are key to determining effective pricing:

- Sales targets
- Maintaining price stability
- Increasing market share and product sales
- Meeting or beating competitor pricing
- Maximizing profits and margins.

Promotion

Communication with existing and potential customers is an important aspect of marketing. Advertising, sales promotion, public relations, publicity and personal selling may be used to communicate with customers.

Sales promotion covers a range of activities to get the message across to the market. Promotional activity involves providing various short-term incentives to stimulate sales of a product or service. It may involve advertising on radio, TV, in newspapers, on the Internet and in magazines. Classified directories such as Yellow Pages and posters may also be used. Alternatively direct mail, which may include letters, electronic mail messages, newsletters, brochures and coupons, may be used. However, many organizations might struggle to be able to afford TV advertising at a local level, although many channels are aiming to making TV advertising more financially viable for all, not just the larger corporation. You may have seen the recent range of TV advertisements using the cast of *The Bill*, the UK television drama series focused on a London borough police station. The cast have been used to highlight to smaller companies the misconceptions about the cost of TV advertising in an attempt to draw them to it.

Sales promotion for SMEs in particular involves generating awareness of the company and its products or services whilst providing customers with reasons to make purchasing commitments. The aim of sales promotion is to attract new customers or gain repeat purchases whilst persuading purchasers of rival products to switch supplier. This is a concept familiar to much larger organizations, and it is increasingly something that SMEs are grasping with some speed.

Implications of implementing the marketing mix for SMEs

Whilst the above are ideas for implementing the marketing mix for SMEs, life is never that straightforward. It is important to understand that SMEs in particular experience a diverse range of difficulties and barriers to implementation not necessarily experienced by large companies, partly because their planning activities are more structured, detailed, monitored and controlled. These difficulties can include the following:

◆ Lack of resources

◆ Lack of money

◆ Poor cash flow

◆ Lack of formal budgeting

◆ Lack of experience

◆ Short-term planning

◆ Entrepreneurial but not contained

◆ Growth unplanned and often unmanageable.

Key websites for advice on marketing for SMEs include:

◆ www.cim.co.uk – Small Business Solutions

◆ www.businesslink.org

◆ www.scottish-enterprise.com

◆ www.businessconnect.org

◆ www.idbni.co.uk

The virtual marketing environment

The evolution of Internet marketing and digital technologies has moved at a rapid pace. Key underlying trends behind the move towards Internet marketing are as follows:

◆ Consumer time poverty

◆ Consumers looking to take control

◆ Convergence of technologies

◆ Shift from physical to digital technologies

◆ Shift from assets to knowledge.

Key virtual trends

There has been a massive growth in online households since 2000. By October 2005, 64 per cent of adults in Great Britain (29 million) had accessed the Internet.

Of the adults who had accessed the Internet in the 3 months prior to interview, 61 per cent had bought or ordered goods, tickets or services. People aged 25–44 were most likely to buy online (67 per cent), while people aged 65 and over were least likely to buy online (41 per cent).

The most common place to access the Internet was at home (86 per cent), 48 per cent accessed at work, 33 per cent at another person's home, 16 per cent at a place of education and 10 per cent at a public library.

Of those adults who have ever used the Internet, 92 per cent had used a search engine to find information, 78 per cent sent an e-mail with an attachment, 32 per cent posted a message in a chat room or newsgroup, 22 per cent had used peer-to-peer file sharing, such as exchanging music and films and 20 per cent had created a web page.

Up to October 2005, 48 per cent of men who had used the Internet had done so for Internet banking compared with 39 per cent of women. But more women (33 per cent) had used the Internet for school, college and university related activities compared with 28 per cent of men (source: www.statistics.gov.uk).

Because there is great innovation and rapid change, it is difficult to forecast the future impact of promotions on technology and comprehend what is to come; however, there is considerable information to be found in many different domains that shows trends in how ICT is going to emerge in the future. Clearly the growth in e-commerce is going to provide many promotional opportunities for all of the ICT modes of communication, but with the major growth anticipated through Internet, interactive and digital communications.

E-commerce is likely to continue to have a huge impact on the way we do business in the future. It has led to dramatic growth in trade, increased markets, improved efficiency and effectiveness and has transformed business processes. One purpose of the survey was as a benchmarking exercise to ascertain what standards other nations are operating at, and identify gaps in the way in which e-commerce is used, to bring the United Kingdom up to a global standard.

One particular strand of the survey into UK business has actually asked businesses about their use of e-commerce and other communication technologies to aid their business. Whilst the outcome of the survey is very long and complex, the basis of it is to measure and predict e-commerce requirements for the future. We know that currently, around 20 per cent of the world population has Internet access and that by the end of 2008 the global access figure is expected to grow to 1.4 billion, compared to 445 million users in 2000.

No other medium has grown in the same way and had the impact that the Internet has appeared to achieve. It is the only medium that has actually taken away slight market share from other media.

It is clear that many businesses, large and small, are consistently increasing their budget expenditure on e-commerce, which illustrates that Internet marketing is very much alive and kicking.

Mobile Internet trends

It is anticipated that should some of the problems associated with WAP technology be resolved that the mobile Internet business could be worth in excess of £20 billion by end of 2005, and that the end-users of mobile Internet technology are likely to spend $150 million (£200 billion) in 2005.

It is known that mobile Internet providers such as Ericsson are planning the next generation improvements for mobile technology and plan to realize a much improved service by 2011.

However, in the last year the latest mobile technology to be launched is the Blackberry. This mobile communications solution is growing steadily, as increasingly people all over the world wish to access e-mails on the go and potentially 24/7.

Case study: The Blackberry

BlackBerry® is a leading wireless connectivity solution, providing access to a wide range of applications on a variety of wireless devices around the world. It combines award winning wireless devices, software and services to keep mobile professionals connected to the people, data and resources that drive their day.

BlackBerry keeps you 'in-the-loop' while you're on the go with push-based technology that automatically delivers e-mail and other data to your BlackBerry device. And with the integrated phone, SMS, browser and organizer applications, you can easily manage all your information and communications from a single, integrated device.

Collaborate and communicate more effectively and enhance your competitive advantage by responding quicker and making decisions faster. BlackBerry is the tool you need to stay connected and take care of business while you're on the go.

Blackberry is on the verge of massive growth all over the world, developing partnerships with organizations such as Google.

Source: www.blackberry.com

Insight: The latest technologies – Podcasts and Blogs

Increasingly in recent years there has been a significant growth in the use of 'podcasts' and 'blogs', both key marketing tools, aiding the growth in virtual, interactive and digital communications channels.

A podcast is a media file that is distributed by subscription (paid or unpaid) over the Internet using syndication feeds, for playback on mobile devices and personal computers. Like 'radio', it can mean both the content and the method of syndication. The latter may also be termed podcasting. The host or author of a podcast is a podcaster.

Though podcasters' websites may also offer direct download or streaming of their content, a podcast is distinguished from other digital audio formats by its ability to be downloaded automatically, using software capable of reading feed formats such as RSS or Atom.

Podcasts can be used to relay a variety of marketing messages to customers and can be downloaded through mobile communications and the Internet. They can be used for selling messages, or key marketing tools, adding value, providing 'knowledge sound bytes' in a knowledge economy. The technology is becoming increasingly competitively priced and will result in much broader use of information in future.

A blog is a user-generated website where entries are made in journal style and displayed in a reverse chronological order. The term 'blog is derived from 'Web log.' 'Blog' can also be used as a verb, meaning to maintain or add content to a blog.

Blogs often provide commentary or news on a particular subject, such as food, politics, or local news; some function as more personal online diaries. A typical blog combines text, images, and links to other blogs, web pages, and other media related to its topic. The facility for readers to leave comments in an interactive format is an important part of many blogs. Most blogs are primarily textual although some focus on photographs (photoblog), sketchblog, videos (vlog), or audio (podcasting), and are part of a wider network of social media.

As of November 2006, blog search engine Technorati was tracking nearly 60 million blogs.

Source of definitions: http://en.wikipedia.org/wiki/Podcasting

Interactive TV trends

It is clearly evident that the Internet may have changed the preconceived ideas about the way in which companies do business and deal with their customers, but interactive TV could take this forward and exploit the new relationships to full potential. By the end of 2005 some 70 per cent of the population had access to interactive TV, and this continues to grow.

Digital TV trends

It is likely, as we know, that digital TV is continuously competing to overtake the PC market as the number of personal PCs within the home reaches saturation point. It has already been reported that HSBC claims to have registered some 1.3 million hits and is enjoying a high level of repeat users. Obviously digital solutions are the way forward.

It is hoped that whilst the scope of ICT is broadening and the range of communication opportunities is growing, organizations do not lose sight of the purpose of various technologies and that they are defined and developed in order to improve and build the scope of customer services and customer care.

It is clear that the shape of advertising, direct and interactive marketing, sales promotions and many more tools will change over the next decade quite considerably. As competition increases due to market saturation, organizations will be looking for new and innovative methods of promotional activities and promotional communications in an integrated way, with increasing emphasis on the integrated. The integrated marketing communications mix in the future is likely to change to accommodate this and more and more organizations are expected to make more of their budgets available to mobile, digital and interactive communications.

After grasping some of these facts and figures you will no doubt realize that the Internet and digital technologies are not only a vital ingredient of the promotional mix, but also a vital component within the realms of direct marketing.

The whole basis of Internet marketing is that it will facilitate an interactive customer relationship online. It will enable frequent, customized and targeted messages to specific customers or customer groups.

What are the business benefits of virtual marketing?

The virtual marketing environment provides a number of significant business benefits to organizations and they can be broken down to four key areas as follows:

1   **Market penetration** – Because of the nature of the Internet and its global communications ability, organizations can now sell more products to more markets, which were not necessarily accessible previously because of cost. The Internet can also be used to create a more broad awareness of the organization, its products and services and give an overall profile of the organization to potential customers.

2   **Market development** – In this situation, the Internet can be used to sell products into completely new markets, taking advantage of low-cost advertising internationally without the necessity of supporting sales physically, in the customer's country.

3   **Product development** – The Internet is excellent for supporting the development of new products and services and testing them out in the electronic world.

4   **Diversification** – In this sector, new products are developed which are sold into new markets. Good examples of this are Dell and Hewlett-Packard, who extended their market considerably. Dell suggests that the Internet supports $6 million worth of sales every day.

The Internet can be used in many ways to support marketing activities:

◆   **Sales** – Achieved through increasing awareness of brands and products, supporting buying decisions and enabling online purchase.

◆   **Marketing communications** – The use of the website for marketing communications is very powerful, particularly as surfing the Net is an increasing activity.

◆   **Customer service** – Supplementing telephone operators with online information. First Direct Bank and Egg are examples of organizations moving in this direction.

◆   **Public relations** – The Internet can be used as a new channel for public relations and provides the opportunity to publish the latest news on products. For example when you log on to AOL.com, a news page and a number of advertisements and banners appear.

◆   **Marketing research** – Earlier in this section we discussed how research collected from websites in addition to the databases available, enabled organizations to acquire a very clearly defined profile of their customers and their customer characteristics.

The advantages of Internet marketing

So far a picture is evolving of a dynamic electronic world that has increased access on a global basis, that is fast-moving, effective and informative. In terms of marketing the key benefits of an Internet presence can be summarized as follows:

◆   **Cost reduction** – Achieved through the need for less resources, less need for actual physical presence, less paper-based activity, particularly relevant to promotional activities and day-to-day business trading.

◆   **Competitive advantage** – Who wants to be a dinosaur? Organizations need to stay ahead of the Internet game and aim to add value through the Internet and introduce new initiatives that will add overall competitive advantage.

◆   **Capability** – The Internet provides new opportunities for the development of new products and services.

- **Communication improvements** – The Internet is a powerful communications tool, with global coverage, and can improve communications for both external and internal marketing.

- **Control** – The Internet may provide better quality of market research information through a range of Internet tracking devices.

- **Customer service improvements** – The Internet contains a number of interactive databases that can provide varying levels of information, at speed, improving customer response times. For the Internet banks, banking can take place 24 hours a day, every day.

The disadvantages of Internet marketing

- **The Internet replaces people** – As we have seen in the financial services sector over the last 2–3 years, there has been a vast reduction in the number of personnel required as a result of the automation of online banking.

- **The possible demise of high street shops** – It has been suggested that within 30 years, retail outlets will be a novelty and will be completely taken over by the Internet. However, this is still to be proven.

- **The loss of the personal touch** – There is the issue of de-personalizing business activity. The electronic world now works on a virtual rather than physical basis. Organizations must ask themselves about the loss of physical control. Is physical control an added value element of the business, or are speed and efficiency more important?

- **Security and privacy** – There are still issues of security and privacy, in addition to general regulation and control of information on the Internet. Under general regulation, there will of course be the issue of data protection. How do organizations ensure that this can be managed satisfactorily? This presents a significant challenge. Organizations must ensure that they are not caught out with the data protection laws currently in place.

- **Accessibility** – Another issue relating to the Internet is that of accessibility by the majority. While there is a significant increase in the number of homes having a personal computer and growing Internet access across different parts of the world, and it is still anticipated that it will grow significantly, will it continue to grow to meet the expectations of industry?

- **Technological defects** – It has been suggested that there is still a long way to go to iron out some of the technical difficulties to overcome customer dissatisfaction with the process.

- **Information overload** – Massive amounts of information make the Internet difficult to work around and hence people spend significantly longer online searching for their information needs. Therefore, the Internet could be perceived as being expensive and time-consuming.

It is suggested that in the future only the most reluctant electronic shopper may still be concerned with these technicalities, but the majority will actually want the new forms of service on offer to them.

From the organization perspective the initial financial investment must be considered. However, many organizations will surmise that they have to invest early on to get long-term profitability and competitive advantage in the future.

The product

The development of product concepts, packaging concepts and associated services will also change as a result of emerging technologies.

Some of the key effects technology has had on the 'product' are as follows:

1   The speed of new product development has changed dramatically; taking a product from concept to reality is more dynamic. With CAD systems, production technology and shorter distribution systems, the product can at times go to market at a rapid speed. This can make a company far more competitive in the marketplace.

2   The nature of packaging could change ultimately. As distribution options vary, packaging will no longer have to be designed for the retail outlet, but be designed for a delivery process that takes it to the customer's door. Therefore, more fragile items will have to have increasingly secure packaging. Foodstuffs might have to have more solid and secure packaging to deal with various delivery methods.

3   The method of delivery will revolve around postage and couriers as delivery comes to you directly, not via a retail outlet.

4   Warranties and guarantees might have to be rewritten to cope with the range of different delivery techniques involved in the process.

Price

One of the significant problems still associated with the Internet and shopping is often the lack of transparency in pricing structure. One of the key elements for successful Internet marketing is transparent pricing, ensuring that customers understand and have clearly explained to them the structure of their purchase, the way it is priced, and the associated delivery and warranty costs.

Price is a central consideration, and as the infrastructure of the world changes shape, so will the economics associated with it, and ultimately so will the way products and services are priced in the future.

Where previously companies would have had to include the cost of the middleman, and the share of the retail outlet, they now have to consider the cost of the Internet server, the customer service infrastructure and the potential change in shape of the distribution costs.

As a marketing manager, you will have to find the balance between increased delivery costs on a more direct one-to-one basis, and the reduction in distribution channel costs. Added to all of this will be packaging costs, and the changing nature of advertising.

Promotion

One of the difficulties that many marketers are currently facing is the greater fragmentation of their existing market. Tesco, when they commenced their online shopping project, had large Tesco stores across the country and then provided an add-on service through

'Internet shopping', effectively allowing time-starved people to shop from the comfort of their own homes, whilst at the same time meeting the demands of the other part of the target audience, who still like to go to the supermarket to undertake their weekly shopping. This has of course been followed by all major supermarket chains, including Sainsbury's and Waitrose, through their Ocado subsidiary.

Whichever way you look at it, there are now two alternative modes of shopping, which require two alternative modes of distribution, pricing to allow for additional delivery costs and, of course, promotions to deal with the different media that shoppers are now using.

Advertising as an element of promotion is undergoing a significant change, with the vast amount of small one-line advertisements ever-increasing on a daily basis. You hear of innovations such as 'interruption advertising'; for example, when you put your computer on, an advertisement suddenly pops up on your screen.

Dynamic marketing

The whole point of this section on virtual marketing has been primarily to enlighten you, focus your attention on the necessity to think about marketing not as a straightforward, theoretical process, but as a dynamic, fast-moving, ever-changing activity. The one thing that is definite about marketing, is that it is subject to constant change and nowhere more so than in this expanding new field of virtual marketing.

Therefore, if we were to summarize some of the impacts of the Internet and digital technologies upon the marketing mix and marketing in general, they would be as follows:

◆ Increased market penetration

◆ Market development – taking existing products to new markets

◆ Product development

◆ Diversification.

Summary

Planning and controlling go together, and in this respect there is no basic difference between the activities of FMCGs, B2B, B2C or virtual environments and those of non-profit-making organizations.

There is more need for charities to be seen to be using their money wisely than there is for commercial companies, as a donor who thinks that money is being wasted may not feel like giving money next time round. Donations to such television marathons as Children in Need improved when some of their successful projects were shown in the course of the programme.

The marketing philosophy is now becoming a permanent feature of not-for-profit organizations. It has been necessary to introduce marketing gradually, so as to highlight a 'customer-centred' focus, which had not previously been noticeable.

For SMEs it is also important to increase the emphasis on planning and the customer-centred focus; often the mere fight for survival (particularly very small businesses) finds them struggling with these concepts. However, SMEs need to ensure that they follow the same basic principles as those larger organizations but on a scale appropriate to their business. There are some key fundamental issues that should be addressed.

Ultimately the virtual environment is changing the way that all sectors do business and the rapidly changing market is presenting many new challenges and opportunities to extend business both locally and globally and increasingly in a more transparent way.

It is clear to see that with the increasing emphasis on digital and Internet technologies, virtual activities will continue to grow and expand to incorporate a range of new and innovative marketing ideas.

Study tip

The importance of not-for-profit-marketing has grown in significance over the past years within the marketplace, and a reflection of this might emerge in the exam paper. In recent years, this particular topic has been the centre of the mini-case study; therefore it is essential to understand the concepts and context of charities and not-for-profit organizations and how they have emerged and become much more marketing-focused.

Further study

To learn more about the evolving power of ICT and potential trends you can look up some of the following websites:

www.statistics.gov.uk

www.cyberatlas.com

www.nua.ie

www.isi.gov.uk

Bibliography

Useful websites include:

www.cim.co.uk

www.wnim.com

Appendix Feedback and answers

Unit 1

Question 1.1

Specific barriers might include the following:

♦ General resistance to restructuring

♦ Lack of co-operation due to scarce resources

♦ Breakdown in communication

♦ Obstructive behaviour

♦ Political barriers

♦ Cultural barriers

♦ Functional barriers – lack of co-operation and agreement among business units

♦ Employee relations issues

♦ High turnover of staff

♦ Political infighting

♦ Management not prepared to change.

Barriers might be created as a result of:

♦ Lack of communication (one of the biggest single factors in creating barriers to change)

♦ Lack of consultation

♦ Autocratic management style

♦ Failure to address the resourcing issue, which can force complete lack of co-operation

♦ Inappropriately skilled staff

♦ Fear of the unknown

♦ Unrealistic targets

♦ Lack of top-down commitment to the planning process.

Activity 1.1

Typical changes might include:

- ♦ New information systems
- ♦ Restructuring/reorganization
- ♦ New management
- ♦ New products/service offerings
- ♦ Diversification – change in direction
- ♦ Mergers/acquisitions
- ♦ Downsizing
- ♦ Changing position on natural resources.

These are just a few of the modes of change that organizations frequently encounter.

Drivers for change might include:

- ♦ Efficiency drivers
- ♦ Stakeholders
- ♦ Competitive forces
- ♦ Evolution of information communication technology (ICT)
- ♦ External drivers of change
- ♦ Political or economic forces.

Unit 2

Question 2.1

Potential opportunities might include the following:

- ♦ Anti-ageing products
- ♦ Provision of nutrients and vitamin supplements
- ♦ Provision of food supplements
- ♦ Opportunities to provide medical bandages, stockings
- ♦ Incontinence pads and so on.

The key to this is that while the example is a healthcare products company, there are so many opportunities available as the demographic trend is that the 'grey market' is living for longer. There are opportunities to provide products that both enhance the life cycle and support it practically.

Question 2.2

As you can see, undertaking a marketing audit is a major task, not only in terms of the volume of analysis to be undertaken and the concepts, elements and components which you are required to understand, but also in ultimately putting the outcome of the audit into the context of strategy development and planning.

A SWOT analysis of your own organization or one you will know well should present many of the components listed within the SWOT analysis grid (Figure 2.4). Clearly recommendations to overcome weakness should highlight a converting of a weakness into a strength, which would potentially see a change in internal marketing objectives to remedy some of the situations your weaknesses currently present.

For example:

Lack of resources should be converted into a strength, by taking a planned approach to increasing the current resource base, through organizational growth and investment.

Aged technology – this could become a strength again, through planned investment.

Weak supplier relationships can also be converted into a strength, by changing the basis of their agreement, incentivizing them, managing them closely and effectively. Be aware of opposing competitive forces, and divert their attention into alternative areas.

Unit 3

Question 3.1

SWOT effectively identifies the key components in relation to the internal and external environment.

It draws a substantial amount of the marketing audit together and provides the basis of the decision-making process by giving a clear insight into the dynamics of the marketing environment.

Strengths of the organization	What the organization does well
Weaknesses of the organization	What the organization could improve
Opportunities for exploitation by the organization	Where the organization can go to
Threats that face them	The inhibiting factors of growth

It provides the basis of strategy development and acts as an indicator when establishing market entry strategies, growth strategies, marketing penetration strategies, new product development and so on.

Question 3.2

Some of the key benefits of a gap analysis might include the following:

♦ It provides an insight into how much there is to achieve between where the organization is now and where it is going.

♦ It provides an insight into exactly how much marketing activity the organization may need to undertake in order to meet the corporate goals.

♦ It provides the basis for strategy development such as market growth, or market development strategies that might fill the gap.

♦ It will provide the basis on which to consider the resources required in order to fill the gap.

♦ It forces the organization to consider carefully the realism of the objectives it has set, versus what is realistically achievable.

♦ It identifies the potential for competitive activity and being prepared to be proactive in order that the competitor does not fill the gap in place of the organization.

♦ In essence it gives the basis on which to formulate a strategy and develop a planned approach.

Question 3.3

Differentiation is a highly significant way of establishing a long-term competitive advantage, in order to retain market share. Therefore, it is essential that the business looks for a number of ways to add value to the product/service in a way that makes its offering more attractive than that of its competitors. The value, however, has to be perceived as such by its customers.

Differentiation therefore provides the foundation on which to compete on price, promotions, product benefits and distribution options.

Question 3.4

Benefits of being a market follower are:

♦ Less perceived risk

♦ Allowing the leader to make the mistakes

♦ The organization works on a follower basis, therefore strategies are generally reactive

♦ Wherever the leader goes you can follow – therefore entry strategies are usually already defined and the groundwork is done for the follower.

Question 3.5

Segmentation and targeting are crucial to the success of any organization. It is a necessary process that enables the organization to understand who its customers are, how they buy, what they buy, their lifestyle and their expectations.

It is important to know where they are, their characteristics, their beliefs and values, in order that you can specifically target their needs and expectations directly through your marketing offering.

The benefits are significant.

Failure to undertake this activity could be catastrophic as you could lose market share, competitors will move in and attack your inability to target the market specifically, and ultimately will erode your competitive advantage in the marketplace.

Failure to undertake segmentation and targeting will mean that the organization is planning in a vacuum, targeting and positioning to an audience who do not necessarily exist.

Therefore it is essential that the organization fully researches the market and understands it in order that it can respond to its needs.

Question 3.6

Positioning statements should reflect issues relating to:

♦ Quality

♦ Service

♦ Price

- ◆ Accessibility
- ◆ Brand image
- ◆ Benefits/characteristics.

Think of the perceptual map and how you would explain the positioning of British Airways against Virgin Express – links to quality, price, service, delivery and so on should spring to your mind.

Question 3.7

Communication is the vital component of internal marketing. It is the bridge between the organization and its employees. It is the very channel that will not only inform and communicate change, but that will also indicate to the organization the employees' willingness and commitment to change.

Furthermore, communication is a vital component to all members of the organization in order that they understand the vision and mission, and what their responsibility and contribution is towards achieving the corporate goals.

Good internal marketing will erode some of the barriers to the implementation of the marketing plan, in order that effectiveness and efficiency can be achieved.

Communications can act as a motivator to the organization, it can act as a tool that conveys inspiration, encouragement and commitment and leadership.

The list of benefits of communicating internally is endless, but ultimately to achieve organizational success, you need to take the 'internal customer' with you. Therefore communicating values, commitment, vision, empowerment and the mission, effectively and efficiently, proactively, not reactively, might enable a smoother transition to new working practices and processes.

Internal marketing should be targeted and planned in order to gain the most success.

Unit 4

Question 4.1

Brand loyalty and customer retention are significant priorities of organizations today. It is a known fact that retaining customers is more cost-effective than gaining new ones.

The basis of brand loyalty, therefore, is through market research, aligning and associating your brand, its values and mission, with your customers.

One of the benefits of brand values is that customers will associate them with inherent values of their own lives and those of the organization. In a business sense these values should be exploited in order to achieve brand loyalty and ultimately develop a brand preference.

Therefore the brand, all that it stands for, image, association, values, assets, should be highly targeted and customer characteristics closely matched.

Question 4.2

Objectives provide definition and direction for the advertising campaign, but they also put into context the marketing strategy and plan in respect of implementation.

Setting of objectives ensures that there is value to the advertising programme that is measurable, achievable, realistic and timebound.

It is essential that the objectives also relate to other elements of the promotional mix, so that the advertising is relevant and complementary to the promotional mix strategy.

Question 4.3

Advertising acts as a support mechanism for the remainder of the promotional mix, in order to create the awareness, interest and desire. Other elements of the marketing mix might then create the incentive to act, or inducement to adopt, and indeed take the decision to purchase.

With more emphasis on direct response advertising, there is perhaps less of a necessity for some other promotional mix activities, but in the main it is helpful to optimize as many tools as possible for reinforcement of the message.

Question 4.4

Typical sales promotional activities from manufacturer to consumer include elements relating to a pull strategy, pulling the products up through the supply chain for adoption and purchase:

Encouraging trial – samples, gifts, trial drives of vehicles – allow customers to decide for themselves.

Disseminating information – information packs on a door-to-door basis, perhaps closely linked with a direct marketing campaign (again utilizing the integrated marketing communications approach).

Trading up – encouraging customers to trade up from their existing models – a typical activity of car manufacturers and white goods manufacturers.

Question 4.5

Typically, sales promotion adds value to advertising by providing the incentive to purchase and the response mechanism, to trial, gain more information, increase sales, encourage repeat purchase and for competitive responses to competitive activities.

Advertising therefore creates the awareness; promotion is the means by which customers have the incentive to respond.

Question 4.6

PR complements the promotional mix in a number of ways – these are just some ways to point you in the right direction:

- It creates a broader awareness of the brand and the organization.
- It increases coverage of principal events and draws further attention to the corporate brand and profile.
- It represents the organization fully in both a negative and a positive response to events.
- It provides the basis for securing greater awareness of product developments and products launched.
- It is a form of advertising.

♦ As a function it might run sales promotion campaigns.

♦ It covers a broader potential audience than perhaps advertising and therefore creates awareness in new markets.

Question 4.7

The promotional mix should take an integrated approach to ensuring successful achievement of the marketing objectives and implementation of the strategy. Therefore, advertising, sales promotions and direct marketing present the opportunity for an awareness-raising, incentive-boosting, informative communications campaign.

As previously suggested, advertising creates the awareness, sales promotion creates the incentive, and direct mail (direct marketing) provides the channel for communication in relation to the promotion, possibly including a voucher.

These three promotional mix mechanisms are very compatible promotional tools.

Unit 5

Question 5.1

The core of the BMW business is the base-line car for the purpose of this question. To take the product from the core to the augmented product will include the development of a range of added value extra components such as stereos, car alarms, superior finish, computerized traffic systems and so on.

Augmenting the product provides the manufacturer with an opportunity to differentiate their products, target different groups of customers with the same core model, but with specification differences, to meet the needs of all customers within the appropriate market segments.

Question 5.2

The contents of the briefing should focus on cars, in particular:

♦ Vehicle modifications – including quality, functionality and style

♦ Differentiation activities, brand and product differentiation

♦ Potential repositioning or re-branding

♦ Increase in promotional activities – advertising, sales promotions, direct mail

♦ A range of different pricing strategies, very specifically targeted for maximum effect

♦ Increase in competitive activity – therefore prepared attacks required.

Question 5.3

The BCG matrix is a highly useful tool in ascertaining both the position of products and their competitive positioning in relation to market share and potential growth opportunities.

In terms of its overall use, it is an extremely useful planning tool, whereby plotting the position of products on the matrix provides you with information to underpin the planning process. Some of the information provided will be:

♦ Competitive position

♦ Stage in the PLC

- ◆ Potential for growth
- ◆ Necessity for deletion
- ◆ Level of investment required to sustain market share
- ◆ The need for repositioning
- ◆ Market development opportunities
- ◆ Market penetration strategies
- ◆ Level of expected profitability from products.

All of the above information, in addition to many more elements, will be fed into the marketing audit process, which ultimately feeds into the marketing strategy. At this stage the contribution that the product will make – proposed changes, new product development strategies, modification programmes and so on – will be decided. Therefore BCG is a planning tool to support both strategic level decision-making and future product planning opportunities.

Unit 6

Question 6.1

The following are some of the key points to be discussed:

- ◆ Seasonal variation
- ◆ Business market rates
- ◆ Services issues of intangibility – if the room is not filled on a particular night the income from that room is lost for ever – should a lower price be charged in order that the room might be filled?
- ◆ Time influences
- ◆ Regional variances
- ◆ Income – state of economy – boom or bust
- ◆ Disposable income levels
- ◆ Customer perception
- ◆ Competitive activity.

Question 6.2

Justifying the value proposition will be quite a challenge and therefore the following marketing activities could be undertaken – these are only some of the activities you could undertake:

- ◆ Product positioning – perceptual mapping
- ◆ Brand development – brand association – establishing brand preference
- ◆ Advertising – promoting benefits and functionality of the products – creating high levels of awareness
- ◆ Market testing
- ◆ Trial programmes
- ◆ Product differentiation
- ◆ Defining tightly targeted groups through the segmentation process

- Establishing quality measures with quality being perceived as a visible component of the purchase
- Price skimming – sometimes pricing might justify quality (however this can be precarious overall)
- Competitive positioning
- Distribution strategies – availability of product, exclusivity of outlets and so on.

Question 6.3

The overall impact of competitive pricing in the 21st century are as follows:

- Intense rivalry
- Competitor warfare
- Profit margins narrowing
- Price reductions unsustainable in the long term
- Industry infrastructure suffering
- A route to mass unemployment
- Saturated markets
- High levels of innovation to overcome competitiveness
- Shorter life cycles – less opportunity for maturity and profit
- High quality/low price.

Question 6.4

It is essential that pricing objectives reflect marketing objectives, in order that the marketing plan can be successfully implemented.

If marketing objectives are based on growth, then pricing objectives have to reflect the ability to achieve growth through appropriate pricing strategies. Similarly, if market penetration is the focus of the marketing strategy, then market penetration activities should be undertaken.

Price will be a key influence in meeting profitability goals (ROI goals), and therefore key influences, costs and external drivers, combined with the marketing strategy, should shape pricing objectives closely in order for successful execution and implementation of the marketing plan.

Unit 7

Question 7.1

Changes in lifestyle have impacted upon distribution in some of the following ways:

- Less time/time-starved individuals
- The need for more convenience products
- The necessity to shop out of hours
- More choice and selection in retail outlets
- Shopping is a highly significant leisure activity
- Direct marketing becoming increasingly desirable

- ♦ The strength and power of the customer and consumer pull the product to market
- ♦ Increasing customer demands
- ♦ Customers more clued into value propositions
- ♦ Increasing debt
- ♦ More flexible payment systems.

Question 7.2

The producer can achieve cost-effectiveness through introducing intermediaries into the channel in the following way. They should be encouraged to facilitate, undertake logistical management and provide transactional management.

Incentivizing organizations to undertake this level of activity, that is through promotional support, merchandising support, profit share and so on, can cost significantly less than resourcing and managing the following functions.

Marketing information	Analyse information such as sales data. Carry out research studies
Marketing management	Establish objectives, plan activities and manage, co-ordinate financing, risk-taking. Evaluate channel activities
Facilitating exchange	Choose and stock products that match buyers' needs
Promotion	Set promotional objectives, co-ordinate advertising, personal selling, promotions and so on
Price	Establish pricing policies, terms and sales
Physical distribution	Manage transport, warehousing, materials handling, stock control and communication
Customer service	Provide channels for advice, technical support, after-sales service and warranties
Relationships	Facilitate communication, products, parts, credit control and so on. Maintain relationships between manufacturer and retail outlets, and customer/consumer

Question 7.3

The basis of your decision and justification should include the following points:

- ♦ It is likely that this will be the basis of selective distribution in the medium term. While palm-tops are highly popular, the diffusion process is relatively slow with the overall prices still being moderately expensive. Therefore, costs of associated valued-added components are also relatively high at this stage.
- ♦ The concept of palm-tops and portable keyboards is excellent, but again diffusion will be slow.
- ♦ Currently this product is not widely available and while it is not sufficiently exclusive to fall under 'exclusive distribution', it is nowhere near a mass market, low price product.
- ♦ In terms of market segmentation and targeting, the likely contenders for the use of this product will be Bs and C1, middle, junior and supervisory managers.

♦ Essentially the uses of these products and the associated technicalities of using palm-tops will require some level of technical support and know-how, which would not typically match against the requirements of an intensive distribution strategy.

Question 7.4

Disintermediation refers to the process of selling directly between the organization and the customer, without the assistance of traditional intermediaries and more in line with the association of cybermediaries.

The benefits of this method of selling, as with companies such as mytravelLite.com, are that the cost of physical and human resources are considerably reduced and the need for significant building of bricks and mortar is less likely.

It speeds up the process of transaction considerably, it closes a sale more effectively, and it provides growth opportunities and cost reductions.

The cost of marketing activities is reduced and the necessity for marketing support to intermediaries will cease to exist.

The process of disintermediation may bring the producer/supplier much closer to their customers. In doing this, with the electronic footprint method of collecting information on an underpinning database, the organization can potentially get much closer to targeting specific customer needs and expectations.

Unit 8

Question 8.1

You will very likely be surprised at the extent of relationships that you are currently involved in within the workplace. The challenge will be to manage them successfully in the true context of relationship marketing.

Question 8.2

Highly motivated personnel are an essential ingredient and should be developed by the organization in order that their skills and abilities are optimized, particularly as they are the frontline people with whom customers actually interact.

Their ability to help, support, guide and service will hopefully turn customers into clients, clients into advocates and advocates into partners, and will be crucial to the achievement of customer loyalty and customer retention within the organization.

Unit 9

Question 9.1

As this question is based upon a country of your choice, you should identify key differences such as the following:

♦ Religion

♦ Education

♦ Place of women in society

- Work ethics
- Social behaviour
- Leisure persuits
- Language barriers
- Values
- Political affinity.

Look at the cultural framework in Figure 9.1 and identify at least two possible options of cultural diversity and discuss them.

Question 9.2

The Internet will aid international trade in some of the following ways:

- Opening up more markets
- Reducing barriers to entry on a country-by-country basis
- Make companies more competitive
- Cost-effective
- Reducing the need for high investment in marketing
- Creating opportunities to establish a more direct relationship with the customer
- Potentially a less risky venture, depending upon the distribution channel
- Reducing the implications of channel management
- Price-competitive and price-sensitive
- Enabling fast response times to transactions
- No time barriers.

The list could go on – see how many more you can get.

Question 9.3

International marketing is an overall strategy that initiates international trade from a strategic level. The process of international marketing then devises appropriate marketing strategies based upon robust market research.

Export marketing is a distribution option available to the organization, that is as opposed to actually having bricks and mortar in a country, exporting is an alternative channel option.

Question 9.4

Economic indicators would include:

- The ability to afford the product being produced
- The exchange rate
- Cost of development in international markets
- Technology – costs of implementing appropriate levels of economy
- Market share
- Disposable income
- Per capita income
- Cost of raw materials

♦ Availability of raw materials

Environmental

♦ Kyoto Agreement and other similar agreements in relation to the use and disposal of materials and chemicals

♦ Packaging

♦ Transportation restrictions

♦ Positioning of plant in respect of environmentally friendly zones.

These are just an example of some of the possible answers you might come up with.

Unit 10

Question 10.1

The following activities are likely:

Once the original interest had been registered by the buyer, it is likely that the consultancy would spend some time understanding the nature and complexity of the project – highlighting that this will likely be a high involvement sale.

The process might include some of the following as an illustration of high-level involvement:

The consultancy would then spend some time drawing up provisional specifications in consultation with the buyer, prior to entering the formal tendering process.

This would involve further meetings, references and information being provided by both organizations, in order to gain a mutual understanding of the situation.

The consultancy is likely to be one of many involved within the tendering process, therefore it will be essential that they understand the full details of the requirements before proceeding to tender.

It is likely that the tenderer will work on partnership arrangements with contractors in order to actually be able to fully price the work, estimate lead times, and draw up resource specifications that will deliver the technical support.

Question 10.2

Typical differences will include the following:

♦ The consumer process could be more impulsive.

♦ Individual decisions can be made without reference to others.

♦ Complexity of the purchase is less.

♦ Number of decision-makers may be one or even a family of four – but not a huge team of decision-makers.

♦ Purchaser is the person who pays for the product.

♦ The user is probably the same person, or passes it on as a gift to the end-user or consumer.

♦ The influencer will vary, but will relate to cultural, social and personal influences rather than organizational.

Question 10.3

Establishing sound and robust relationships with buyers is essential to achieve some of the following:

♦ Gain preferred supplier status
♦ Gain trust
♦ Collaborate and establish partnership agreements that are mutually beneficial
♦ Flexibility
♦ Respect, honesty
♦ A stronger likelihood of quality and delivery.

Question 10.4

Customer uncertainty relates to the gap between understanding the customer and their expectation, and what the service deliverer actually provides.

The gap, so to speak, can cause a range of different behaviours in the customer as a result of the gap in delivery and their expectation, and thus highlight 'customer uncertainty' in respect of what they have received, as opposed to what they expected.

Question 10.5

The additional 3Ps of the marketing mix are imperative to enable the successful execution of the services marketing campaign. The original 4Ps of the marketing mix fail to take into account the service deliverables, that is the people, the processes and, where appropriate, the physical evidence. As services are very people-oriented, these mix elements need to be introduced.

They are vital to enabling service delivery, service success, and give a basis on which to develop a service-based strategy.

However, the 4Ps do have a function, indeed the elements are complementary to the 3Ps in order that the mix may be priced, promoted and delivered.

Question 10.6

The basis of evaluation of services delivery could be along the lines of the following:

♦ To ensure that quality delivery is taking place
♦ To identify the gaps in delivery performance and delivery goals
♦ To identify the gap in expectations between the consumer and the delivery
♦ To be able to implement a programme of continuous improvement
♦ To ensure that quality prevails as a core denominator in the programme
♦ To ensure that customer uncertainties do not continue to arise and that the perception gap is filled
♦ To be a learning organization
♦ To understand customer dissatisfaction
♦ To ascertain levels of satisfaction
♦ To ensure that the design criteria are successful
♦ To measure the effectiveness of administrative and peripheral elements of the services mix.

Unit 11

Question 11.1

Three methods of gaining funds for charitable donations might include some of these:

♦ Charitable event organization

♦ Door-to-door collections

♦ Selling of merchandize

♦ Internet

♦ Major appeals – Red Nose – Children in Need

♦ Sponsorship of participants in major events (London Marathon)

♦ Corporate sponsorship

♦ Corporate donations

♦ Bequests from wills

♦ Direct debits.

Question 11.2

Targeting for charities

Target donors – This is in order to continually remind them of the need for their donations; they are in the main the backbone of the financial support needed in order that the charitable objectives can be achieved.

Target volunteers – In order that fund allocations can be maximized, charitable work is therefore carried out by volunteers. The more volunteers, the less funds are committed to the running costs of the charities.

Clients/users – They are targeted in order that the organization can carry out their works to a target audience who need their services, their support and their financial contributions. Therefore, clients might be homeless, disabled, suffer from MS, starving, blind, to name but a few. They need to be aware that there are resources available to make their life easier.

Question 11.3

Not-for-profit organizations differ from commercial organizations in the following ways:

♦ Not-for-profit means profit is not the focus, though income generation is

♦ Objectives will be based around making people's lives better, rather than making money to benefit shareholders and the board

♦ Highly accountable to their members and donors

♦ Less resources available to do the job well

♦ Target market very broadly based (geographically and culturally diverse nations)

♦ Measurement and control less easy to implement and monitor

♦ The nature of the marketing audit will focus on very specific areas

♦ Heavy reliance on stakeholders

♦ Donors give money for nothing in return, rather than receive anything for their contribution.

Question 11.4

You should be thinking along the following lines.

♦ An advertising agency would be inappropriate for the following reasons:

♦ Too costly, this might be an inappropriate use of funds – agency costs historically high

♦ Work can be done by professional volunteers without a fee attached

♦ Agencies would need to understand the nature and culture of charities, this could be time-consuming and possibly not achievable

♦ Charity work is capable of achieving its own publicity, and can be managed in-house more satisfactorily overall.

Index